Love You to Death

Love You to Death

The Unofficial Companion to **The Vampire Diaries**
Season 5

• CRISSY CALHOUN *and* HEATHER VEE •

ecw press

Published by ECW Press
2120 Queen Street East, Suite 200, Toronto, Ontario, Canada M4E 1E2
416-694-3348 / info@ecwpress.com

LIBRARY AND ARCHIVES CANADA CATALOGUING IN PUBLICATION

Calhoun, Crissy, author
Love you to death : the unofficial companion to the Vampire diaries, season 5 /
Crissy Calhoun, Heather Vee; foreword by Kevin Williamson.

ISBN 978-1-77041-227-9
Also issued as 978-1-77090-638-9 (PDF) and 978-1-77090-639-6 (ePub)

1. Vampire diaries (Television program). I. Vee, Heather, author II. Title.

PN1992.77.V34C345 2014 791.45'72 C2014-902543-2
C2014-902544-0

Editor: Gil Adamson
Text design: Melissa Kaita
Cover design by Risa Rodil (risarodil.tumblr.com)
Printed and bound in the United States by United Graphics 5 4 3 2 1

The publication of *Love You to Death — Season 5: The Unofficial Companion to The Vampire Diaries* has been generously supported by the Government of Canada through the Canada Book Fund for our publishing activities, and the contribution of the Government of Ontario through the Ontario Book Publishing Tax Credit and the Ontario Media Development Corporation.

Canada
Ontario
Ontario Media Development Corporation

Contents

In loving memory
of Mary Ann Kackley

Foreword

(be warned: season five spoilers lurk herein)

There's a scene in *The Vampire Diaries*' first episode that to this day still gives me goosebumps. It's the moment when Julie and I knew this show was going to be special. Whether or not it would find an audience, whether or not it would be a hit, we both knew that it was going to be something very special to us on both a professional and a personal level. It was the moment when Elena and Stefan meet face to face in the graveyard. Their eyes meet, they are connected. We had chemistry between our two leads. It was there and was felt by everyone on set. It's an introduction that includes a line from Elena that perfectly defines the mythology of the show: "We have History together." A beautiful moment between two broken but strong souls in what can best be described as, and what soon became our buzzword for everything *TVD*, *epic*. It was the beginning. One hundred and eleven episodes later, the romance and mystery of Mystic Falls are stronger than ever, and I love every minute of it.

However, it's no secret I was reluctant at first to join Julie in adapting the book series into a TV show. I didn't want to create another vampire love story knockoff. It was already overdone. I felt sure this would be the final nail in the coffin of the vampire genre that had taken the world by storm. But as I gave the books a chance, I realized this was much more than just a love story about a vampire and a mortal — *TVD* was about loss and grief. It was about people and family. It told the story of how even the hopeless and lost can find a way to live and love. It's about family and second chances and all the sad and happy truths that come with life and death. It was truly epic. So, here we are five years later, and I couldn't be more proud and fulfilled to be a part of the *TVD* world. I was dealing with great grief and loss in my own personal life, and working with my dear friend Julie and all the wonderful cast and crew — this show brought me back to life. It saved me in ways you will never know.

Season five was a huge milestone for us. We took Elena, Caroline, and Bonnie out of Mystic Falls and dropped them into Whitmore College, a place with mysterious ties to the Gilbert family. We delved deeper into the history of the doppelgängers and introduced new mythology through the Travelers. The Originals moved to New Orleans, Bonnie anchored the Other Side, and Katherine came face to face with the daughter who was ripped from her arms after childbirth. Stefan dealt with his shadow self, Silas, and lost his mind in the process. Damon went off the rails, redeemed himself, got the girl, and sacrificed himself to save Mystic Falls. And if that wasn't enough, we celebrated our 100th episode, a true testament to the incredible work done by our cast and crew over these past five years. I couldn't be prouder of Julie and Caroline Dries and their creative team for keeping the series going twist after twist. Their hard work and dedication is in every fiber of this show and it's because of them that we have been so incredibly successful around the world.

The Vampire Diaries would be nothing without its eternally loyal and hardcore fans. You've stood by us from the very beginning, keeping tabs on Julie and me and all of our fabulous writers as we deviated from the books and developed our own version of Mystic Falls. And through it all, Crissy and Heather have been our biggest cheerleaders. We first met them through the popular Vampire-Diaries.net, which connected us to you in ways we could never have imagined. I was floored when I saw how devoted the Vampire-Diaries.net team was at keeping up with us as they built their incredibly comprehensive website. With their Love You to Death books, they've spent countless hours breaking down and analyzing each and every frame of season five. They bring you close to the action through insightful interviews, analysis, and witty commentary — sometimes even calling us out on our mistakes! Their books serve as a perfect companion to the show and are a must-have for any *TVD* fan.

Thank you for being part of what is a truly special fandom family. Stay tuned for season six of *TVD*. There's so much more twisty fun to come. So many more epically epic stories to tell . . .

Much love,

Kevin Williamson

Introduction

"I'm in." "Me too." "Absolutely." "Count me in." "Done dealio." This spring, very shortly after we sent out interview requests for this here volume of Love You to Death to a list of *TVD* crew, our inboxes filled up with these quick and keen replies. As it turns out, the talented folks who work on *The Vampire Diaries*, just like those who watch it, are more than happy to talk about it. Which makes this season five companion a Super Edition: we have more insights and voices herein than in the previous four books combined. (See the sidebar for a rundown of who's who.) From the revealing backstories that informed what we ended up seeing on screen, to the lighting and framing and stunts, to the perspective on the season as a whole now that it's in the rear-view mirror, this group of writers, directors, producers, cinematographers, production designers, and editors together provide a candid (and often funny) oral history of this season. We hope you find it as illuminating and entertaining to read as we did to put it together. After all (to paraphrase Ferris Bueller), *The Vampire Diaries* moves pretty fast. If you don't stop and look around once in a while, you could miss it.

In the episode guide, each write-up begins with a bit of dialogue that stood out either because it captures the episode in a pithy few lines or it was just too well written to ignore. From there, we dive into an analysis of the episode, exploring its main themes, the character development, the questions it raises, or, in some cases, providing a critique. Next, we present these sections:

COMPELLING MOMENT Here we choose one moment that particularly stands out — a turning point, a heartbreaker of a scene, or a shocking twist.
CIRCLE OF KNOWLEDGE This is the section in which you'll find all the need-to-know info — the details you may have missed on first watch, the cultural references, and motifs or recurring elements. If an episode's title is a play on another title (of a film, book, song, etc.), those references are explained here.
HISTORY LESSON The only class at Mystic Falls High School that ever got considerable screen time is history. History, both real and fictional, is important in this series — so, for the characters' historical quips, the town's history, and subtle references, "History Lesson" is your study aid.
THE RULES Any work of fiction with a supernatural element has its own particular spin on how that world operates. Here we catalog what we've learned about what goes bump in the night.
PREVIOUSLY ON *THE VAMPIRE DIARIES* History repeats itself in Mystic Falls, and here we outline the incidents, motifs, and key moments that are revisited or echoed in each episode.
OFF CAMERA We leave the fictional world behind to hear what the cast and crew have to say about an episode; you'll also find background details on guest stars.
FOGGY MOMENTS Elena, surprised by Stefan in the cemetery in the pilot episode, tells him the fog is making her foggy. "Foggy Moments" is a collection of confusing moments for these viewers — continuity errors, arguable nitpicks, full-on inconsistencies, and conundrums that may be explained later.
QUESTIONS *TVD* fans *love* to theorize about what will happen next or what motivates a certain character. In this section, we raise questions about characters, plotting, and mythology and leave you to consider them as you watch the season unfold.

Wherever sister show *The Originals* got into a little crossover action with *TVD* this season, we include a brief rundown of what went down in the Big Easy in the section entitled "Meanwhile in New Orleans . . ." Make sure you watch an episode *before* reading its corresponding guide — you will encounter spoilers for that episode. The timeline included in previous volumes of Love You to Death is updated to include season five's info on the past 2,000 years in the *TVD* universe. As well, a song-by-scene guide is included at the back of the book.

Enjoy the trip back to Mystic Falls,
Crissy Calhoun and Heather Vee
July 2014

Brett Matthews, writer and producer. Joined *TVD* in season four, after having worked on little-known shows like *Firefly* and *Supernatural.* (!!)
Caroline Dries, executive producer, writer, showrunner, badass painter. She joined the writing staff in the midst of season one.
Darren Genet, cinematographer on the series since season four. Don't freak out (like we did) but he worked on *Kings*. Genet directed his first episode of *TVD* this season.
Garreth Stover, production designer with the series since season one. Expect to hear a lot of love for Garreth and his work in these here pages.
Joshua Butler, director. His work on *TVD* began back in season one as an editor, and he's also worked on all of your favorite shows (e.g., *FNL*, *PLL*, *The OGs* . . .).
Julie Plec, cocreator, executive producer, and writer. Mad genius. Excellent conversationalist.
Holly Brix, writer and producer, who joined the *TVD* family in season five.
Kellie Cyrus, associate producer and director. Kellie joined the series in season one as script supervisor.
Marc Pollon, editor. A season one veteran, Marc is another Whedon alum, having worked on *Angel*.
Matthew D'Ambrosio, writers' assistant and writer. Matt's been with the show since season one; in addition to an episode this season, he cowrote issues of DC's *TVD* comic.
Melinda Hsu Taylor, writer and producer. New to the series this season, Melinda's IMDb page boasts such credits as writer/producer for *Lost*, *Medium*, *Falling Skies* . . .
Michael Allowitz, first assistant director and director. A beloved *TVD* veteran, Michael has been with the series since episode two and directed his first episode last season.
Michael Karasick, cinematographer. New to *TVD* in season five, Michael has been shooting TV and film for the better part of two decades.
Neil Reynolds, writer and producer. Joined the writers' room in season four.
Paul Wesley, director and actor. The one and only Stefan Salvatore. (Also, Silas.)
Rebecca Sonnenshine, writer and producer. On the writing staff since season three; has a penchant for horror that we adore.
Tony Solomons, editor. With the show since season four and has an impressively varied résumé — from *Californication* to MMA reality series to *ANTM*.

We are all strangers in a strange land, longing for home, but not quite knowing what or where home is. We glimpse it sometimes in our dreams, or as we turn a corner, and suddenly there is a strange, sweet familiarity that vanishes almost as soon as it comes.

— *Madeleine L'Engle*

Episode Guide

Season Five
October 3, 2013–May 15, 2014

CAST Nina Dobrev (Elena Gilbert/Katherine Pierce), Paul Wesley (Stefan Salvatore/Silas), Ian Somerhalder (Damon Salvatore), Steven R. McQueen (Jeremy Gilbert), Kat Graham (Bonnie Bennett), Candice Accola (Caroline Forbes), Zach Roerig (Matt Donovan), Michael Trevino (Tyler Lockwood)

RECURRING CAST Raffi Barsoumian (Markos), Chris Brochu (Luke Parker), Rick Cosnett (Dr. Wes Maxfield), Olga Fonda (Nadia), Janina Gavankar (Tessa), Jasmine Guy (Grams Bennett), Marguerite MacIntyre (Liz Forbes), Michael Malarkey (Enzo), Sabrina Mayfield (Diane Freeman), Caitlin McHugh (Sloan), Penelope Mitchell (Liv Parker), Kendrick Sampson (Jesse), Shaun Sipos (Aaron), Lana Young (Mrs. Douglas)

Damon: If I hear the word doppelgänger one more time, I think I'm actually going to have to learn how to spell it.

5.01 *I Know What You Did Last Summer*

Original air date October 3, 2013
Written by Caroline Dries **Directed by** Lance Anderson
Edited by Tony Solomons **Cinematography by** Darren Genet
Guest cast Max Calder (Student #2), Jesse Haus (Student #1), Claire Holt (Rebekah Mikaelson), Hayley Kiyoko (Megan), Hans Obma (Gregor), Rick Worthy (Rudy Hopkins)
Previously on *The Vampire Diaries* Paul Wesley

It's college move-in day for Caroline and Elena, and Damon tries to keep things in check at home with human Katherine, extra strong Silas, and Little Gilbert.

While the season begins with its characters all over the map (underwater, on the Other Side, in the mountains of Appalachia . . .), the episode manages to unite the storylines through each character's desire to hold on to some form of normalcy after a summer that held them in various states of limbo — some of them *way* more fun than others.

Some opt for fresh starts in new surroundings, but Matt chooses the good ol' reliable world he knows. He's back in his Grill T-shirt because he needs a paycheck, and Rebekah's "one more chance" to go with her to New Orleans doesn't even tempt him. Tyler, a character fated to another thin season, literally phones it in this episode, leaving Caroline a voicemail wherein he chooses to focus on his supernatural side (helping a wolf pack) over freshman courses at Whitmore with his girlfriend.

On the opposite end of the spectrum, Caroline and Elena struggle with their new normal in a storyline that explores that tension between a fresh start and bringing the past with you to the dorm, along with the small appliances. That conflict is created by doomed-from-the-start Megan: how will the girls manage to keep their supernatural secret from a vervain-water-drinking roommate? Determined not to be outed as vampires on their first day at college, the roomies have amusingly opposing reactions, with Caroline suggesting the old route (capture, compel) and Elena successfully arguing for a diabolical alternative: act like normal and fun-loving human college students, a.k.a. fake it 'til you make it. "What's the point in going to college if we're just going to recreate what happens in Mystic Falls?" asks Elena, convincing Caroline to give it the old college try. These two as roomies is highly entertaining so far, and Caroline's hilarious and sweet turn in this premiere signals a more Caroline-heavy, and nuanced, season than we saw in season four — from her neurotic control freakiness over the Megan situation to the perfect mix of emotions Candice Accola gives us as Caroline reacts to the news that Tyler won't be joining them at college.

Remember back in season one when Elena told Damon that she "used to be more fun"? Well, gloomy graveyard girl is on hiatus in "I Know What You Did Last Summer." Bonnie is right: Elena does look happy at Whitmore — thanks to a summer of lovin', free of supernatural drama. Elena's ignorance is her bliss, and her "normal college experience," quite expectedly, is short-lived. The girls can't even enter the party house, thanks to being vampires. Pretend as they might, they can't deny what they are or outrun the past. What at first seems like a simple touching moment turns out to be a hint at a mystery to come: Liz tells Elena that her father fell in love with medicine at Whitmore College, and by episode's end Elena has found a photo of her dead dad on her dead roommate's cell phone. What does the vampire-hating good doctor Grayson Gilbert have to do with Megan?

Before Bonnie's father is rudely interrupted (and then murdered) at the town's end-of-summer barbecue, Mayor Hopkins says that family is one of the core values of the Mystic Falls community. But "I Know What You Did Last Summer" gives us families splintering and separating, which forces the characters to find connection outside their bloodlines. In the least tragic of situations, Caroline is treated to her empty-nest mom in tears, and then sheds some of her own. Lying in a strange new bed, her parent no longer a room away to console her, she relies on the comforting presence of her roommate and friend to get her through the heartache. It's about as normal as it gets on *The Vampire Diaries*, especially Caroline's earnest "I'm really glad you're here," said through her tears. By episode's end, Liz Forbes is the only living parent of the core characters, and she acts as a surrogate parent to Elena when she moves the girls into their dorm room. Between the schlepping of boxes, the adorable "mom ears" comment (overhearing Caroline say that Damon and Elena have been "shacking up" all summer), and her tearful embrace of Elena, Liz acts as a stand-in for Grayson and Miranda Gilbert, reminding Elena that attending Whitmore is part of her family tradition.

The new Gilbert tradition? Struggling through the end of high school orphaned. It's not clear what Jeremy did all summer (other than forge emails and postcards for Ghost Bonnie), but it's obvious that Elena was way more focused on fooling around with Damon than on being her little brother's keeper. (Which, fair enough.) The Gilbert siblings' rehearsal of what lies to tell the school about Jeremy's death and the Gilbert house fire are certainly necessary but a far cry from "normal." With Elena off to college, and his actual little brother M.I.A., Damon is in the position of surrogate older brother, so he steps into Alaric's old role as unofficial official guardian to Jeremy.

Now with two little brothers, Damon feels like he's failing, and when he learns from Silas that Stefan has been suffering all summer long, he realizes he has. Silas's suggestion that Damon has just been deluding himself into thinking that everything was fine, that Stefan would ever just leave and not get in touch, that it would be *that easy*, hits a nerve. While his initial reaction to being alone with Jeremy is that this guardianship will be very hands-off, by episode's end, Damon shows just how much his feelings about Little Gilbert have changed since the beginning of the series. This episode offers a few choice callbacks to earlier seasons, tweaked for the new era that is season five, but none so poignant as Damon saving Jeremy and giving him a little hug as he comes back to life — now his protector, not his murderer.

Resurrected Jeremy struggles with the return to his old life, managing to get expelled on his first day back at school. Picked on for being the freak who faked his own death, he reacts as if he is battling a supernatural creature and not a run-of-the-mill teenaged jerk. Jeremy's unaccustomed to his hunter strength and agility and the necessary secrecy that goes along with being mystically endowed, but his new roomie Damon is already teaching him the ropes. The tension between these characters has always made for great TV, and, awesomely, Jeremy is not too shy to bring up the whole "you killed me" thing. With Elena away at college but still very much present in their lives, their dynamic takes on new complications. Damon is keen to keep the darkness away from her; he withholds the truth about Katherine, about Silas and Stefan, about Jer's expulsion and near death, so that she can go on enjoying her new college life. It's as close to being a normal, supportive boyfriend as Damon is capable of, given the circumstances. And though it's likely to blow up in Damon's face at some point, Jeremy goes along with it. He's used to keeping major secrets.

Bonnie Bennett shares Damon's motivation. She refuses to drop the ruse that she's still alive, forcing Jeremy to dupe her loved ones. It's another lie

© Andrew Evans/PRPhotos

that's sure to be revealed soon with the way these *TVD* writers like to blaze through storylines. Bonnie's putting on a happy face in the first half of the episode: she tells Jeremy that she feels lucky to be able to talk to her best friends from beyond the grave, she wants Elena and Caroline to have their happiness, and when she stands beside them at college, unseen, it's a bittersweet and lonely tableau. She's there, and they have no inkling that she's dead. As the episode progresses, an increasingly frustrated Bonnie hits the limitations of her ghostly existence: she can't help Jeremy convince Damon that Silas is back, she can't help Jeremy when he lies dying in the road after the car collides with a telephone pole, and most heartbreaking of all, she can't do anything to stop Silas from murdering her father in cold blood. While, on an intellectual level, she knows she is dead, knows that she's present but unable to truly be a part of what's going on, her new reality is brought painfully and horrifically home when she witnesses Silas's demonstration of strength in the town square. Unaffected by his mass mind control but unable to stop him, she watches as Silas slits her father's throat.

The episode's "Previously On" narration says, "We've all made sacrifices," but true suffering is visited upon Bonnie and Stefan. Characters who have been punished rather than rewarded for their selflessness and sacrifice, they struggle to hold on under the weight of excruciating situations. Though Bonnie is (for the most part) alone on the Other Side, she has found ways to still be a presence in her loved ones' lives, and in an inverse of that situation, Stefan finds a way to keep his loved ones with him, even as he is alone in a nightmare. The horror of being trapped for *months* in a coffin-like prison, waking, drowning, dying, and then doing it all over again with only his own tormented thoughts for company, is a little too much for anyone's brain to handle. Stefan basically mind-whammies himself, as we've seen vampires do to others in the past: he hallucinates his home — open space and daylight and sustenance — and, in the shape of his brother, Stefan tells himself to give up and turn off his emotions. While he'd still be in physical pain in the underwater safe, if he flipped his switch, he would lose all the emotional torment. And he very nearly does choose that option. Stefan may have a literal, external shadow self in Silas, but he also has split selves within: the conflicting voices in his head arguing for this or that course of action, which he personifies as Damon and, finally, Elena. Stefan seems surprised by her appearance in the final hallucination (though it's his own imagination that has conjured her), and he draws from her words the strength he needs to hold onto his humanity, just as he did during their brief phone call on the night of her 18th birthday when he was tethered to Klaus and on the path back to ripperdom. Stefan well remembers the last time he flipped his switch, and his Elena apparition urges him not to let go. "Your humanity is the one thing that makes you who you are" — sage advice from one doppelgänger to another. While there are some differences in physical ability between Silas, the original immortal, and his vampire knock-off, what makes Stefan *Stefan* and not just Silas's "shadow self" is his humanity, and Stefan knows it. He finds a way to experience light in the darkness, and the hallucination sequences are masterful from a technical standpoint, as are the stark transitions in and out of those moments. While "Graduation" had Stefan resolving to let go — of Elena, of Mystic Falls — here he chooses to hold on to what his love for Elena inspires in him. It's a poignant reminder that the people you love are with you even when you're alone.

But what if you've spent 500 years deceiving, using, cheating, killing, and making enemies and running from them? Enter Katherine Pierce, Human Edition. She now understands how much work mere mortals put in to looking even one percent as good as she normally does, and Katherine remains delightfully Katherine in "I Know What You Did Last Summer." Like the girl who hung herself to escape Klaus and Rose and Trevor, Katherine solicits help from Damon but as soon as she realizes she's reached the limit of his goodwill, she scrambles to save herself. The scene in the car with Jeremy is a prime example: Jeremy goes along with the rescue mission but gives her the silent treatment (after all, he's been ordered to protect the person who fed him to Silas, left him for dead, and unleashed all kinds of hell on earth), but when he turns that car around to deliver her to Silas, Katherine kicks into high gear, negotiating for her life with all she's got. When her pleas fall on deaf ears, Katherine Pierce doesn't accept her fate: she changes it. Crafty and quick thinking, she crashes that car and leaves Jer for dead — again. Still integral to Silas's plan (for reasons yet to be revealed), our girl is back on the lam, bruised and bloody, in a bathrobe and bare feet, no less. *TVD* may have lost a villain we loved to root for when Klaus left to be King of New Orleans, but Queen Katherine is proving more than capable of filling that role this season, scrambling to survive no matter who she has to leave in her dust.

With Katherine as willing as ever to kill off Jeremy to serve her own interest, it's a good thing Damon is in Hero Mode, because with his brother trapped in the quarry, Bonnie dead, Matt brain-zapped by mysterious and sexy foreigners, and the college coeds out of town, he's leading a lone charge against the impressively villainous Silas. Introduced last season wearing all manner of disguises, Silas reveals his true self and personality in "I Know What You Did Last Summer" — a snarky, all-knowing villain who hits where it hurts, and not just with physical violence. He casually reminds Damon that Stefan has historically been the Chosen One when it comes to their shared lady loves; he points out to Katherine just how vulnerable and weak she is; even poor Liz Forbes gets a dig ("Eating your feelings?") before being sliced into. Silas is clearly experimenting with the limits of his abilities — chugging blood all summer. But the biggest question isn't how many people he can dupe in one go, it's the one he flat-out refuses to answer: what is his plan? What does he want with Katherine? As the one who consumed the Cure, she's got very special blood running through her veins. A bold new villain wearing a hero's face, Silas seems intent on not only compelling the townsfolk into helping him find Katherine, but on revealing the self-delusions that plague the characters.

Damon has deluded himself into thinking that Stefan really would just disappear for three months, cool with his big bro shacking up with Elena, and send nary a text message to assure anyone that he'd not spiraled into ripper mode. Elena herself has been plagued by unease and dread — something's wrong with Stefan, and she can feel it — but she's been pushing those feelings aside, assuming they are just the workings of her guilty conscience, as Caroline argues. And Caroline is herself deluded about her relationship with Tyler. Silas hints at a season-long concern when he asks Damon, "How well do you know your brother?" In a season full of characters *not* knowing those closest to them and not recognizing when something is terribly, terribly wrong — like a loved one is imprisoned in a safe underwater or has been dead for three months — the gang is unable to admit how far from okay their reality is for fear of losing the little glimmer of happiness they are experiencing.

No normal college party free from murder-by-vampire. No pleasant town event without the Mayor's shocking death. No threesome in Europe without supernaturally dicey consequences. Whether a few hours away at Whitmore College or back home in Mystic Falls, the gang's drama-free summer has come to a brutal and bloody end.

COMPELLING MOMENT Silas murdering the Mayor in front of the silent and still crowd, Bonnie's screams and cries as her father is slain the only sounds. Absolutely chilling.

CIRCLE OF KNOWLEDGE

- Tyler doesn't appear in this episode, but his voice is heard when Caroline picks up his voicemail.
- *I Know What You Did Last Summer* is a 1973 young adult suspense novel by American writer Lois Duncan. Nine months after a hit-and-run accident that kills a 10-year-old boy, the four teens who were in the car are confronted with their past sin as a vengeful Someone Who Knows escalates from creepy notes to violence. Julie James, a happy senior whose love for cheerleading and socializing disappeared after the life-changing incident, plans to escape the past by attending college far from home. Her ex-boyfriend Ray Bronson comes back to town after a year away, having realized that you can't outrun your past. The 1997 film adaptation, starring Jennifer Love Hewitt, Freddie Prinze Jr., Sarah Michelle Gellar, and Ryan Phillipe, was penned by *Vampire Diaries* cocreator Kevin Williamson, who reimagined the story as a straight-up slasher film.
- In the threesome scene, Nadia says to Rebekah in Czech, "I want you." Rebekah and Nadia's smooch is the first same-sex kiss on the series.
- Bonnie's email has one line that we don't hear in the voice-over but is visible onscreen in Elena's Gmail: "And I'm assuming no one's heard from Katherine since you shoved the vampire cure down her throat?"
- It wasn't until most of our characters had graduated for the series to give us Mystic Falls High School's principal. Principal Weber calls the Salvatore house to report Jeremy's hallway brawl. Damon later uses compulsion on Principal Weber (offscreen) so Jeremy won't be expelled from school; he gets a "generous three-day suspension" instead.
- Silas prefers to use the term "shadow self" over doppelgänger, which pulls in the Jungian concept to the relationship between Silas and Stefan. Swiss psychologist Carl Jung (1875–1961) wrote about the "shadow" as the darkness within each individual's "self" that is cut off from his or her conscious being. "We carry our past with us," said Jung in 1937. For someone to be cured of a looming shadow self, Jung said, "it is necessary to find a way in which his conscious personality and his shadow can live

> "Usually the episode writer gets to pick the title. The titles usually emerge at some point in the break [of the episode] and we're all present and give it our stamp of approval. I like the slightly funnier/ironic ones. I usually pick existing movie titles. I have veto power on titles and have used it a few times . . . I won't say on which. And Julie vetoed one of mine once too — [what became] 'The Murder of One' [3.18]. Not that I'm still thinking about it or anything."
>
> — Caroline Dries

together." The idea being, if one ventures into the "darkness" of the self and brings the self and shadow into a "precarious unity," then it's possible to assimilate the dark side rather than be overwhelmed by it (which Jung felt was the inevitable result of denying and repressing it). "The hero's main feat is to overcome the monster of darkness," wrote Jung, referring to the victory of the conscious self over the subconscious urges. In *TVD*, Silas and his shadow self are a peculiar inverse of this concept — with Stefan as a carbon copy of who Silas was before his crime against Nature (the immortality spell), a shadow of the self that is arguably *less* evil and dark than the original or prime consciousness.

- The lady doppelgängers share a fondness for baths: at the start of the episode, Elena indulges in a bubble bath while Damon plies her with champagne and asks her to stay; later, Katherine takes a bubble bath in the same tub, only her experience is much less relaxing . . . since Silas tries to kill her.

THE RULES Bonnie can communicate with Jeremy, because he can see ghosts, but they can't touch each other. Her death undid her spell that encased Silas in stone ("The Walking Dead," 4.22). As a ghost, Bonnie has no magic.

Silas unloads a lot of important fun facts regarding his capabilities. First of all, do not call him a vampire. He's an immortal; vampires are just perverse knock-offs of him. He is unkillable and has vampire-style healing abilities (though a little slower, judging by his recovery time from Katherine's retaliation), he needs to drink human blood in order to sustain himself, he does not have super speed, but he does have super psychic abilities — mind control, mind reading — and the more blood he drinks the greater his ability. (R.I.P. mayor #3.) And while there haven't been any psychic powers the likes of Silas's, Bonnie's spirit-magic abilities first manifested as psychic (like her uncanny ability to correctly guess what's in the Gilbert kitchen drawers in "Friday Night Bites" [1.03]); through physical touch, she was able to learn that Mason and Katherine were a secret item and that the moonstone was hidden in a well in "Plan B" (2.06).

When Jeremy touches Silas, he gets a chill where his hunter's mark used to be — akin to the way a witch can tell someone's a vampire by touch.

Silas states that the creation of a shadow self, or doppelgänger, was Nature's retaliation for him becoming immortal: a killable edition.

PREVIOUSLY ON *THE VAMPIRE DIARIES* Tyler's excuse for missing his first semester at Whitmore is a familiar one: he tells Caroline that he's helping a wolf pack in Tennessee. After Bill Forbes told Tyler how he must break his sire bond to Klaus in "The Ties That Bind" (3.12), Tyler left town and later returned to Mystic Falls a changed man in "Heart of Darkness" (3.19), having broken free of the bond by turning deliberately a hundred times in the Appalachian Mountains. When Klaus and Stefan searched for werewolves to turn into hybrids, they found a pack in the Appalachian Mountains ("The Hybrid," 3.02).

Jer's excuse about faking his death plays into his character, albeit the one we were introduced to in season one: erratic, a drug user, troubled.

We first saw Whitmore College in "The Five" (4.04), when Bonnie, Elena, and Damon went to scope out the school and met the professor who took over Sheila Bennett's Occult Studies class, Atticus Shane.

Silas reminds Liz that they "met before" when he impersonated her daughter — a moment we didn't see from "Pictures of You" (4.19): by the time we see Caroline returning home, Silas was role-playing as Liz.

By forcing the car crash, Katherine nearly kills Jeremy — again. She attacked him in "The Sacrifice" (2.10), when he attempted to retrieve the moonstone from the tomb where she was trapped, and she killed him in "Down the Rabbit Hole" (4.14) by feeding him to Silas.

Silas taunts Damon, refusing to tell him what he's up to because it'll be more "fun" that way; not a far stretch from season one Damon, who irked his brother with his smart-ass villain comments like in "The Night of the Comet" (1.02), "That's for me to know and you to dot dot dot."

Last time Stefan was missing for a summer, Damon and Elena spent every waking moment trying to track him down ("The Birthday," 3.01), but they spend this summer assuming Stefan has left town of his own volition, as he told them in "Graduation" (4.23).

OFF CAMERA Caroline Dries calls "I Know What You Did Last Summer" her proudest writing moment of the season, "because it felt funny and fresh and like a really good start to the season. Also, every department was 'on' — all the actors were fresh, the directing was inspired, the editing was fantastic. Everyone kind of nailed it."

This episode marked Claire Holt's final recurring guest star appearance on *The Vampire Diaries* as she made the transition to a regular on *The Originals*. She admitted to *ET Online* that she was surprised at Rebekah and Matt's European adventures when she read the script. "Even when we were filming [the threesome scene], I thought, 'Are we allowed to do this?' We're getting very risque in the 8 p.m. hour . . . All bets and clothes are off!" Olga Fonda revealed that it was the very first scene she shot when she arrived on the Atlanta set. "I call it an ice breaker," she told *E! Online*. "I got to tell you, Claire and Zach are amazing. They made that scene so easy and so fun and so wonderful that I'm very thankful for them."

Kat Graham was excited about Bonnie's lack of powers now that she's dead, particularly the moment where she can only watch helplessly as Silas murders her father. "You're going to see a character who is already vulnerable because her power got taken away," she told *Zap2It*. "But I also think you're going to see a side to her that's a bit more powerless. She's wanting things to change and realizing the reality of the situation she's in now."

As for Silas, who returns to Mystic Falls masquerading as Stefan, Paul Wesley provided insight into the Big Bad's cocky nature. "[Silas] isn't intimidated by anything," he told *TV Guide*. "He's 2,000 years old and finds himself to be supremely more interesting and sophisticated." As for Silas's unusual method of drinking blood, which we see him perform on Sheriff Forbes, Wesley explained, "He doesn't feed on people, he thinks it's gross and primitive, so he manipulates people into cutting themselves and pouring their blood and then he drinks it; he's a little snobby."

FOGGY MOMENTS The lid and straw to Liz's drink cause some continuity problems, disappearing and moving from shot to shot, as Silas is mopping up her wound before walking away. But perhaps more curiously: why did no one in the town square see Silas cut Liz's wrist and drain it into the cup?

We see how Bonnie is able to email her friends from the Other Side (thanks to Jer) but how does she send postcards that are (a) in her own handwriting and (b) postmarked from all over the country?

Back in "The Five," Elena and Damon were able to waltz right into a party at Whitmore College, their only invitation a flyer, but here Elena and Caroline are barred from entry because they haven't been invited in by the homeowner, even though they have a flyer and the verbal invite from Jesse. So only some frat houses at Whitmore have legitimate tenants?

Why does Caroline care if the authorities hear the voicemail Elena left for Megan? It was a deliberately innocent-sounding message about leaving the party.

QUESTIONS

- In "The Walking Dead" (4.22), Silas's victim, whom we saw in the hospital drained of blood, had his wrists slashed, and Silas gives Liz a slice at the block party in this episode. Does Silas have fangs and refuse to use them, or did those come with the vampire upgrade too?
- Where did Silas get the large volume of blood he consumed over the summer?
- The mystery of poor Megan! When was that photo taken of Megan and Elena's dad? How did they know each other? How did she end up as the girls' roomie? Did she know they were vampires, or did someone give her that vervain-laced "protein water" to protect her from her roommates? Who killed her and why?
- Matt's eyes turn black after Nadia's friend performs some sort of spell. What did he do to Matt? What language was he speaking? Are Nadia and her friend witches? Did she know what the Gilbert ring was when she stole it? Will she be returning Rebekah's earrings as well?
- Resurrected Jeremy is still a hunter, Silas still lives . . . Does that mean there are still four other hunters (or hunter potentials) out there?
- Katherine is reluctant to try turning into a vampire for fear she will just stay dead. What *would* happen to Katherine if she tried to turn?
- Who will volunteer to be the next mayor of Mystic Falls?

- Tyler says he is "helping" a wolf pack. How? Unless the entire pack of them are newbie werewolves who need help sorting out how to handle the full moon (and the psychological ramifications of realizing you're a werewolf), Tyler has no skillset to offer them — no hybrid bond to break. Does he just not want to return home after Klaus lifted his exile in "Graduation" (4.23)?

Darren Genet on *TVD*'s Cinematography

On bringing his own spin to *TVD*: Coming in in the middle of the fourth season like I did, the show pretty much had a look and a world that they had discovered over the years with the other [cinematographers]. My decree was to try and take that look and sort of elevate it to another level and bring it a little further. So I had long conversations with Julie and Chris Grismer about some of the things that they liked and what they didn't like. And a lot of it was compositional, and it was really refreshing to come in and have such a good conversation and good connection with Julie, visually, and we could talk very specifically about what the look should be and what they were hoping it would be. We got to literally sift through and watch episodes and see what we liked, what was working, and what wasn't working. Julie has always been really good about encouraging me to push the envelope and to expand the mythology in a visual language a little bit. So since then we've been doing that, and it's been a really good collaboration with Julie and with myself and the production designer.

On shooting in digital: It has its pros and cons. I mean, one thing that you gain with shooting digitally is that you can play with darkness a lot more, because the cameras are so sensitive to light. You can use a lot less light on the set, and it really reads into the shadows a lot better and more than film does, in theory. So you can really play with darkness and you can really kind of *push* it. But the reverse of that is with digital, you're always struggling against that super-clean digital look. We're always trying to take that video edge off things, and one of the things that's been very important to both myself and to Julie is to keep that video look at bay.

One of the ways we do that is by using longer lenses, so there's more out of focus in the frame. One of the drawbacks of video is that everything is in focus. So we try to limit the focus to have really nice out-of-focus, blooming highlights and what's called "bokeh" in the background — when you get these really out-of-focus, shimmering spots and shadows. So that's one way we combat video. Another way we do it is we keep it moving, whether it's the camera or the people. We don't let the image just sit static for too long, because when it does your eye starts to wander and you start looking for the creases. That's been one thing in terms of battling against the digital: try to keep it still cinematic. But these cameras now are so good that I see it as an advantage, where some people try to fight against it, I try to kind of embrace it.

One thing I do like about digital is that we get to see it on the set exactly how it is, so we're not hoping that some colorist at 4 a.m. is seeing it the same way that we did. We don't have any of the negative issues — with scratching negatives or lab issues or any of that stuff — so we can really dial it in on set, and that's exactly what the dailies look like and down the line that's exactly what it will look like. So we have a lot more control on the set than we ever had with film, which is a good thing, I think. As these episodes are being color-timed, we're not able to be there, so what we do now is just take little stills from the cut and we give our little notes, but having been able to do it on the set with the digital imaging technician and have the dailies look pretty close to what we want, the notes tend to be pretty minimal. We end up streamlining that whole process tremendously, which is great.

On embracing the darkness: The big challenge with [a show] like this, with the darkness and gothic nature, is to try and keep it as dark as possible and yet be able to see everything, so it's that movie-dark. What we're always striving for is riding that line — you still want to see people's eyes and people's faces. But we're shooting, basically, a horror movie every week, so the trick is to ride that line between being too dark and too bright. Because the last thing you want is that night stuff to be too bright. So that's the big challenge, keeping it really dark and feeling really dark without losing what you need to actually tell the story, which is the faces, people's eyes when they're talking, that kind of thing. We're always struggling to keep depth since we are working in a 2D world. It's always about giving depth, especially at night. If you have too much darkness in the frame, you look like you have a head floating in nothing. It's sprinkling just enough light to feel the environment and feel the depth and to feel the tone of the scene without going too far or not far enough. My favorite part of the show is that line, living in that space. When you get that right, it's really satisfying.

Where you have fun is in the background and in the big wides and things like that, where you can really play with contrast. That's something I'm very hyper-aware of is just making sure that even when we're in really, really dark environments, like caves where there wouldn't be any natural light or in forests with people just walking around in the middle of the night in the woods, that you can see just enough to know what's happening, but not feel like you're looking at a movie set that's been lit up with lights.

Then also taking a little bit of license because we are in a world where vampires and werewolves roam the earth. We have a little bit of authority to make it look cool and to look scary and all of those things, so we can do shafts of light at night and things like that that really help make it feel scarier, make it feel isolated, and all of those tools that we have. Because, really, the only way you know if something's dark is if there's something light as well in the frame. If you have too much darkness, it just turns into a mess. The key is to balance that with contrast. That's something that we like to play with, and I in particular like to play with. I came out of that independent feature world where it was all about darkness.

On the show's various realms: We're the shepherds of those looks and what we do is we pitch ideas and discuss with the director and producers and everybody on board, to see what works story-wise and what we can manage in terms of the grammar of the show, something we can be consistent about. We do testing and we show them things and we talk about things and it goes back and forth for awhile, and then we settle on something that we like, and then we have to make sure that we're consistent with it. For me, it's really important to be consistent with our language. So if there is something that is very specific to an episode — like the Other Side is a great example because that's one of the things that's been a bit of a through-line this season. We wanted to do something visually that lets you know immediately that you're not in the "real world" but it has this otherworldly feeling. We did a lot of testing, we basically threw the kitchen sink at it with lenses, with lighting, with color-timing, and techniques, and we ended up settling on a combination where we do a bit of lighting and blooming the highlights so things feel like they're in another world. We looked at infrared photography as an influence where the skin tones kind of glow and the trees and flora and fauna would glow. It has this whiteness to it, which is really interesting, and then we took it from there and Mike [Karasick] and I found something really interesting where it feels almost like a carbon copy or an inverse of the real world.

And with flashbacks we do the same, but we're pretty much placed in charge of that. We usually just set what we like — they usually leave that to us. Sometimes there are very specific notes about it, how it affects the skin tones of our beautiful people in those scenes, so we just make sure that people — I think the big concern on the producers' end, the writers' end, is that people look good. That we don't change the images so much that it's unflattering. But within that there's a lot of freedom to suggest, and as long as it comes from a place of story, then you can't really go wrong. And then it's just a matter of taste.

On working with a director's unique vision: That's the beauty of having an episodic, where you have different directors. They can bring — working within the grammar of the show — a little something to it. For instance, there are a couple of episodes where we played a lot with flaring the lens. We would let the light hit the lens and create these big flares, and that would help with our transitions in and out or would just give it yet another layer of abstraction, which is cool. Directors come in and they have ideas about how to work within the language but to make it their own; we love that. We're sort of charged to be the policemen of the overall tone of things visually — we bring their ideas in but make sure it sits with everything else in the season. That's fun — adding little personality and tics to what's there, so we can elevate that way too.

On his favorite type of scenes: I really like flashbacks, I like the Other Side stuff, 'cause, again, it gives us something to play with visually — we're not tethered to reality as much. But I like anything that takes me out of the normal coverage of scenes. Which you have to do, but I like to do any kind of scene that is new or different or a challenge. Scenes that are fun for me — which may not be fun on the day, but looking back that's some of the best work — are in the caves, scenes where you have to figure out how to make something look natural where there wouldn't be any natural light. And then we've had some scenes where the camera moves around so much that we have to hide light and any time we're orchestrating camera work it's fun. We've done a bunch of that in the Scull bar.

I remember specifically episode 4.15 ["Stand By Me"], the first episode I shot, we had one scene and it was the whole axis of the episode and it was all one shot essentially, one long Steadicam shot that we had to do through a whole scene. Of course, we ended up shooting other stuff to cut into it but just making that shot work was a real challenge and something I've had a lot of experience doing and it's always fun. You just have to get involved and figure it out technically and also storytelling-wise, finding the best place to be at the time and make it all fluid. And the sets are great. Garreth's a brilliant production designer and he makes these beautiful sets and it's really fun to get in there and work within those sets.

On the show's cinematic feel: That's always been the goal is to make this feel like a movie — that we're watching an hour-long movie every week. And to play with scope and not to get caught in the middle visually, so wide shots should be *really* wide and tight shots should be *really* tight and play the gothic, play the darkness, play the negative space. I always try to imagine — whatever framing we're doing or whatever shot we're doing — I always try to imagine it on a 40-foot screen. I try to keep things in a movie sense, cinematic — even with the way we move the camera. We're always trying to make it feel like you're watching a movie. A 22-hour movie, every season.

Jeremy: I can't leave Matt.
Katherine: Wait. How do you think I survived 500 years?
It wasn't because I was a vampire, it's because I never looked back.
Don't be dumb. Survive.
Jeremy: That's why people treat you like an object and not like a person.

5.02 True Lies

Original air date October 10, 2013
Written by Brian Young **Directed by** Joshua Butler
Edited by Marc Pollon **Cinematography by** Michael Karasick
Guest cast Ammie Leonards (Woman), Hans Obma (Gregor), Hunter Smit (Student), Russ Tiller (Cashier), Rick Worthy (Rudy Hopkins)
Previously on *The Vampire Diaries* Paul Wesley

With the aid of the Gilbert-Donovan Brain Trust, Katherine's on the run from Silas and his team of brainwashed townsfolk. Silas makes a pit stop at Whitmore College to mess with Elena and Damon. Bonnie mourns her father.

Another great episode marked by peppy dialogue, snark aplenty, and some unexpected heroics, "True Lies" goes beyond its titular references to honesty and deception to explore how our choices shape or destroy our humanity. It's a theme that *The Vampire Diaries* loves to explore, tossing its characters into all manner of impossible scenarios to see how they'll react — but thanks to the ingenuity of the writers here, and the characters' constantly changing states of mind and relationships, it feels far from stale.

What would a hero do? What would a reformed serial killer do? Elena takes on the case of "Nancy Drew and the Creepster Professor," but what she's willing to do to reach her goal differs wildly from her "reformed serial killer" boyfriend's and her doppelgänger's modi operandi. She rejects compulsion, violence, torture, and threats, opting in the end for a little frank conversation — which Damon declares a hero move. She believes that she and Caroline have to protect themselves from exposure at Whitmore College and offers Damon's proactive infiltration of the Founders' Council in season one as a good model for survival. Her enthusiasm for an authentic college experience has been doused by Megan's death and by the revelation that her father is somehow connected to her. While her conversations with Damon about how to approach the mystery are comical at the outset of the episode, their differing philosophies take on a dark edge when Silas gets involved. Pissed with Silas, Damon arrives on campus in a violent mood — he attacks a college student and Caroline admonishes him — but he's forced from aggressive vampire mode into hostage negotiator mode when Elena reveals herself to be under Silas's compulsion. It's a great role reversal, with Damon as the level head, talking Elena down from a rage-induced frenzy to a calmer, sadder place.

With his super-psychic abilities, Silas can turn anyone (save hunter Jeremy and "occupied" Matt) into a weapon that will do his bidding, but he makes it more personal than, say, a shotgun blast to the chest. Tattletale Silas is keen to pit Elena against Damon, playing on her guilt about ditching Stefan and elaborating on Damon's actual lies about Jeremy. As we saw last season, Elena has a powerful rage inside her and Silas uses that to try to take out Damon. The Silas trance that Elena must fight through allows her to voice her buried feelings: about Stefan and about Damon. Stefan's prolonged suffering is in part a consequence of the secrets Damon has been keeping from Elena. As much as she loves Damon, he is a self-proclaimed reformed serial killer who makes questionable and often violent choices. But unlike last season when Elena's will was not fully her own and she struggled with her new vampire identity, freshman Elena has the space from the brothers Salvatore to be the hero herself, in ways that are both moral and self-preserving. Elena is clever with her seduce-and-destroy attack on Damon and equally so when she physically restrains herself from attacking him. That it is her love and concern for Stefan that brings her out of her rage is fitting given this trio's history and strong feelings. As much as Damon says he's okay with her connection to his brother, time will tell how honest he's being, especially once Stefan is back among them. Which should be soon, considering that Stefan's special hell ends, somehow.

The last of his visions is of being with Elena, peaceful by the waterside . . . until she starts drowning. He watches her suffering, unable to help her. Before the fantasy turns nightmarish, he says it's the simple moments that keep him from falling apart — that keep him human. Arguably, it's a simple moment that makes Katherine turn back and help Jeremy despite the risk it poses her. When she's sitting by the fire, miserable from her first sinus infection in 500 years (maybe ever!), Jeremy puts a blanket around her to keep her from shivering. Katherine literally spooks in reaction to the gesture of human kindness, but his small action, combined with his keen insight into why she's being treated like "the frickin' moonstone," clearly affects her. Like his big sister, Not-so-little Gilbert demonstrates what a hero would do, as he plays the white knight with his trusty BFF at his side. Katherine cautions him *not* to play the hero, to look out for himself over anyone else and never look back, but Jeremy proves he possesses wisdom in his youth, flat-out telling Katherine that she should stop running. Using her wiles and her vampire powers to survive at any cost has meant that Katherine has never felt enough remorse (if she felt any) to stop using people for leverage and gaining from others' suffering. But with her hilariously human weaknesses, Katherine is vulnerable and the kindness of others (letting her pee like a lady, buying her medication, and giving her the truck keys to aid her escape from Silas) motivate her to act in kind. She no doubt realizes that having a super-strong hunter as her protector gives her a better chance at survival, given she's alone on the lam from an immortal psychic, but Katherine could easily have kept running. The boys act decently toward her, because they're decent people, and Katherine seems to learn (a little) from their example. While she's far from "even" with Jeremy now, when she shoots Silas and saves Jeremy, she takes a teeny step toward earning the good treatment she's been enjoying, and perhaps no longer being an object to barter. Whatever happens with Katherine as she's forced to face the grim limitations of mortality, "True Lies" gives us plenty of instantly classic Katherine moments, thanks to Nina Dobrev's comedic instincts. Pairing her with the two mortal characters in the show provides for some nice commentary on what makes us human and allows Matt and Jeremy to quickly come into their own this season.

Damon gets the gang in trouble by keeping secrets, but it's Jeremy who doesn't change his ways by episode's end. He's been somewhat amusingly feeding Bonnie's insight about Silas's plans to Damon, and when Bonnie asks him to continue keeping her massive secret, he vows to help her, to lie away her death in a time of supernatural insanity and personal tragedy. They both know they can't keep up the ruse forever, or for long, but Bonnie just isn't ready to accept the fact that she is dead and trapped in supernatural purgatory. Her stoic insistence that it's not *so* bad is transparently false to Matt, when he finds himself briefly on the Other Side. In a heartbreaking moment, he embraces her, tells her it's not okay, and allows her to grieve what she has

> "I love the first run of Katherine being human and having Matt and Jeremy kind of being her punching bags but then standing up for themselves and protecting each other from her, but also ultimately protecting her. I loved those three together in those early episodes. I loved Damon with her and just being so like, 'I could give a shit about you.' But it was so fun. The Katherine-being-human storyline and everything that orbited around it and all the characters that played a part in it, I loved."
>
> — Julie Plec

lost. It's a beautiful friendship moment between these two characters who have grieved together before, and Bonnie experiences catharsis thanks to his acknowledgment of her death. But that solace is temporary. When Matt returns to the Land of the Living, he doesn't remember his time with Bonnie or the secret that she and Jeremy are keeping. It's a strange circumstance layered onto a very human and relatable experience of grief. The opening scene when she recounts her father's murder to Jeremy reinforces just how isolated Bonnie is and how much tragedy she's experienced in her short life (and afterlife). There may be nothing she can do to change her situation, but Bonnie is just as Elena describes Stefan: scared, lonely, and in a lot of pain.

Bonnie isn't ready to accept that she's dead or that her father was brutally murdered, and it makes her choice to lie about it (and to make Jeremy keep up her lies for her) understandable, just as Damon's lies to Elena were rooted in a desire to protect her, a hopeless bid to safeguard her happiness. As Jesse says in his insightful conversation with Caroline in the wood shed (because college quads totally have wood sheds), we are just unwilling to hear certain truths; we won't believe them until the undeniable happens. That self-delusion is what makes Silas's emotional manipulation and psychological insight such a powerful weapon: he forces these moments of reckoning, in a manner reminiscent of master-manipulator Katherine. "Cockiness masking fear. How transparent," says Silas to Damon, and that's the kind of insight Katherine Pierce is wont to take advantage of herself. While it's a pleasure to watch the delightfully devilish Silas interact with (and emotionally eviscerate) anyone, the interactions between Silas and Damon are particularly charged and entertaining (not least thanks to Damon's "you've never had sex with me" comment). Silas is ruthless in the grand tradition of *Vampire Diaries* villains, snapping Matt's neck and on the brink of killing Jeremy, and just as cagey about his plans as Damon once was. Katherine's longevity came down not to weapons, or even to the physical prowess of being a vampire, but to her ruthlessness, and Silas is proving a worthy opponent because he lacks what Katherine now possesses more than ever: a fear of dying.

COMPELLING MOMENT Matt giving Bonnie a moment to grieve while he's on the Other Side.

CIRCLE OF KNOWLEDGE

- No Tyler in this episode.
- *True Lies* is a 1994 American action-comedy, cowritten and directed by James Cameron, about a man living a lie. Harry Tasker (Arnold Schwarzenegger) is not a boring salesman who travels a lot for work but a secret government operative. Soon his wife and daughter are entangled in his international spy intrigue and their lives are endangered; harmony in the marriage isn't restored until Mrs. Tasker (Jamie Lee Curtis) is in on the action — a parallel to Damon and Elena's lies-cause-chaos plot line in this episode.
- Dr. Maxfield, who doesn't seem overly fond of bonfire parties, starts his microbiology class by talking about the rancid smell in corpses and quizzing the chatty girls in the back about the bacterium that causes it. When an animal or human body dies, the process of decomposition begins immediately: bacteria in the intestine begin to feed on the intestine itself (instead of just its contents), which causes the release of the body's enzymes as organ tissues break down. Decay spreads to the surrounding organs and tissues thanks to the chemicals released and the bacteria's new all-you-can-eat buffet options. The body itself releases its gases — methane, carbon dioxide, and hydrogen sulfide — and the bacteria also produce gas as they chomp through the corpse. Maxfield implies there is one specific bacterium that causes the stink, but in fact all your released internal bacteria conspire together to produce that super duper terrible smell that insects adore.

- On the phone with Elena, Damon talks about compulsion, threats of violence, torture, and describes himself as a "reformed serial killer" right in front of the Mystic Falls police department. Ain't no thing.
- At the bonfire party, Jesse tells Elena about rumors that "Dr. Dickfield" is part of a campus secret society. "What, like middle-aged men at an Elk lodge?" asks Elena, referring to the Benevolent and Protective Order of Elks, one of the most well-known fraternal orders, founded in 1868. Requirements for membership are being over 21 years old and an American citizen, having good moral character and a belief in God, and initiates into the Order must pledge to conceal the secrets of the Order, protect their fellow brothers, and uphold the Constitution.
- "I'm the leverage. I'm that thing that everyone wants. I'm the frickin' moonstone," says Katherine in a killer callback to the ultimate *Vampire Diaries* MacGuffin from season two. Now a mortal doppelgänger, Katherine is a bargaining chip, sought by powerful immortals. This puts her in a role reversal with Elena. In season two, Elena was "the doppelgänger," more object than person, of great import to Klaus and used as valuable leverage. Both women have been treated like the moonstone, something to be acquired and destroyed, and they share a strong distaste for such objectification.
- When Silas grabs Matt's head to speak to the "occupant," he asks, "Why are you watching me, Traveler?" and then, in Czech, says, "Answer me."
- When Nadia and Gregor corner Silas in the convenience store, he says, "Oh, the gypsies are here," but then snarkily acknowledges that gypsies is not a PC term compared to "Travelers." The term "gypsy" has historically been used to describe a class or ethnic group that maintains a nomadic lifestyle, such as the Romani and other tribes of South Asian origin, while Travelers described groups of European origin. However, "gypsy" is now considered to be a derogatory term and a racial slur, suggesting illegal activities and cultural peculiarity, so when Silas mentions killing Gregor's host, the "blond-haired, blue-eyed" Matt Donovan, there's an undercurrent of racial tension.

HISTORY LESSON Mister "Call Me Dr. Maxfield" tells his class that Whitmore College was founded as a hospital during the American Civil War (1861–1865). While camps had field hospitals to provide immediate medical aid to those most egregiously injured, hospitals provided longer-term, convalescent care for the sick and wounded. Roughly two-thirds of the Civil War's 620,000 casualties were from disease, not from wounds inflicted in battle. Poor hygiene, filthy and overcrowded camp conditions, inadequate diet, exposure, virus-carrying bugs, and contaminated water all contributed to the rapid spread of disease among soldiers. If they didn't die from infections and gangrene as a result of their wounds, soldiers had a good chance of contracting one of the following maladies: yellow fever, tuberculosis, smallpox, swamp fever, malaria, pneumonia, scarlet fever, whooping cough, measles, typhoid fever, chicken pox, and mumps. Dysentery, which causes pain and swelling of the intestine, severe diarrhea, and fever, was the most common cause of death in Union and Confederate soldiers. Disease and infection was so widespread, in fact, that soldiers did not have much confidence in doctors at all, and it was not unheard of for a wounded or sick man to refuse medical care. Mid-19th century doctors were woefully under-trained and had little practical knowledge of sanitation or how disease spread, and they often unintentionally infected patients themselves. Contrary to Dr. Maxfield's assertion that disease was such a problem that bodies were rounded up and burned once a week, the primary method of body disposal at the time was burial, not burning, largely due to the prevalence of Protestant Christian beliefs.

THE RULES Through magical possession, a Traveler can use a human's mind as a host, in this case to spy on Silas through Matt's eyes. Silas cannot read the minds of the possessed nor can he compel them since there's already someone "in there" blocking him.

We learn why the Gilbert ring was taking longer and longer to resurrect Alaric (and it wasn't because Esther had been chatting him up on the Other Side). The wearer of the ring awakens on the Other Side further away from his body each time he dies; he only returns to life when he reconnects with it. Matt is unable to remember his interaction with Bonnie (although he did remember talking to Vicki after he resurrected from a "natural" death in "The Reckoning," 3.05). Bonnie describes the feeling of being on the Other Side as a "void" and "emptiness." Despite his ability to see ghosts, Jeremy doesn't see Matt when he and Katherine run past his spirit; this is because of the lack of a push-and-pull from both parties, the necessity of which we learned about in season two during Jeremy's "spiritual" relationship with Anna.

As a hunter, Jeremy is impervious to Silas's psychic powers. As seen in the

© Andrew Evans/PRPhotos

"In my experience, we editors have the freedom to experiment with sound and picture as we want. However, there is one thing we don't do: slow motion! If something has been established as mythological rule (e.g., transitioning to the Other Side, when and how we see ghosts — they're there, then not there . . .), we try to be consistent. But when we're assembling scenes, we're free to try and be as creative and original as we please. Sometimes it works, sometimes not!"

— Marc Pollon

previous episode, Silas is weaker and slower than a vampire, and it takes him longer to recover from serious injuries (like two shotgun blasts).

PREVIOUSLY ON *THE VAMPIRE DIARIES* Elena compares the vampire death cover-up at Whitmore College by Dr. Maxfield to the Founders' Council's practice in Mystic Falls, where doctors such as Meredith Fell forged death certificates ("The New Deal," 3.10). Elena suggests mimicking Damon's season one strategy: he kept his vampire status a secret by infiltrating the council in "162 Candles" (1.08), cozying up to Sheriff Forbes, offering Zach Salvatore's stash of vervain, and taking credit for killing vampire-problem Logan Fell ("The Turning Point," 1.10).

Caroline's choice of drama as a major is a change from her pre-vampire career goal: she expressed interest in TV journalism in "The Turning Point."

Sheriff Forbes aids Damon here in his search for Stefan, just like she helped him track Stefan down in "The Birthday" (3.01).

Katherine has always been a sucker for Matt Donovan's blue eyes, first falling under their spell in "The Return" (2.01): "His eyes are so blue!"

Whitmore College boasts a consistent hiring policy: handsome but creepy. Dr. Wes is this year's model of last season's Professor Atticus Shane (4.04–4.14).

Damon walking in on Caroline in a towel and saying, "No one cares," recalls one of his greatest lines from "Children of the Damned" (1.13) when he interrupts Stefan and Elena in bed: "If I see something I haven't seen before, I'll throw a dollar at it."

When Silas sees Damon on campus, he greets with him with a traditional "Hello, brother," which we first heard Damon say to Stefan in the pilot (1.01).

Elena is shaken out of her Silas trance when Damon spits vervain water on her, much like Caroline was awoken from her Silas trance in "The Walking Dead" (4.22) when Rebekah slapped her across the face.

In order to avoid being killed, Damon gets Elena to think about something more powerful than her rage against him, namely her concern for Stefan, and this helps her resist Silas's mind control. Similarly, Stefan resisted Klaus's compulsion to kill Elena by focusing on his love for her in "The Reckoning."

Jeremy's ready lie that Bonnie is grieving her father's death by withdrawing with family will ring true since that's exactly what she did after Grams died in "Fool Me Once" (1.14).

OFF CAMERA Dr. Wes Maxfield, hot-but-arrogant microbiology professor and signer of suspicious death certificates, is played by Zimbabwe-raised Rick Cosnett, an actor and voice-over artist based in Sydney, Australia, and Los Angeles. Cosnett has appeared in a handful of Australian television shows and short films and had a small role in *The Trojan Horse*, a Canadian miniseries. The role of Dr. Maxfield was his first recurring guest star role on an American TV series, as well his first opportunity to road test his American accent. He was subsequently cast as Eddie Thawne on The CW's 2014 *Arrow* spin-off, *The Flash*. "With Dr. Maxfield, we had a very clear vision," says Caroline Dries. "So when our casting team — Lesli [Gelles-Raymond] and Greg [Orson] — mentioned [Cosnett] was available, we were like, 'Actually we're creating this Dr. Wes guy that he may be perfect for.' And it worked out."

Speaking with *TV Fanatic* prior to his character's introduction, Cosnett described Dr. Maxfield as neither helpful nor kind, but a very intelligent man: "It's safe to say he might know more than anyone else [about the supernatural world]." He also had an interesting way of describing his character. "I describe him as Indiana Jones with a house in Nantucket," he told *ET Online*. "He's a really smart, incredibly driven, hands-on professor who knows a lot about everything." Despite his character's immediate shady status, Cosnett found the passionate fanbase of *The Vampire Diaries* endearing, and he claims a love for genre film and television fan culture.

Director Joshua Butler on "True Lies"

On working with writers: The great thing about television is how much the studios, networks, and producers value the writers. I always have the pleasure of being on set with the writers of my episodes, and they are incredibly valuable to have around — not just for moral support, but also for instant on-set collaboration when questions arise. It was a pleasure to go back to Whitmore for the first time after "The Five," and Brian Young's script for "True Lies" was so fun and funny and romantic. I was so excited to direct that episode.

On his background as an editor: I think editing is an extremely valuable skill to have as an episodic television director. The episodic television pace is so much faster than on most traditional feature films, and we're often asked to shoot six to eight pages of the script during the allotted hours of the shooting day. In a way, the whole enterprise is a big mathematical equation — how many shots, takes, angles, variations do we have time to get and still "make our day"? As the director, I have to make sure I stage scenes efficiently and only shoot what is necessary, while still getting options for the writers and producers, who might want to try different things in the editing room. I have to approach that task with editorial choices in mind instead of just "hosing it down," which is how we describe shooting anything and everything without having a vision for how it will come together in editing.

On the Other Side: The challenge of creating different "worlds" in an episode like "True Lies" is to make sure the audience accepts the reality of what they're seeing when they're seeing it. Michael Karasick, my brilliant director of photography on that episode, and I decided reality would simply be the gorgeous, deep, rich palette that *TVD* is known for. In Stefan's dream sequence, Mike used filters to glow the sunlight coming off the water in the quarry and we "warmed up" the images, giving them a truly magical feel. For the Other Side, we went the opposite direction. There are cold colors (blues and greens) and we made sure to make the woods a lot more smoky and sparse than they usually appear in the world of *TVD*. Plus, I worked with my awesome editor Marc Pollon to create a sound design for the Other Side that would be truly haunting. In a way, all of the creative decisions were stemming from Bonnie's plight and her extreme loneliness wandering in a world where she can't interact with the people she loves. I think we achieved that feeling, and Kat Graham certainly dazzled us with her performance.

On the fun of doppelgängers: I thought Paul Wesley was absolutely incredible as Silas. He gave Silas a bemused worldview and a sharp wit that so beautifully differentiated him from Stefan. My favorite scene is when Silas confronts Nadia and Gregor in the convenience store at the end of "True Lies." Paul just *knew* how to convey a world-weary guy who has been alive for a couple of millennia and has little tolerance for those who threaten him in any way. The fight with Jeremy was also hugely entertaining to shoot. Both Paul and Steven displayed such physicality in those moments, and they both brought their A-game, even though we were shooting that scene in the middle of the night. On a side note, Brian Young cleverly added Jeremy's line to Silas — "Plus, I work out" — which was, yes, commenting on how buff Steven was when he started season five.

On the art of making TV: I think that the common misperception about directing for television is that because shows are shot so much more quickly than feature films, episodic television is in some ways a "lesser" medium. I believe the exact opposite: we are in a golden age of television, and even feature film directors are crossing over because they want to be a part of it. Yes, the money is usually tighter and the hours are sometimes longer and the shooting schedules a lot more demanding, but that doesn't mean we make an inferior product. We use limitations to make us more creative and prove that it is possible to make great art under more challenging circumstances.

On the challenges of shooting this series, cinematographer Michael Karasick says, "*Vampire Diaries* is lots of nights; that's just a general challenge. We do a pretty good job though of keeping a reasonable schedule, just so that everyone does make it through the marathon, so to speak. There's lots of heavy scenes, lots of emotional scenes, so some days it can be pretty heavy duty on set — because of the emotion of the scene. I mean, there's always weather to deal with! Those guys are like kings of the weather — [producers] Trish [Stanard] and Pascal [Verschooris] are amazing at predicting the weather now; they have this amazing skill."

FOGGY MOMENTS Why didn't Elena just go talk to Dr. Maxfield instead of changing both her and Caroline's course loads?

Where did Matt and Jeremy get all their camping gear? Jer's house burned down and Matt doesn't seem to have much of anything he can call his own. Pit stop at the camping goods store while on the run from Silas?

Whitmore College doesn't mind students setting up a *bonfire* in the center of the quad?

Setting aside the fact that Caroline and Elena's giant dorm room *has* a fireplace, why is there a gas line leading into a wood-burning fireplace?

Damon steals back Stefan's daylight ring from Silas. Two questions. How the heck do you steal anything from a super-psychic, let alone a ring that is on his finger, without him knowing? And since Damon and Elena expected to find Stefan in the safe when Sheriff Forbes brings them to it in the woods, why the heck did they open it in broad daylight, knowing that Stefan didn't have his daylight ring on and would burn?

QUESTIONS

- Silas says to Damon that he is more like a "distant nephew" to him than a brother. Are doppelgängers blood-related in the traditional human sense (i.e., continuous bloodline running from 2,000 years ago through to Stefan), or are they only blood-related in a mystical, magical, woo-woo way?
- Is the connection between Stefan and Elena due to them both being doppelgängers?
- Stefan can't get far without his daylight ring. Where is he? Did he kill the man in the safe? Who is the man in the safe?
- Does Jesse know more about vampires than he is letting on, or is he just fond of holding would-be stakes in casual conversation about secret societies?
- Is Dr. Maxfield in a secret society and is it akin to Mystic Falls' Founders' Council? Was Grayson Gilbert in the secret society? Does the college that was originally a Civil War hospital have a long history of dealing with the undead?
- Silas tells Damon that he has a soft spot for brunettes. Was his one true love (the one Qetsiyah killed) a brunette?
- What is Nadia's agenda and why does she say she doesn't consider herself a Traveler? Can *any* Traveler possess a human or only some of them?
- Nadia says that all the Travelers have ever wanted is for Silas to be in the tomb, forever imprisoned. Since this is only a very recent escape he's made, what have they been doing for the past 2,000 years? Are they witches or something else? Do Travelers consider hunters their enemies since the hunters want Silas dead, not imprisoned? Why don't they want him dead?
- Does Silas still have Elena's phone?

Tessa: You and I are the same, Damon.
The obstacle standing between two fates. Silas had his true love and Stefan has Elena. We're merely the conflict that makes it interesting.

5.03 *Original Sin*

Original air date October 17, 2013
Written by Melinda Hsu Taylor and Rebecca Sonnenshine
Directed by Jesse Warn
Edited by Joel T. Pashby **Cinematography by** Darren Genet
Guest cast Alyssa Lewis (Elena Double), Briana Laurel Venskus (Jo)
Previously on *The Vampire Diaries* Paul Wesley

Stefan learns Qetsiyah's side of the story — complete with flashback Silas hair! — while Damon and the lady doppelgängers try to track him down. Nadia tries to out-maneuver Silas.

"It doesn't sound crazy. It *is* crazy," says Damon to Elena when she wants to follow the clues from her psychic dream to find Stefan. He's right: the whole thing is crazy — and that's part of the charm of *The Vampire Diaries*, its willingness to stick a wig on its lead actor and zip him back 2,000 years in a love-triangle-gone-wrong story that parallels the ongoing tension between Stefan, Elena, and Damon. In "Original Sin," the series takes us as far back in time as it's ever been to a settlement of mystical people in Ancient Greece: an epic tale of soul mates, spells, love, destiny, and destruction. Taking its title from the Old Testament story of man's fall from grace, the episode introduces us to a character we'd only heard about in season four, giving us Qetsiyah's side of the story in a he said/she said situation that has had far-reaching and long-lived consequences. But you never can trust what you hear from supernatural baddies, and trust issues abound in "Original Sin." Qetsiyah, a questionable and biased source if ever there was one, says she has trust issues, thanks to the "original sin" that set her on the course of revenge she's been on for two millennia.

Duped into thinking he loved her as much as she loved him, Qetsiyah was ready and willing to spend a literal eternity with her "soul mate," unaware that he believed his soul mate was another woman, Amara. Qetsiyah describes herself to Stefan as a "lovesick idiot" with the wisdom of 2,000 years of hindsight, and she's right: she created a spell that bred mass destruction and discord, all for naught. The image of Qetsiyah left at the altar, the decay around her spreading as a result of the immortality elixir she created, is a potent one: the paradise she knew has been poisoned, irreparably. But even before the betrayal, the crazy was there: neither Silas nor Qetsiyah could possibly have been sane, rational, well-adjusted people to toy with their power and with eternity like that. The Salvatores have done some pretty kooky stuff in the name of love (first for Katherine, then for Elena). They've killed. They've been killed. Turned against each other. Gone back to *high school.* But Silas and Qetsiyah set a new high-water mark for intensity. Doing anything for the one you love means "bending the rules of possible," as Qetsiyah tells Stefan. And outside her ancient tale of doomed romance lie parallel storylines. The Stefan-Elena-Damon triangle gets harangued on all sides by people claiming one match or another is meant to be, while Nadia tells Gregor she would do anything for him, so strong is her love, and she's plotting to find a way for him to escape death. It's an impossibly romantic and terribly unrealistic ideal that is front and center in "Original Sin": true love, soul mates never parted — not even by death. And the real crux of the story of Silas, Amara, and Qetsiyah is its moral about the consequences of doing *anything* in the name of love. To spend eternity with the one *he* loved, Silas pulled a long con on Qetsiyah, fooling her into thinking he loved her and wanted to marry her, so he could take advantage of her power and get her to make an immortality elixir. Silas leaves her stranded at the altar, flowers wilting, her heart broken, the elixir stolen, and her humiliation public. Not cool, dude.

There's a thin line between love and hate, and Qetsiyah's passion quickly found a new outlet — her dedication to vengeance is unrivaled. It's a very deliberate choice to have Stefan be the audience to Tessa's tale: not only is there a layer of mystical weirdness with her telling her story to a man who has the same face as her betrayer Silas, but Stefan can relate to the core of Qetsiyah's experience. Stefan once believed that he was Elena's one true love ("It's you and me, Stefan — always") but Elena changed her mind. While she has, of course, every right to change her mind, the pain of losing an eternity with someone you thought was your soul mate remains the same, no matter the manner in which the dumper leaves the dumpee. He also shares Tessa's burning desire for revenge on Silas; mere hours before hearing that the original version of him has been a total dick for 2,000 years, Stefan had been entombed underwater in extraordinary pain, the months passing like an eternity, because Silas put him there. Though in the final moments of the episode, we see Stefan's plan may be thwarted thanks to Tessa zapping his brain free of memories, Stefan very clearly states that he wants to be *himself* when he gets his revenge on Silas. He didn't flip the switch, and not because his Elena vision told him not to, but because he needs to know the full satisfaction of killing Silas.

That intensity is but a shadow when compared to Qetsiyah's. Her initial intention with the immortality spell was to make her and Silas's love "last forever," but the consequences were an eternity of vengeance, the love between Silas and Amara echoing over millennia in the form of their doppelgängers, and Silas and Amara themselves kept apart. Stefan is told that the "second chance" Qetsiyah offered Silas is the Cure: to drink it and spend a long mortal life with her, knowing full well he would refuse and she would play her trump card, holding up a human heart and telling him she cured and then killed his beloved Amara. It's the perfect punishment, foiled only because Silas is her equal when it comes to stubbornness and determination. While Qetsiyah was willing to create an elixir for her and Silas, Silas takes it one step further: his love for Amara is perhaps the only earnest thing about him, and his devotion prevents him from giving in to Tessa's plan. He would rather suffer for 2,000 years than drink the Cure and wind up on the Other Side with her. And now they are back on common ground thanks to their desire for the Cure: she wants Silas to consume it, and what could he want it for other than to consume it himself?

Like Tessa who is willing to placate Stefan with the promise of a daylight ring and keen to manipulate Damon with tales of the doppelgängers' destiny, Nadia, the other newbie badass in town, displays just such ruthlessness and single-mindedness. Nadia plays all sides. She tells Matt to trust her. She tells Gregor she will do anything for him and will find a way to make him permanent in Matt's body. She strings Silas along while she goes after Katherine and she disobeys his clear instruction to kill Matt. Matt's life is under her protection as long as Gregor lurks inside him, but Nadia has proven she's willing to go to great lengths with seemingly no qualms. She has hijacked Matt's body to use as a vessel for the boyfriend she stabbed in the neck, all for a dangerous alliance with Silas, one she breaks the first chance she gets at nabbing Katherine. Nadia may not be forthcoming about *why* she's doing what she's doing, but she's clear about the *how*: by any means necessary.

The fruit of the original sin — arguably both Silas and Amara's sin for

Writer Melinda Hsu Taylor on "Original Sin"

On setting Silas and Qetsiyah's origin story in Ancient Greece: That was a practical consideration, because we wanted it to be more or less the year zero, so we needed a place that was somewhat civilized at that time, or somewhat recognizable to a TV audience. A lot of times you pick things because it is a shorthand, people are going to get that instantly — for economy of screen time, do the quickest possible "we're in the storybook now, we're in Ancient Greece." People understand those costumes and what that setting is.

But in terms of the geography, we wanted something where people could be ethnically diverse because the Bennett line of witches is African American and we've had a lot of witches of color; not all of them, but we wanted to allow for that possibility. And that was one reason we were so delighted to find Janina, who is a terrific actress and of Indian descent but also, you know, she looks like a lot of different kinds of mixed cultures, which was what we going for. But at the same time, it had to be a place where someone who looked like Paul Wesley could hang out, and it couldn't be so exotic that you'd be like, "What's this white dude doing here?"

I did a little bit of Wikipedia-ing and Google-ing and found out that that part of Greece — if you pointed on a map, *this* part of Greece — had been colonized by the Romans at a certain point, so in the backstory in my head, Silas was a member of this kind of Roman government arm that was living with the locals, had gotten accepted as a prominent leader, and was very established in this kind of society that Qetsiyah lived in, so it was very natural that they would marry. Kind of the heads of their respective social groups. So we just didn't want any of that to be an issue, so — Ancient Greece.

On the backstory we didn't see: What we talked about in the [writers'] room was: there's always been magic in the world, from ancient times, before Qetsiyah, there were people who could do simple spirit magic, people who we think of now as witches. But then Qetsiyah and Silas doing their thing created an imbalance and they were clearly pushed out of normal witch society for that and forced to wander the earth as the Travelers. So in a way, Qetsiyah's family became the original Travelers. Like, all the folks at the wedding, they sort of became Travelers — even though they had nothing to do with it and it wasn't their fault, they sort of guilt-by-association got kicked out.

In fact there was a character, her brother, who fit in really well but unfortunately ended up on the cutting-room floor for length, but her brother had a whole scene with her in the script, in the writer's draft, where he freaked out on her after what she'd done and killed her over Silas's headstone, which is where she'd been mourning and that's how the blood got into the headstone.

But that was just the writer's draft and we just didn't have room for it, because it was a script that was quite a bit longer than what we were able to shoot on our schedule, so we had to trim it down. But that was the idea — that he was horrified, he killed her with one of those Traveler knives, but it was just too late, and the land around them was withering and they were packing up. But in that piece of dialogue between Qetsiyah and her brother, there was mention of her brother's family. So that was the idea — that there was a whole family unit that was going off to wander the world.

On using Tessa as a storyteller: It was something that I had to work on a lot. Because Stefan, in my first draft, was a little too passive. There was a lot of him listening, taking things in, reacting to things she says, but not a lot for him to do. In the second draft of the script, I had to go through and figure out what he was doing both in a physical way and also character actions. If the actor asks you on set, "Why am I saying this to her?" I prefer to be prepared with a response like, "You are punishing her for what she just said." It's like if you, as the writer, can orient yourself in what the character or actor is doing, it makes the words come more easily in the dialogue, and I think it's easier for the actor to play it. At least they can have a conversation with me, even if it's not working for them. At least you have a starting point to say, "In this scene . . ."

With Tessa and Stefan, I went through and did a lot of that sort of thinking. What is she doing? She's trying to tell her side of the story; she is in a way stalling, because she has no intention of freeing him, but she is expositionally laying the track for a lot of what's going on in the plot. But for Stefan, he's stuck and he does want to know what's going on and he's humoring her a little bit, and then he makes a break for it. In every scene, there's a kind of a central thing going on between them and if you can make them in direct opposition to each other, the two characters, it's helpful to the scene.

consuming the elixir and Qetsiyah's for creating it — are the doppelgängers. According to Qetsiyah, they are star-crossed lovers fated to be together by "the universe." The sudden reference to forces greater than any individual's will is jarring for the characters. Tessa's biblical storybook tale that is literally ancient history has very immediate implications, ones that Damon and Elena rail against. *The Vampire Diaries* has a near obsession with the idea of choice — of free will, of deciding one's fate, of choosing how to react to whatever hellfire and grief is thrown in one's path, of deciding on which version of oneself to be. A lot of those choices have been intricately tied up with the characters' choices of who to love. Damon's speech to Elena at episode's end perfectly encapsulates that spirit of defiance; it's a John Locke "Don't tell me what I can't do" moment. But how do you defy the universe? We've long heard of "Nature" as a force in the magical world of *TVD* — it balances, it provides power to witches — but the universe is a new player, and Qetsiyah is openly derided by the Salvatores and by Elena for believing in its willfulness. But what qualifies as crazy? Is it any crazier or freakier for the universe to have a plan than for Nature to make shadow selves of immortal Travelers? Whatever power there is to the universe's will, however fixed the doppelgängers' destiny is, the romantic triangle is again complicated. What greater force must true love overcome than the frickin' will of the universe? Or, if you prefer the other pairing, what greater validation of It Was Meant to Be than the frickin' will of the universe? However you slice it, Elena is, as always, in the center, pulled in two directions. We will see if her will can triumph over influence, after last season's adventures with the sire bond.

There's an inherent danger in Damon's romantic notion that Elena is his sole purpose in life, as he says she is in his passionate speech. What happened to Qetsiyah when her life was Silas, and he took that away from her? The cautionary tale of this original love triangle doesn't seem to have yet sunk in, and Damon and Elena brush off the idea that the doppelgängers' wills might not be their own. Damon and Elena are confident that they can subvert this crazy idea of fate but their will is clearly subject to powerful forces, like a resurrected, vengeful witch. Tessa is capable of subverting anyone's will should they get in her way or betray her. She plants the psychic dreams in Katherine and Elena to draw them to her (though it's unclear what she needed Elena for), and in her biggest move of all time, she created a supernatural purgatory to force Silas into, an eternity of payback on him for eluding an eternity with her. Since he thwarted that plan she has come up with another, and she breaks Stefan in the process. With no memory, he becomes what Tessa said she wanted to make Silas into: an immortal nobody.

The curious and hitherto unanswerable question of just how similar the doppelgängers would be without their unique experiences could now, perhaps, be put to the test. Stefan's capacity for violence, his penchant for vengeance, his determination, and his unlimited capacity to love a doppelgänger are all traits he shares with Silas. While human Katherine is still delightfully (and thankfully) Katherine in all her shit-disturbing ways, she's also displaying glimpses of the humanity that Elena says she wanted Katherine to rediscover in herself. Katherine rather hilariously describes Elena as boring, self-righteous, and condescending, but she thanks her . . . and she seems to mean it when she says she's glad to know that Elena cares. Katherine-as-mortal has been an opportunity for comedy gold and subtle pathos as she experiences the mundanity of being human. She's cold, she's hungry, she's slow, she gets carsick in the backseat. Who in the world ever expected to see Elena come to Katherine's aid, protecting her from an assailant and ordering her to run? As Katherine became reliant on Damon, Elena, and company for protection from Silas, and as their interests align, the dynamic between the characters shifts in entertaining and revealing ways. And now with Stefan waking up from Tessa's spell with no memory of who the two most important people in his life are, he's going to have a ton more to catch up on than just who drank the Cure.

COMPELLING MOMENT The beautifully filmed cold open, with Stefan staggering, pre-dawn sky behind him.

CIRCLE OF KNOWLEDGE

- No Tyler, Jeremy, Caroline, or Bonnie in this episode.
- While *The Vampire Diaries* tends to skirt around religion, the concept of "original sin" is particular to Christianity with parallels between Adam and Eve and Silas and Amara. Their sins (both committed in gardens) are responsible for the fall of man and the warped supernatural world order of doppelgängers, respectively. From Qetsiyah's perspective, the sin lies in the betrayal, like that of Adam and Eve betraying God's rule. The sin against Nature that causes the ripple effect is the immortality spell itself — committed by consuming the forbidden-fruit of an immortality elixir.
- When Stefan stumbles into Jo's Bar, Jo the Bartender tells him that last call was four hours ago; last call in Virginia is 2 a.m., so it's about 6 a.m. during this scene. Jo's Bar is located along U.S. Route 29, which runs through Virginia and, according to the map Bonnie used to locate Elena after she was kidnapped by Rose and Trevor in "Rose" (2.08), it's very close to where the fictional Mystic Falls is located.
- Nadia is a vampire, and there are two clues leading up to the reveal: even though she's working with and in love with Gregor, she said to Silas she

"never really considered herself" a Traveler in "True Lies," and her lapis lazuli daylight ring is visible on the index finger of her right hand when she grips Matt's face to call forth Gregor in this episode.

- Qetsiyah and Stefan both get dialogue mileage out of casting her as the "woman scorned," which originates from the 1697 play *The Mourning Bride* by English playwright William Congreve: "Heaven has no rage like love to hatred turned, Nor hell a fury like a woman scorned." Professor Shane also used the phrase when telling the Silas-Qetsiyah story in "We All Go a Little Mad Sometimes" (4.06).
- Qetsiyah snarks about the hunters failing in their task to kill Silas. Lady, if you want a job done, maybe don't involve mystical tattoos that gradually appear as you kill more and more vampires, only to lead to a "map" appearing in pieces and featuring clues written in Aramaic. Just light a path in blue fire for your mystical hunks to follow to the tomb.

HISTORY LESSON Ancient Greece 2,000 years ago means Qetsiyah, Silas, and Amara lived during the period of Roman rule commonly referred to as — wait for it — "Roman Greece." When our original love triangle of doom happened, Rome was ruled by its founding emperor, Augustus, from 27 BCE to 14 CE. Despite the strong influence of the Roman Empire, Greek culture — from religion to commerce to literature — had spread as far as Britain, and Greek trumped Latin as the language of educated, cultured people.

THE RULES Gregor made himself a "passenger" inside Matt, and now that Gregor's body has been killed, he is trapped. The passenger inside a host doesn't seem to have any power over when they appear, rather another person must call them forth, as Nadia does with her special Czech phrase (which means . . . come forth). When Gregor is in control, Matt loses time and does not remember what happened to him (and totally misses the rest of his shift at the Grill). The passenger spell is a poor-man's version of Klaus's old favorite, the body-jump spell, wherein he can enter someone else's body and retain complete control until he decides to return to his own.

You know a witch is serious when she makes *blue* fire . . . Living up to her reputation, Qetsiyah proves to be a powerhouse: she created the immortality elixir and the Cure, and she plants dreams in Katherine's and Elena's subconsciouses to draw them to her. She wants Katherine because she knows

© David Gabber/PRPhotos.com

Katherine has the Cure running through her veins, and her plan is to weaken Silas, then force him to take the Cure — a.k.a. drink Katherine's blood.

Using a variety of local flora, fire, molten metal, and some incantations, Qetsiyah erases Silas's psychic abilities via a spell performed on his doppelgänger. Silas's powers are gone and Stefan wakes up amnesiac. Qetsiyah tells Stefan that Silas's abilities were not always so strong and that he has honed them over the past two millennia.

When Silas and Amara consumed the immortality elixir, the life around them — the pretty wedding setup in particular — all died. Qetsiyah explains the consequence of the immortality spell: all living things must die, so an immortal thing violates the natural law. The doppelgänger is Nature's way of creating balance — a mortal iteration of the immortal. Silas cannot be killed, but his doppelgänger, or shadow self, can.

PREVIOUSLY ON *THE VAMPIRE DIARIES* In season four, we learned from Professor Shane that Qetsiyah lived 2,000 years ago ("After School Special," 4.10) and that Silas had been entombed on an island for 2,000 years ("Down the Rabbit Hole," 4.14).

In the flashback, Silas says, "When I look at you, Amara, all I see is an angel." If only Katherine knew that she could use it in her argument that she and Stefan are meant to be: in the 1864 flashback in "Memory Lane" (2.04), smitten Stefan says to Katherine, "I look at you and I see an angel."

OFF CAMERA Before her turn as scorned witch Qetsiyah, American actress Janina Gavankar was perhaps best known for her role as Papi on Showtime's series *The L Word*, but she's also had memorable turns on ABC's *The Gates*, FX's *The League*, HBO's *True Blood*, and The CW's *Arrow*. Fans of the site *Funny or Die* will also recognize her from several of the site's shorts. Gavankar is an accomplished musician: she was a member of the singing group Endera, has had her songs licensed for the screen, and has performed on film scores.

"I *loved* Janina," says Caroline Dries. "We saw so many actors for this role. We looked and looked and needed someone who felt contemporary but could play ancient witch mythology. We finally asked The CW if they had any ideas and they suggested Janina. I remembered her from *The L Word* and I thought, huh, really? And I watched her reel and thought she was hilarious in *True Blood*. She just had a way of delivering fun lines. So we decided to go

> "This will sound lame, but I love a lot of act one scenes that set up what the conflict and stakes of the episodes are. One that stands out is 5.03's Elena/Damon scene in act one where they decide they have to go on a road trip and then Katherine pops in and says she's coming. Rebecca [Sonnenshine] wrote that. The reason I liked it was that it very simply and clearly set up stakes and touched on the episode dynamics in the clearest possible way. As a writer, you're always striving to be as clear as possible in the most economical fashion — [to avoid] the tediousness of reset — and Rebecca's stuff was really enjoyable to watch."
>
> — Caroline Dries

with her and hope for the best. And sure enough, she brought a cool energy to the show and had a lot of spunk. Her character really popped."

Gavankar told *TV Guide* that her casting was last minute. "I got a call that *The Vampire Diaries* wanted me to do an arc, but if I wanted to do it I had to leave tomorrow. So I got on a plane and flew to Atlanta. As usual I said, 'Fantastic. Let me read the material.' They send me sides, which give me no information, but when I got a script it ends up being 18 pages of monologue. I was ushered to my dressing room with a bunch of DVDs in hand and stared at the wall for a second like, 'What have I gotten myself into?'" She sat down with episode cowriter Rebecca Sonnenshine to get a handle on the character and backstory. "It was definitely a crash course," says Sonnenshine. "We had about an hour. Janina is very, very smart and engaged. I just tried to give her the simplest, cleanest version of the mythology without making it sound too crazy! Imagine someone trying to absorb all that info the day before shooting. She was really fun to work with. She brought a lot to Tessa — an unhinged streak, a deep emotional woundedness, and excellent comic timing." After that mythology lesson, Janina "had more hair tests and makeup tests than any other show." While she thought fans would understand Tessa's motivations, she admitted they'd also find her to be "a bit extreme and ruthless. So, people will either love her or despise her."

Melinda Hsu Taylor enjoyed writing for Nadia and she found her scene with Matt-as-Gregor "huge fun to write because I had an imagined version of what their relationship was like in Europe and how they'd come over to the States and what their love life was like, essentially, in that brief snippet that you see between them in the alley."

FOGGY MOMENTS Silas doesn't entirely trust Nadia, thinking she may have only killed Gregor to gain Silas's trust and that Gregor may still be alive thanks to Matt's immortality ring — and he's right. Why doesn't he know all of this for certain, since he is a super-powerful mind reader? Wouldn't he have picked up all of that when he read Nadia's mind at the gas station in "True Lies"?

Stefan says Silas is a bloodthirsty immortal who has killed more people than he can count. When did Silas do all that murdering? The people who visited the well to get a vision of their beloved dead didn't all die (as Qetsiyah confirms, saying Silas fed on mere drips of blood from thousands). Silas has been inert for 2,000 years, the only feeding rampage he went on that Stefan knows about was pre-graduation day and he left a relatively small body count (when it comes to these things). Also, *thousands* of people managed to make it to that really-hard-to-get-to location in remote Nova Scotia and dripped blood down to Silas?

Why is Silas's tomb on a remote Nova Scotian island if Silas, Qetsiyah, and their people were in Greece? How did they get to North America — the magic of the *Travelers*? While magic makes anything *possible*, the geography on this is far from plausible. In "Into the Wild," the language on the hunters' tattoos and on the sword is Aramaic, which Klaus theorized was the native tongue of Qetsiyah and Silas. Since we now know it wasn't, why *was* Aramaic used in those contexts?

Gregor says that Nadia slit his throat; to be more precise, she stabbed him in the neck. No slitting. Though Gregor starts their conversation in Czech, Nadia continues it in English. Why wouldn't the two continue speaking in Czech, especially if they're talking about something they don't want overheard?

The bartender says she saw a woman — Qetsiyah, who's been dead and on the Other Side for 2,000 years — throw Stefan in a truck and drive away. When did Qetsiyah learn how to drive? Is that what she's been up to since she was resurrected three months earlier?

Tessa implies to Damon that she's been watching his and Elena's summer of lovin' from the Other Side, but she crossed over before Elena made her post–sire bond choice to be with Damon.

Why did Tessa plant the psychic visions in Elena's head as well as Katherine's? She wants Katherine for her Cure-laced blood, but she has no use for Elena. Did she double-doppelgänger the spell in order to lend credence to the dream, knowing the two were cohabiting with Damon?

QUESTIONS

- Qetsiyah is responsible for Katherine and Elena's dreams of Stefan outside the bar, but she doesn't claim responsibility for or even have a motive for Elena's bad vibes about Stefan all summer. Are those doppelgänger connection feelings, provided by the universe? Did Katherine have them too?
- Why is Qetsiyah so sure that the doppelgängers fated to be together are Stefan and Elena, and not Stefan and Katherine? Or is she simply trying to get Damon to feel so insecure about his relationship that he'll leave his baby brother behind with her?
- Qetsiyah took advantage of the moment Bonnie brought down the veil just before graduation day. How did she stay on the living side when the veil went back up? What has she been up to all summer? Looking for Stefan?
- Could Qetsiyah create another dose of the Cure? What spell is she performing in her last scene of the episode, sitting cross-legged on the cabin floor surrounded by candles and dripping her own blood into a bowl?
- In the flashback scene where Qetsiyah brings Silas those charming wedding gifts, we see a bleeding heart, a lot of blood, but no body. Was Amara killed or was Qetsiyah just tricking Silas into thinking she'd murdered his one true love? Is that why there have been Amara doppelgängers?
- When did Qetsiyah die and how? When did she create the Other Side? Qetsiyah explains the creation of the Other Side as a part of her vengeance plan: Silas would take the Cure and then die, expecting to be reunited with Amara but instead find himself in supernatural purgatory. But by the time Silas sent Professor Shane on his mission, Silas knew about the Other Side and wanted it destroyed. At what point did Silas learn about the Other Side?
- How much of the Silas-Qetsiyah origin story did Esther know when she cast her spell turning her husband and children into vampires? Was she

aware that Tatia was a doppelgänger of Amara, and thus her blood was more powerful than the average person's?

- Qetsiyah tells Damon that the universe has been trying to get the doppelgängers together for *ever*: is she implying that the universe had its hand in Silas and Amara falling in love? Or is she just keen on hyperbole? Nature has a motive for creating doppelgängers: to restore balance. If the universe is drawing them together, what is its end goal? Is it a punishment for Qetsiyah's role in creating the elixir or for messing with the afterlife?
- Why does Gregor need to know where his body is? Since Matt's boots are muddy when he wakes up, can we assume that Gregor found it? Will Nadia be true to her promise to find a way to make Gregor's presence in Matt's body permanent?
- Silas is right not to trust Nadia, who clearly has some other agenda in mind. What did Silas mean when he said Nadia was playing out a "twisted fantasy" with Katherine?
- Just what are Travelers? Silas doesn't seem to consider himself a Traveler, but Tessa refers to them both as part of the powerful people called the Travelers. Is Silas unique among them for having psychic abilities? What was the fallout in Traveler society in the wake of Silas's betrayal and Qetsiyah's revenge?
- Silas tells Katherine that her face makes him want to vomit, yet he told Damon in "True Lies" that he understood why Damon was in love with Elena, sharing a soft spot for brunettes. Is Silas anti-Katherine and pro-Elena? Or does Elena's face make him want to barf too?
- Qetsiyah says she's seen everything now that she's seen Stefan, a vampire doppelgänger with a conscience. There's an implication that, just as Katherine and Elena are different, Stefan and the previous iterations of his doppelgänger form are different. What does that mean for Stefan now that his memories are gone? (Permanently? Temporarily?) Will he still be Stefan-like?

Caroline: Part of me just wishes that I could trade places with you.
Because without all the memories, maybe it wouldn't hurt so damn much.
Stefan: It's okay.
Caroline: It's not.

5.04 *For Whom the Bell Tolls*

Original air date October 24, 2013
Written by Brett Matthews and Elisabeth R. Finch
Directed by Michael Allowitz
Edited by Tony Solomons **Cinematography by** Michael Karasick
Guest cast Gregory Chandler (Patron), Amanda Powell (Waitress)
Previously on *The Vampire Diaries* Paul Wesley

Damon and Elena try to jog Stefan's memory on Remembrance Day in Mystic Falls. When the gang is desperate for Bonnie's help, Jeremy can keep the secret of her death no longer.

With a peculiarly morbid, drunken, and only-in-Mystic-Falls backdrop of a celebration of the beloved dead, "For Whom the Bell Tolls" is this season's "Memorial" or "Ghost World" — a moment to pause and remember, to acknowledge the past and the lost, to examine one's choices and relationships, and to reaffirm the purpose of being decent without reward.

The central tension of the episode comes from throwing an amnesiac Stefan into a day of memorializing. The opening scene is a lot of fun, playing off Stefan's usual intensity, propensity for introspection (even when he was a ripper, as his diaries from the '20s suggest), and guilt-driven sense of morality. But now? He's a blank slate, and who are you without your past? His humorous misinterpretation of himself as "the fun brother" and Damon as "the safe brother" is quickly corrected by Damon spectacularly flipping that stolen car, but Damon — while still fun — is a lot more of a safe brother than when he first sauntered into Mystic Falls. He used to push so hard for Stefan to have blood straight from the vein, but here he encourages restraint, yanking Stefan off the Mystic Grill waitress to keep his brother from unleashing the ripper, from adding more guilt he would later suffer. Stefan without his memories reveals to us just how much Damon has changed. And blank-slate Stefan himself is keen to reshape his identity: he postulates that his tendency to be a serial killer may not be some innate, biologically hardwired behavior, but a reaction to the double-whammy trauma of being a vampire who killed his own father.

While we're unlikely to get a definitive answer to the nature vs. nurture debate on the ripper question, Stefan does manage to change the framework of trust displayed in the cold open. Damon tells him, "Trust me," to which Stefan replies, "Do I have a choice?" By episode's end, Stefan has been through a day of remembrance, and he has figured out a couple of key things he doesn't want in his new, weird existence — Damon and Elena. In attempting to do the impossible — teach someone who they are and their long life history while simultaneously preventing them from being that person and giving into a vampire's instinct to feed and kill — Damon and Elena brush over the more recent developments in their triangle's relationship in a way that misleads Stefan and breaks his faith in them.

What do you do with a newbie vampire? Distract and sublimate. Elena learned those tactics from Stefan himself, who tried to take care of her last season as she became accustomed to her new identity. Faced with a person she knows intimately but who doesn't remember a thing about her, Elena is unsettled. As much as she wants him to gain his memories so he'll regain his sense of self, she wants him to remember *her* so her own identity is restabilized, defined as she is in part by how he feels about her. While he smiles and flirts, she responds in kind; the roles they'd grown into and their history is wiped clean. And though she walks him through her tragic past, their "collision" outside the boys room at Mystic Falls High, the site of her near death and human death, even the vague cause of their breakup (*it's not you, it's me*), Elena seems almost happy to be able to begin again with Stefan. To have him compliment her strength and character without any of the hurt and confusion of their complicated romantic past. And the sublimation works; with Elena as his guide, Stefan doesn't want to feed. While he doesn't remember the halcyon days of when they fell in love, she definitely does. Caught up, Elena begins to reenact the turning point in her relationship with him, and with the help of Sara Bareilles' "Gravity," the echo is made just as nostalgic for us at home. But Elena fails to make Stefan remember her or their love: instead she only reminds herself of what they once shared, and she succeeds in drawing this new Stefan to her again, however intentionally, only to push him away. She's with Damon. That withheld truth breaks the tether Stefan felt to these two kindly strangers. He doesn't want to be the Stefan they knew.

> "I love so much of this season, [but a favorite moment] I immediately thought of is Elena and Stefan in 5.04, 'For Whom the Bell Tolls,' by the side of the river and in a way reliving some of their first connection, you know, and she touches his cheek. And it was such a delicate moment. In the room, some of us — or as least I thought — oh my gosh, she's such a tease [laughs], like why didn't she just blurt it out? Just tell him they're friends. But then when you see the moment onscreen, and it's written beautifully, and it worked perfectly, and you don't feel like she's a tease; you feel like she's trying so hard to tell him, and the connection between them is so natural that it just happens in the best way. And of course he's terribly hurt once he realizes what the truth is and off he goes, and it's the end of an act.
>
> And so it propels you into a great act-out and the rest of the story, which is the best kind of moment in my opinion. When it comes from this really honest place, it's completely visual and emotional and engaging on its own merits, but then [it] serves an entirely crucial function in the story."
>
> — Melinda Hsu Taylor

Though Stefan is alive and in Mystic Falls, he is absent in a way that echoes the lost loved ones the people of Mystic Falls mourn on Remembrance Day.

While Damon and Elena's somewhat accidental secret keeps biting them in the butt and drives Stefan away, Jeremy's revelation of his summer-long deception only brings the gang closer together. With everyone banging down his door to get Bonnie to magically fix everything again, Jeremy reaches his breaking point. As much as he wants to support Bonnie and her choices, he can't deny the truth or be alone with this secret any longer. In a telling move, he doesn't text Elena or Matt to open up to, he texts Damon. It's stunning how different the relationship between these two has become, and Damon's reaction to Jeremy finally admitting that Bonnie is dead, as Damon and Bonnie each beg him not to say it, is particularly powerful. In the past, Damon's grief has manifested as anger and hurt, he's lashed out and he's isolated himself from his fellow mourners. Here he chooses a different path. Thinking of what Jeremy has been through, what he has shouldered alone,

Damon doesn't shoot the messenger but hugs Jeremy, embracing the role of big brother to Little Gilbert.

As odd as it is, the Mystic Falls' tradition of getting wasted in a cemetery and ringing bells is, at its heart, about community — mourning collectively and drawing strength from each other. And the impromptu memorial for Bonnie does just that for her group of friends. Bonnie's there to watch her own funeral like a witchy Tom Sawyer or Huck Finn; the ceremony allows her to accept the fate she's been denying for months and to recognize what she still has. With Jeremy as a medium for her to communicate through, Elena, Caroline, and Matt get what so many have dreamed of after the passing of a loved one: a message from the Great Beyond, reassurance, the blessing to go on living.

All Bonnie wants is for the gang to be together, to be there for each other, to attempt happiness despite the horrible, terrible, violent, and trying circumstances they struggle with every other day. And though Stefan doesn't remember Bonnie, or himself, he proves he does know the answer to the question he poses while in a feeding frenzy, Jesse's blood dripping down his face: What's the point of being good? It's not to be rewarded, or to be guaranteed a fair and just fate. Stefan's dedication to doing right by those he loves hasn't been rewarded, nor has Bonnie's. Caroline's kindness to Stefan and his opportunity to return that friendship shows this blank slate of a vampire that, as hard as it is, connection and community are what makes soldiering through the heartache worthwhile. And perhaps that's why the lone wolf returns: Tyler Lockwood rejoins the group as they mourn Bonnie, providing comfort to Caroline when she most needs it.

An episode with very little plot shenanigans but a heck of a lot of heart, "For Whom the Bell Tolls" presses pause on the Silas Of It All and lets Katherine chill out with her kidnapper in order to remind us of the characters at the core of this series and the unending grief that unites them.

COMPELLING MOMENT An episode rife with callbacks to seasons past culminates with Bonnie's emotional memorial in the old cemetery. Try not to cry when Elena brings the feathers, acknowledging a private pivotal moment between the girls. And then, even in her afterlife, Bonnie looks after her friends.

© David Gabber/PRPhotos.com

CIRCLE OF KNOWLEDGE

- The phrase "for whom the bell tolls," most famously used by Ernest Hemingway as the title of his 1940 novel set in the Spanish Civil War, comes from metaphysical poet John Donne, who published *Devotions Upon Emergent Occasions* in 1624. "Meditation XVII" contains this well-known phrase alongside another: "No man is an island." In the meditation, written during convalescence from a serious illness, Donne hears the ringing of a bell, which signifies death, or impending death, of someone in his community. His observation is that, since we are connected ("every man a piece of the continent, a part of the main"), the death of any individual affects the whole: "Any man's death diminishes me, because I am involved in mankind; and therefore never send to know for whom the bell tolls; it tolls for thee." The bell reminds him of his own mortality, and, as a religious man, he is inspired by that knell to make peace with his god.
- Remembrance Day is an actual holiday observed every year on November 11 in Commonwealth nations. While Mystic Falls' version commemorates anyone who has passed away, the actual holiday was dedicated by Britain's King George V in 1919 as a day for memorializing members of the armed forces. The holiday's date of observance stems from the Armistice of Compiègne, the agreement between the Allies and Germany that brought an end to fighting and went into effect on November 11, 1918. Though World War I would not formally end until the Treaty of Versailles was signed in June 1919, Armistice Day (another name for Remembrance Day) is widely considered to be the end of the war.
- Keeping with the morbid town tradition, the first shot of the episode is a cross at the side of the road, marking the site of a deadly accident. Moments later, Damon forces the car they are riding in to flip several times and land in a fiery heap in the middle of the road. So disrespectful, Salvatore.
- While discussing Stefan's amnesia over the phone, "Dr. Forbes" warns Elena that victims of retrograde amnesia, or other brain injuries, can turn volatile, displaying changes in personality, intense anger, and unpredictable behavior. In the same conversation, Caroline quips that she's been brushing up on *Gray's Anatomy*. Henry Gray's 1858 illuminated text is widely regarded as the most influential work on human anatomy and it continues to be revised and republished. Then there's ABC's *Grey's*

The Writers on Joining *TVD*

Brett Matthews on his road to *TVD*: I majored in film studies at Wesleyan University and moved out to Los Angeles shortly after graduation. I searched for an entry-level job while writing my own material and eating way too much ramen, and eventually found work as a production assistant on *Buffy the Vampire Slayer*. During that time, I was lucky to get to know Joss Whedon, who I basically owe my entire career to. I was his assistant for a year when he gave me the opportunity to write an episode of *Firefly*. Every writer needs that first person to give them a break, and mine just happened to be a genius. Strangely enough, it all seemed completely normal at the time. Looking back, I see what an ignorant kid I was. But what a mentor, and what an experience to watch him run his shows. He just does it right. Joss is the best.

Matthews on his first impressions of *TVD*: I appreciated the pace, the show's utter devotion to the story it was telling, and most of all its willingness to make big moves. The best shows know what they are, and *TVD* clearly does. Those were the things that were attractive to me as a writer. And its visuals looked almost feature quality. I really loved the look of the show as well as the writing.

Melinda Hsu Taylor: I always thought it was a great idea for a show. I first started watching it in earnest when I actually had an interview for a job on the show after season two — or going into season two? I forget. But I quickly had to catch up on episodes because I didn't watch it in season one. But I tuned in to the episode "Founder's Day," and Elena shows up in period costume, looking like Katherine; Stefan and Damon are in a shot looking back at her and she does a little curtsey and she's not really sure what to make of the whole thing. And there's this moment where Damon is just really struck by *Oh my god she really does look like Katherine* and it so summed up the show in 10 seconds of visual, and I was like, *Oh*. Triangle. Brothers, good, bad. You've got a doppelgänger, she's an innocent modern girl. I get it. I get this show and I liked how concise it was with its language. So ever since then, I've been on board.

I think that as a writer it's really fun also to work on something where you don't have to worry about the rules of evidence or somebody's day job or anything like that. [laughs] It's just "magic doesn't work like that," or if there's a spell sealing them inside the house, then can one other person come in? Is it like a roach trap, like you can't get out? These "magic doesn't work like that" conversations that we have are so much more fun than "That wouldn't be admissible in court." I've worked on procedurals too, and the rules of reality bring me down sometimes.

Holly Brix: When I was asked to interview to write for the show, I watched all of *TVD* in a month. I got so hooked after, like, the fourth episode, that it was one of the better months of "work" I ever had in my life. I fell in love with how smart the show was. I was recommending it to everyone I knew, even the checkers at the market. "Have you seen *The Vampire Diaries*? You've got to check it out."

Neil Reynolds: I hadn't [watched *TVD* before interviewing for it], although enough of my friends and colleagues had recommended it that I was curious. I marathoned three seasons in two days. I fell in love with the characters almost immediately, and connected to their young, human vulnerability so directly that at times I forgot it was a vampire show. Happily, I also enjoyed the vampire hijinks, copious amounts of blood, and frequent heart-pulls — and appreciated how elegantly those fast-paced stakes fueled all the heightened emotions.

Matthews on what might surprise people about working on *TVD*: How genuinely nice everybody is and how much we laugh during the average day. And just how incredibly hard everyone works to make the show we all love. It's just a huge undertaking and it kind of consumes us for 11 months out of the year. Also, we can never get the temperature in the writers' room right. It's like Goldilocks' porridge — always too hot or too cold.

Anatomy (2005–present), an American television drama that follows the shenanigans of sexy doctors at the fictional Seattle Grace Hospital.

- While Damon insists they should let his brother be "fun, drunk Stefan," Elena points out that the younger Salvatore's blood addiction could be hardwired into his brain, part of his biology. Damon snarkily calls Elena the "queen of nature versus nurture," referring to the scholarly and popular debate about how an individual's physical and behavioral traits are shaped: by their genetic material or by their experience. Amnesiac Stefan is rather hopeful that it's his traumatic experiences that made him the Ripper of Monterey and that without his memories, he'll be able to live a normal vampiric life.
- Damon mentions that Mama Salvatore (first name still unknown) died of consumption, which is the old-school term for pulmonary tuberculosis. The disease, which targets the lungs, was widespread in mid-19th-century America. Symptoms include a fever, weight loss, fatigue, chills, and coughing up blood.
- Togavirus causes congenital rubella, "whatever that is." Let us explain it for you, Caroline! Togavirus is any of a family of single-stranded RNA viruses that can cause German measles, and congenital rubella is when

the fetus of a pregnant woman contracts rubella, a.k.a German measles. As for Red Queen Theory, it's not actually a theory (an established principle) but a hypothesis (a specific prediction that can be tested) that describes two similar ideas based in coevolution. Caroline describes it as "the contradictory relationship between predator and prey," establishing that the weaker species will stay one step ahead out of fear of extinction, like a rabbit running for its life from a fox who just wants its dinner. The hypothesis is named for the Red Queen in *Through the Looking-Glass* (1871) by Lewis Carroll. Finally, aplastic anemia — the prime topic to talk about in the aftermath of an awkward kiss — is a disease that damages blood marrow and stem cells, and it can be caused by drugs, infection, radiation, and heredity. But definitely not by kissing.

- When Gregor is called forth from Matt by a phone call, he says to the person on the line, in Czech, "Thank you, Kristof. Traveling safely."

HISTORY LESSON According to Damon, Remembrance Day in Mystic Falls began during a cholera outbreak in the 1820s. Daydrinking must've made Damon a little fuzzy on the details: the first documented case of cholera in the United States didn't occur until 1832, during what is referred to as the second cholera pandemic (1829–1849). Scholars believe the disease spread from Europe to the United States via Irish immigrants fleeing the potato famine in 1832 and entering the country in Detroit and New York City.

As for the holiday's rather nightmare-inducing bell-ringing tradition, its origins lay in the fear of being buried alive, which was particularly pervasive in Western culture throughout the 18th and 19th centuries. The first known "security coffin" was ordered to be built in 1792 by a German duke, Ferdinand of Brunswick. In his book *Buried Alive: The Terrifying History of Our Most Primal Fear* (2001), author Jan Bondeson describes the coffin's specifications: "a window that let in light, an air hole to prevent suffocation, and a lid with a lock-and-key mechanism instead of being nailed down." Keys to open the coffin lid and the burial vault were tucked within a pocket sewn into the shroud. Since most security coffins were elaborate contraptions designed and built by skilled tradesmen, only the wealthy could afford to have them, but that didn't prevent cheaper, homemade alternatives, similar to the scenario Damon describes: "tie a string connecting a bell to the finger of the buried person."

THE RULES Jeremy does all those push-ups after his run to work off the extra adrenaline he has as a hunter. Jeremy reminds Damon that Nature demands a balance — there is no resurrection without a cost, a life for a life. Leaning over a microscope, Dr. Maxfield proclaims there to be vampire blood in Jesse's system, meaning its cellular properties are somehow distinct from human blood.

PREVIOUSLY ON *THE VAMPIRE DIARIES* In the car, Stefan reads a March 12, 1922, diary entry, which Damon has clearly read before (he mouths along with the "I feel alive again" part); in "The End of the Affair" (3.03), Elena read this entry as she and Damon tracked Stefan down in Chicago. Stefan mocks Honoria Fell's name but is told he killed the poor woman, as seen in "The Dinner Party" (2.15).

Elena tries to recreate important moments from her relationship with Stefan in order to jog his memory: their first meetings in the cemetery and in the hallway at Mystic Fall High School from the pilot (1.01); when Stefan whooshed Elena to the top of the Ferris wheel at the Mystic Falls carnival in "Brave New World" (2.02); when Stefan rescued Elena from the Wickery Bridge car crash that killed her parents (revealed in "Bloodlines," 1.11), and again in "The Departed" (3.22). "Gravity" by Sara Bareilles, the song that played over Stefan and Elena's first kiss in "The Night of the Comet" (1.02), is reprised here as Elena touches Stefan's face, recalling her touching his face and telling him not to hide his vampire nature in "The Turning Point" (1.10).

Matt's right — his blackouts don't have to do with the Gilbert ring, but to answer Jeremy's question, Matt has died twice while wearing it: when Damon snapped his neck to trick Elena into turning her humanity back on in "She's Come Undone" (4.21), and in "True Lies," when Silas realized Matt had a passenger and couldn't mind-control him, he snapped his neck.

In a heartbreakingly real moment, Elena breaks down when she can't find anything to wear to Bonnie's memorial; she burned down her house, and her funeral clothes with it, in "Stand By Me" (4.15).

Bonnie's memorial in the woods is as tragic as Jenna and John's funeral in "The Sun Also Rises" (2.21), complete with a tear-provoking Birdy song. Caroline and Bonnie were on the cheerleading squad together ("Friday Night Bites," 1.03), and Caroline brings pom-poms to the memorial; Matt and Bonnie spent the summer before we met them lifeguarding together ("The Reckoning," 3.05) and he has a lifeguarding whistle; when Bonnie revealed

> "The whole concept [of shooting a TV show] is it's a marathon not a sprint. You really have to pace yourself for the general rigors of the whole season, because it's so long and it's demanding. It is a good steady gig. TV shows can be very, very hard, and if you don't have people on the same page and committed, it can be a struggle, and *Vampire Diaries* is not one of those shows. It's really a good show to work on. It has a lot of the same attributes as a feature, because of that."
>
> — Michael Karasick

to Elena that she was a witch, she floated pillow feathers ("162 Candles," 1.08), and Elena pays homage to that moment; and Damon brings Emily Bennett's grimoire, which Stefan unearthed from Giuseppe Salvatore's grave in "Children of the Damned" (1.13).

OFF CAMERA This episode is a favorite in the writers' room. "It was such a great emotional episode," says Matthew D'Ambrosio. "Damon and Stefan brother bonding. Stefan relearning about what Elena did. Damon hugging Jeremy. Bonnie's funeral. People drinking in cemeteries. It had it all." And Julie Plec also counts it as a highlight, specifically Bonnie's funeral, "which I just *loved* beyond all compare and I've never cried so hard."

One of writer Brett Matthews' favorite season-five moments is in "For Whom the Bell Tolls": "I've just always enjoyed writing and truly collaborating with Finchie, and Bonnie's funeral really hits us both hard every time. . . . I lost my dad last year, so that was a big part of where the event Remembrance Day came from and what makes the episode special to me. I think Julie pitched the idea of a feather, and on the day on set we decided to use a mess of them because it just felt powerful and right. They're actually the same exact feathers that were used in ["162 Candles"] too. Joe Connelly, our prop master, still had a giant bag full of them from season one."

The cold-open car crash was, according to director Michael Allowitz, something "that came together quite nicely considering. After much planning and Special Effects executing a test on the day of the shoot, we got ready to place the cameras. For many safety reasons, the camera placement was dictated by these limitations. Nevertheless we figured it out. Then when we finally shot the car roll, it didn't do anything like it was supposed to. So we took the smashed car and did it again. We were able to put the two takes together in post and deliver a great stunt sequence."

Jesse, the hot college guy with a crush on Caroline, is played by Kendrick Sampson, an American actor, writer, and producer. Sampson has a handful of TV series credits, including *CSI*, *Greek*, and *Days of Our Lives*. Since his recurring role on *The Vampire Diaries*, he was cast as Dean Iverson on *Gracepoint*, the 2014 American remake of the British TV miniseries *Broadchurch*, starring Scottish actor (and tenth Doctor Who) David Tennant. Like many other guest stars this season, Sampson found himself on a plane to Atlanta within hours of being cast and told *The Hollywood Reporter* that filming a supernatural TV show was a surreal experience. "The craziest thing is getting used to people walking around in their supernatural costume — their wardrobe, their fangs. It's a little freaky. And the blood. There's so much blood!"

This episode originally "had an entire Nadia/Katherine storyline that was lifted and put into 5.05," says Caroline Dries, "because we had no room in 5.04 and we didn't want to cut anything. The scenes from 5.05 that we lost appear in the DVD extras."

FOGGY MOMENTS Guess that waitress at the Grill never drinks the coffee, which is regularly laced with vervain so the customers and staff aren't, you know, accosted by vampires in the back room.

How can Matt Donovan afford all those fancy cameras? Has he been selling off Carol Lockwood's antique furniture?

When Damon and Elena realize that there is way too much temptation for Stefan at the Grill, why do they take him to a cemetery full of drunk people instead of taking him home to the empty Salvatore mansion?

At the Salvatore crypt, Damon rhymes off the family members buried there and includes Papa Salvatore. Giuseppe Salvatore is actually buried outside the crypt, as seen in "Children of the Damned."

QUESTIONS

- What happened to Bonnie's body after she died on graduation day? Did poor Jer have to sneak her body out of the tunnels and bury her in an unmarked grave?
- While Damon hadn't yet got to the Elena part of Stefan's past, did he explain the whole Katherine situation? Stefan knows that his mind was

fried by a witch, but does he know that Elena and Katherine are doppelgängers or that he is Silas's shadow self?

- What made Tyler return? (And who told him there was a makeshift funeral in the old cemetery?)
- What's so special about the knife Gregor has left in Matt's possession?
- Dr. Maxfield told Elena in "True Lies" that he had studied her father's research; was Grayson Gilbert the one who discovered that vampire blood was detectable through some scientific process? What sort of mad-scientist business is Dr. Maxfield up to, and has Jesse been demoted from lab assistant to lab rat?

Caroline: Love me more than you hate him.

5.05 Monster's Ball

Original air date October 31, 2013
Written by Sonny Postiglione **Directed by** Kellie Cyrus
Edited by Marc Pollon **Cinematography by** Darren Genet
Guest cast Alyssa Lewis (Elena Double)
Previously on *The Vampire Diaries* Paul Wesley

At the Whitmore Historical Ball, Damon teams up with Silas, Caroline finds out why Tyler came back, and Elena makes a new sullen friend, Aaron. Nadia tells Katherine who she is.

Katherine Pierce was once the Big Bad in Mystic Falls, the most ruthless, the most hated, the villain who our gang plotted to kill — and seemed justified in doing so. In "Monster's Ball," she's a compelling contender for most human and most vulnerable. On *The Vampire Diaries*, the diabolical ones never quite read as all evil, and the final moments of this episode prove that the moral ground on which the "heroes" stand remains shaky.

Though the season so far has been hampered by its chronic and heavy recapping — let's explain again the possible scenarios in which Silas becomes mortal and where he'll end up if he dies! — "Monster's Ball" finds its strength in moving its characters around the dance floor with cruel acts committed in the name of love . . . or love long lost. As Elena tries to distract herself from her grief over Bonnie's death by focusing on her investigation of Dr. Maxfield, Tyler proves true the common platitude: we all grieve differently, which Elena tells survivor-guilt-ridden sad-sack Aaron. While Caroline and Elena do what their lost bestie wants them to do — move on from past hardship — Tyler has allowed his grief over his mother to fester, in the nine-or-so months since her violent end, into a white-hot need for revenge. Though for a while he allows Caroline to believe he might do so, Tyler won't return to a "normal life," knowing that Klaus got away with stone-cold murder. He puts his own need for vengeance ahead of his love for Caroline, ahead of her need for him in the wake of Bonnie's death. Tyler seems unaware of the selfishness of his action, and how it makes him similar to his nemesis Klaus. Caroline is right on point when she tells Tyler that he sounds like Klaus — determined to ruin his chance at happiness by chasing vengeance. Tyler's distance (both physical and emotional) has been torture for Caroline, and for him to return to town to hop into bed with Caroline for the better part of four days only to break her heart again plays as needlessly cruel. The breakup scene is a great reminder of just how powerful Michael Trevino can be when he's given *something* to work with, but it's been thin pickings for Tyler for most of the series (save for season two), with his here-today-gone-tomorrow character arcs.

While Tyler's cruelty to Caroline is not malicious, Silas *definitely* enjoys tormenting his former fiancée, once again fooling Qetsiyah as he did two millennia ago. He leads her to believe it's his doppelgänger romancing her, and he plays on Tessa's former fondness for him in order to lull her into a false sense of security and control. While Tessa claims her quest for revenge is not rooted in a lingering love for Silas, that she has no desire to hold on to the bond she thought they once shared, her tears as she stops his heart and desiccates his body tell a different story. Vengeance can be as all consuming as love, and she is determined to reveal Silas's true self that lurks behind the handsome face — the lies, the deception, and the capacity for cruelty. It's unclear why she wants to find the mystical Anchor herself: the Travelers don't seem to have any wish to destroy the Other Side, and they've had the Anchor and access to power for the past 2,000 years. Still, her locator spell conveniently puts that MacGuffin in the game: she knows where it is, and Silas knows where it is. And thanks to Damon Salvatore, Silas is no longer out of commission . . . nor is he immortal.

> "[In-episode recapping is] a network request, but it does help to orient the audience — at least, I think I does. I have a hard time being objective because I know everything [that's going to happen]. I like watching the show with non-regular viewers to see what they understand.The challenge of a serialized show is pushing forward without boring viewers who already know what's going on. And it's not easy for actors to say 'reset' dialogue, because it's not really natural. It's tricky as a writer to sneak it in. And when it doesn't work, it really doesn't work and we end up cutting it out."
>
> — Caroline Dries

The insane things people do for love! Jeremy ignores Bonnie's very sensible suggestion that they not team up with the evil killer, that they not risk lives to use untested, powerful magic that *always* comes with dire consequences. His foolhardiness is akin to (and in parallel with) Damon's. Jeremy loves Bonnie, and he wants her back in the Land of the Living, while Damon wants to restore Elena's happiness and he thinks it'll come in the form of a teenage witch back from the dead. Neither of them care how high the risk is, or what alliances must be forged, and they both go rogue with their secret plan. Damon, in particular, has thrown all sense out the window. He has no concept of right and wrong, of sensible and reckless, of what Elena would actually *want* him to do. It's crazy to team up with the Big Bad and agree to temporarily kill your amnesiac brother, who's already experiencing serious trust issues, without even asking Silas *why* first. It's crazy to stone-cold murder the woman you were in love with for 145 years, who happens to look absolutely identical to your current love, to turn said Big Bad into an incredibly powerful witch. It's crazy, and it's *so classically Damon*, a character whose M.O. has always been "be bad with purpose," as he told Klaus in "A View to a Kill." He believes a noble purpose makes rash actions forgivable. And it's forgiveness that Damon expects from Stefan when he wakes up from his snapped-neck. Noble purpose is behind Elena's tacit agreement when Damon bites into Katherine and lets Silas drain her of her blood — knowing it will kill her. But the definition of a noble cause has only become broader and broader as the series progresses and now excuses murder, violence, and

© Andrew Evans/PRPhotos

betrayal, with Damon, Elena, and company deciding which individual's happiness is more valuable than another's.

From a storytelling perspective, does a character get any more valuable than Ms. Katherine Pierce? With the epic overhead shot of her lying motionless, that trademark "This character is dead" moment, it felt *possible* that Katherine Pierce — a character who has only become more compelling as a mere mortal — was a goner. And what a loss it would've been. As Katherine's discovered the doldrums of being human, it's been hilarious and poignant. And the twist that Nadia is her very-long-lost daughter has only deepened that journey. In "Katerina," we saw Katherine as her newborn was taken from her, we saw her return to Bulgaria to find her family slaughtered, we saw the devastation of her early life. But it is no surprise that the character who has run for 500 years chooses to stay with Nadia. Though they've spent centuries estranged, Nadia undeniably shares that same Petrova fire; she is her mother's daughter — a determined badass with a soft spot for family. How fitting it is that only when Katherine is human again they are reunited for the first time since the day Nadia was born. That quiet emotional scene between the two of them in the hotel room, as an understated bond forms with the tea offered and accepted, serves to make Katherine's later pleas for her life to Damon agonizing. This is a woman who has survived, who is a fighter and who (thank the Powers That Be) lives to see another day. For whatever mystical juju reason, Katherine is the Timex of doppelgängers and, complete with a sassy quip, she rises to die another day.

In his Dr. Jekyll costume, Wes says, and maybe even believes, that he is not responsible for the actions of his darker half, but his cold, detached "scientific" treatment of Jesse dehumanizes him and only reveals the monster within Dr. Maxfield. Like the other wrongdoers of the episode, Wes is not only responsible for his monstrous actions but is defined by them. It's the determination and ruthlessness with which he pursues his ends that make him a threat, just as Silas — whose evil master plan is to kill himself with lots of collateral damage — is a viable threat because of his unflinching willingness to see his plan through to the end *no matter the cost.* When our heroes' actions mimic those of the villains, not even a "Damon-sized" rationalization can excuse their dark sides.

COMPELLING MOMENT While Katherine's background shenanigans (eating chips, flopping off the bed, despairing over the contents of the mini fridge) were comedy gold, the perfect Katherine Pierce line upon returning from the dead — "Am I in hell?" — takes the cake, even in an episode full of classic KP moments.

CIRCLE OF KNOWLEDGE

- No Matt in this episode.
- A monster's ball is a prisoner's last night before his execution, a term that's been around for centuries. It was used as the title of the 2001 film in which Halle Berry plays the wife of a death row inmate who develops a relationship with her husband's executioner (Billy Bob Thornton).
- Poor Damon spent about nine hours in the car, driving back and forth between Mystic Falls and Whitmore College, just to have brief conversations with people. Considering 2011 (in *The Vampire Diaries* timeline, it's still 2011) saw gasoline prices reach a national average of over $3.50 per gallon, the highest on record at the time, it's a good thing Damon can use his vampire compulsion to avoid paying at the pump.
- As Katherine notes before calling her bluff, Nadia's story is full of inconsistencies: she starts off by saying she has been tracking Katherine for 500 years, but then sets her story in 1645, 366 years ago, and says she has a Parisian mother, Lily Atoma, when Nadia's accent is clearly *not* French.
- At the Whitmore Historical Ball, other costumes include: Robin Hood, the notorious and beloved outlaw of English folklore, notable for "robbing from the rich and giving to the poor" (though it's still widely debated whether he is based on an actual person); a Playboy Bunny, originally waitresses at Playboy Clubs from 1960 to 1988, who wore bunny ears, corsets, and cottontails inspired by the tuxedo-wearing bunny mascot of *Playboy* magazine; Marie Antoinette, the deposed Queen of France and Navarre (1774–1792), who was tried for treason and executed by guillotine in 1793 during the French Revolution; and the iceberg that took down doomed British passenger liner RMS *Titanic* on April 15, 1912.
- Dear Dr. Maxfield, stick to bio, not history. His costume is an odd choice for the historical ball, given that Dr. Jekyll is a literary character. Robert Louis Stevenson's 1886 novella *Strange Case of Dr Jekyll and Mr Hyde* has been referenced on *TVD* before; Damon slipped a copy of it into Alaric's lock-up care package when he was going through his split-personality problem in "Heart of Darkness" (3.19). The costume is a brazen choice

> "We were so excited to see Katherine's daughter this season and how Katherine would react. Olga Fonda was great. One of the best Nadia scenes was one where Katherine put Nadia to bed after she nearly killed her in 5.05, and explained how she didn't abandon her but went looking for her, and then ended it with 'Nice to meet you.' I think it was originally written that Katherine was somewhat sarcastic and bitchy, and Julie rewrote the end with a very simple tweak and made Katherine loving and warm when she said, 'Nice to meet you.' And it was such a wonderful moment and a great learning experience for me as a writer to see how character moments form when showing tiny glimpses of humanity."
>
> — Caroline Dries

for Dr. Wes, who all but admits by his choice that he has a problematic dark side ready to pop out at any moment.

- In the *Beverly Hills, 90210* season two episode "Halloween," Brenda Walsh and Dylan McKay attend a party as Bonnie and Clyde, as Caroline and Tyler do here — relationship drama is sure to ensue when those two are your pop-culture predecessors!
- Damon uses Timex's iconic advertising tagline to express his awe of Katherine's continued durability: "Takes a licking and keeps on ticking." From the 1950s to 1990s, American watchmakers Timex maintained a popular ad campaign meant to emphasize the fortitude of their watches and often enlisted celebrities to put the watches through "torture tests."

HISTORY LESSON Damon and Elena attend the ball as King Henry VIII (1491–1547) and Lady Anne Boleyn (1501–1536), his second spouse, Queen of England for three years, later beheaded (with a sword) officially for treason and incest but unofficially for neglecting to give birth to a son. Elena is wearing a replica of the "B" necklace often seen in portraits of Anne Boleyn. The original necklace is believed to have been passed on to Henry and Anne's daughter, Elizabeth I, but it's also been suggested that Henry had the necklace sold or recut after Anne's execution.

Caroline and Tyler are Bonnie Parker (1910–1934) and Clyde Barrow

(1909–1934), notorious American outlaws (not serial killers, as Tyler says) who terrorized the central U.S. with a string of robberies and murders during the Depression and were later killed in a hail of gunfire by officers in Louisiana. Stefan is James Dean (1931–1955), an American actor who appeared in such classic films as *Rebel Without a Cause* (1955) and *East of Eden* (1955) but achieved legend status only after he died in a car accident at the age of 24. And Qetsiyah selects her near-contemporary Cleopatra (69–30 BCE), the last great pharaoh of Egypt and the Ptolemaic dynasty. Cleopatra formed an alliance with Marc Antony, an antagonist of Octavianus, who would later become Augustus, the first Roman emperor. Upon the defeat of his forces at the Battle of Actium, Antony committed suicide, and Cleopatra followed suit, killing herself, as legend tells it, with an asp bite. With the exception of Henry VIII, all of the above historical figures have something in common: they died violently or unnaturally.

Elena mistakes Dr. Maxfield's Dr. Jekyll costume for Abraham Lincoln, most likely due to the stovepipe hat commonly associated with the 16th American president.

Qetsiyah expresses a fondness for Phoenician wine. Wine growth and production as we know it today was cultivated by the Phoenicians, an ancient civilization whose major cities were located on the Mediterranean coastline and whose culture and prosperity centered on maritime trade. In their early days, Phoenicians traded mainly with the Greeks — their name derives from the Greek word for "purple," for their purple dye, which was highly prized — but they soon spread their knowledge of wine production throughout modern-day Spain, Portugal, Egypt, Italy, and elsewhere. Qetsiyah also laments missing out on bacon for so long, saying, "No one thought to cure pig fat." While a form of bacon existed during the Roman era, the cured form of bacon as we know it today originated in 17th-century Britain.

THE RULES Nadia tells Katherine that in order for Silas to be cured by drinking her blood, he has to drink *all* of it. (Not clear how she would know that — maybe the Travelers told her?) Qetsiyah uses one of her old pendants to amplify her power and do a locator spell to find the "mystical Anchor" that binds the Other Side spell. Silas rightly assumes that if the link between him and Stefan is broken by Stefan's (temporary) death, his psychic powers will return. Bonnie reminds Jeremy that spells are often bound with something powerful like the moon, a comet, or a doppelgänger.

PREVIOUSLY ON *THE VAMPIRE DIARIES* As she does here with Stefan's and Tyler's costumes, Caroline often puts herself in charge of outfitting her friends for special events: she provided Bonnie's Halloween costume (witch, naturally) in "Haunted" (1.07) and ordered gowns for the gang in "Graduation" (4.23). High school may be in the rear-view mirror, but *TVD* keeps up its tradition of big theme school dances, even without Caroline officially on the planning committee: the gang has also dressed up in '50s ("Unpleasantville," 1.12), '60s ("The Last Dance," 2.18), and '20s ("Do Not Go Gentle," 3.20) costumes.

There's also a *TVD* tradition of finding mystical jewelry at big parties: like Tessa here getting her pendant while at the ball, Damon tracked down the necklace with the tomb-sealing crystal when the Mystic Falls historical society had objects on display at the Founders' Ball in "Family Ties" (1.04). Professor Shane got Silas's headstone, full of Qetsiyah's calcified blood, from the Whitmore collection that also holds Tessa's pendant ("We All Go a Little Mad Sometimes," 4.06).

Wes tells Elena that he couldn't very well blame Megan's frat-party death on a mountain lion; Damon used a mountain lion as his patsy for his early season one spate of murders ("Family Ties").

Tyler reminds Caroline that Klaus killed his mom ("O Come, All Ye Faithful," 4.09) and that Klaus granted them permission to be together as a gift to Caroline in "Graduation."

Damon holds Katherine's neck to feed Silas, just like Katherine held Jeremy's neck to feed Silas in "Down the Rabbit Hole" (4.14). Both of their deaths were temporary, as it turns out.

OFF CAMERA Katherine's daughter Nadia is played by Russian-born actress Olga Fonda. A model since 2007 when she was discovered by a scout while vacationing in L.A., Fonda has appeared in TV series like *How I Met Your Mother*, *Melrose Place*, *Nip/Tuck*, and *Entourage*. Her film work includes roles in *Little Fockers* (2010) and *Real Steel* (2011). While season five was airing, she could be regularly seen in TJ Maxx commercials as "The Gifter." In an interview with *Extra TV*, Fonda said she learned she was cast as Nadia the day after her audition, with four hours to jump on a plane to Atlanta. She also admitted, "I was a little bit nervous when I just got the job, because [the cast has] been working together for so many years, and I was kind of the new kid on the block," but the cast was "wonderful and loving, kind and helpful.

> "Kevin [Williamson] and I always knew that we'd bring Katherine's daughter into play at some point, back even when we were doing season two, when we made up [Katherine's] whole backstory, and what had led her to become the person she became. We knew that the daughter was an element out there in the ether, that we could play with at some point or another. And so this year, when Katherine was human, we figured it was now or never . . . and what better way of exhibiting the human side of Katherine than by thrusting this responsibility and emotional relationship at her?"
>
> — Julie Plec

They're a great family." Like the audience, Fonda was kept in the dark about the fact Nadia was Katherine's daughter; the information was not included in casting sides or mentioned during the audition process. "I actually didn't find out until I received the script from production. The producers and writers are very careful about storylines, and for a good reason!"

Explains Caroline Dries, "We try not to tell actors too much in general, because things change so much all the time and we don't want them to dig into anything or play into anything, in case it changes. But when it's a huge casting objective like finding someone who looked like Nina, we let the casting folks in on the secrets."

Fonda and Nina Dobrev did not discuss the reveal beforehand, which Fonda believed made the actual scene more genuine. "That moment was the first time we were experiencing each other's emotions and hearing each other's lines, which plays out perfectly for the scene. Nadia and Katherine don't have a relationship beforehand, so preparing it in that way really helped once we got to set." But after they filmed the scene, "we were both so tied up into the moment that we hugged each other. The writers are great at developing these characters and you can get really lost in the moment."

The timeline error in this episode (Wes, Elena, and Damon establish that it's been three days since the previous episode's events, but Silas says to Nadia on the phone that she's had Katherine just one night) is the result of the Nadia-Katherine hotel room scene being filmed as part of "For Whom the Bell Tolls" by director Michael Allowitz, and inserted into this episode.

Episode director Kellie Cyrus says Katherine's death scene was "originally scripted in act five but it got moved to the last scene, so I just tried to make it feel like the episode was ending with a crane shot up and then the crane came back down as we hear her heart beat, and it ended with some comedic dialogue."

FOGGY MOMENTS Damon refers to Silas's dead true love as Amara, but Qetsiyah told the whole story to Stefan, whose memories were then erased. Unless Qetsiyah told Damon the story offscreen, he shouldn't know Amara's name.

Last season, the gang knew that Silas wanted to destroy the Other Side so he could pass on and be with Amara, but when Bonnie recaps that information here, Jeremy and Damon react like it's a revelation. Similarly, Elena and Damon were already aware that Dr. Maxfield knows about vampires, since he covered up Megan's death-by-vampire, but Damon acts surprised to hear that Wes is in on the supernatural secret.

When Stefan wakes up after the first time Damon snaps his neck, he makes a crack about a "Damon-sized rationalization" . . . but with no memories of his brother, how is he capable of making such an on-point observation about Damon's behavior?

QUESTIONS

- Where was Nadia when Katherine came looking for her in 1498? Why doesn't she remember where she was when she was eight years old? How did Nadia find out about vampires? Katherine didn't know about them until she got to England (as far as we know). Was it Klaus's minions' slaughter of the Petrova family that brought them into Nadia's world? Who did Nadia get to turn her, and where did she get a daylight ring? She knows details about the night Katherine turned that likely only Rose and Trevor knew — since they were alone in that cottage and then on the run. Did Nadia meet them at some point?
- How did Nadia become mixed up with the Travelers? Does she actually love Gregor or was she using him to track down her mother?
- Are Dr. Maxfield and trust-fund-kid Aaron blood related, or is Wes just his legal guardian? Why does everyone around Aaron die? Is he linked to Elena's dad in any way, like Megan was?

- Who are the people watching Elena and her friends at Whitmore that Dr. Maxfield warns her about? Are they the secret society we learned about in "True Lies"? Will Caroline and Elena cut and run back to Mystic Falls?
- Dr. Maxfield says Jesse is a perfect candidate — for what exactly?
- How did Katherine come back to life?
- Qetsiyah says that the Travelers hid the Anchor after they killed her. Why did they kill her — for creating the immortality elixir, or for her vengeance on Silas and Amara? Where and what is the mystical Anchor?
- Will Silas resurrect Bonnie? Will there be consequences? Will Jeremy's crazy question "What could be worse than this?" be answered?

Damon (to Silas): You do realize that by destroying the Other Side, you are personally moving heaven and earth to be together? That's not fate, you idiot. It's you being a crazy person.

5.06 *Handle with Care*

Original air date November 7, 2013
Written by Caroline Dries and Holly Brix
Directed by Jeffrey Hunt
Edited by Joel T. Pashby **Cinematography by** Michael Karasick
Guest cast Jacinte Blankenship (Waitress), Kyle Russell Clements (Rene), Dean West (Kristof)
Previously on *The Vampire Diaries* Paul Wesley

Jeremy takes a road trip with two guys who've killed him to find the mystical Anchor in a warehouse in New Jersey. Elena spends her day trapped in a cabin with Amnesia Stefan and Qetsiyah, while Katherine impersonates her on campus.

As Katherine sits down to an epic breakfast, the soundtrack of Sleigh Bells sings out that it was "the best of times, it was the worst of times": as for Katherine, so for the episode at hand. While "worst" may be a bit too harsh, "Handle with Care" is again bogged down by first-act rehashing of plot, motivation, and character, only to be pushed along by a flimsy narrative motivator: Elena wants to have a good day. That's nice, dear. It comes off as both harebrained and selfish in light of the heightened danger. Everything goes to hell in a handbasket over the course of a day that starts off not half bad, and the episode thankfully has some clever twists and lively pairings to balance out the doldrums, as it explores questions of fate and faith, free will and hope.

While Tessa's one-note, woman-scorned character grows tiresome by episode's end — despite the excellent performance from Janina Gavankar — her ironclad confidence that Silas will be unable to destroy the Anchor even if he finds it turns out to be delightfully founded. There were some strong hints in "Original Sin" that Amara did not die 2,000 years ago, but the reveal that *she's* the mystical Anchor, bound to the existence of the Other Side, is a classic *TVD* twist pulled off with aplomb. Welcome, Amara. The day was intended to be Silas's last and a day of resurrection for Bonnie, instead a woman long thought dead is revivified . . . only to reveal that she is more than ready to die. Silas long ago accepted her death, and he plots to find his own soon enough, while Jeremy and Damon refuse to accept that Bonnie's death is final. For Jeremy, it's an issue of faith. Jeremy earnestly believes that if they are fervent in their denial of the permanence of Bonnie's death, they have the ability to change it.

Amara's actions also seem to put a vote in for free will over destiny. If the universe is conspiring to bring Silas and Amara together, well, why does she put her desire for death over her love for him? Damon's theory on the Doppelgänger Destiny issue is that it's not fate, it's just the actions of each individual, pointing out that Silas is "moving heaven and earth" to be with Amara, much as Damon is willing to do for Elena. Over at Tessa's cabin, Stefan saves Elena from Tessa, and Elena reads his actions as specific to *her*: Stefan always tried to save her, to protect her life, and therefore Amnesia Stefan's choice reflects some significant connection between the two of them. The more obvious explanation — that he's just a halfway decent person who isn't down with murder — doesn't spring to Elena's mind. Like his sister, ever-hopeful Jeremy Gilbert's happy day is soured. Despite his determination, and his ability to get Bonnie on side with his "will it into being" attitude, words and will are not enough to outfox Tessa. Bonnie remains a ghost because Elena's life once again hangs in the balance, used as leverage.

Elena's fate, if she has one, is perhaps to test how far her loved ones will go, and how often, to ensure her safety. Damon and Jeremy are forced into making a choice where there is really only one path forward for them: they can't resurrect Bonnie, or Elena will die at Tessa's hand. As with Damon's point that it is each individual's determination that shapes their fortunes, not a prophecy or the universe, so it is here: Tessa is the one pulling their strings, and her mission is vengeance. She extends her revenge to Stefan, angered when he comes to Elena's rescue, which from her perspective replays the choice Silas made 2,000 years ago — Amara over her. Her punishment for Stefan is a diabolical one: she gives him his memories back, knowing that the horror of his own experiences is plenty painful. His sheer existence is a trial, as seems to be the case for Amara — driven mad over two millennia and desperate for the end to come.

While Team Resurrect Bonnie flounders, the College Detectives have a little more success. If you throw a bad day at Katherine, she rallies. Gray streak ruining her breakfast? She just dyes her hair and moves into Elena's dorm room. Threatened by a girl she turned into a vampire? Make a compelling case for Caroline needing her help. And in turn, Caroline lights up when she's given a mystery to solve and a partner in crime. There's a special magic that Katherine Pierce brings to the screen, and here, as when she was partnered up with Matt and Jeremy, the Caroline-Katherine twosome brightens the episode. And while the sandwich-police scene with Aaron is epically hilarious, it takes a stomach-turning twist when Katherine coughs out a bloody tooth. (*Horrifying.*) Even as she is physically falling apart, Katherine breathes new life to the Whitmore College scenes, as do the new plot complications — a secret society called Augustine complete with its own murderous vampire . . .

"Handle with Care" may not be the standout episode of the season but it has the thankless job of teeing up all the plot shenanigans to follow — at least it delivers them in an entertaining package.

COMPELLING MOMENT Wandering crazy-eyed Amara, muttering and disoriented, is amazingly distinct from Katherine, girl detective, cheeky winker, and sandwich (and scene) stealer. Hats off, once again, to Ms. Dobrev for delivering vital and compelling characters, no matter what the writers throw her way.

CIRCLE OF KNOWLEDGE

- No Matt or Tyler in this episode.

> "My favorite moment that I wrote is in 'Handle with Care,' when Damon shows Elena who he has tied up in the trunk — a mentally unstable third doppelgänger, Amara, whom Elena didn't know existed — and Damon introduces the two. 'Elena, meet Crazy Pants. Crazy Pants, meet Elena.' It was the only line I wrote that made it in the best lines list they did in *Variety* for the show's 100th episode."
>
> — Holly Brix

- Damon isn't impressed that the Anchor is in New Jersey, a.k.a. "Snooki's backyard." Nicole "Snooki" Polizzi was one of the stars of the American 2009–2012 MTV reality series *Jersey Shore*, for which Caroline expressed a fondness in "The Return" (2.01). Snooki's backyard is about a six-and-a-half-hour drive from Mystic Falls, heading north on Interstate 95.
- Katherine injects Dr. Maxfield with etorphine, an opioid (a psychoactive chemical) that is 1,000 to 3,000 times more potent than morphine; it's most commonly used by veterinarians to immobilize large mammals, like elephants, but seems to work equally well in sedating microbiology professors with massive egos. Caroline does some quick blood volume calculation: the typical adult does indeed have between 4.7 and 5 liters of blood in their body, and Caroline's "4.7 pints" conclusion seems to be the amount of blood they believe they can drain without killing him, though Maxfield (quite rightfully) disagrees — that's nearly 50 percent of his blood volume.
- Once Dr. Maxfield is vervain-free, Caroline compels the name of Whitmore's secret society from him: Augustine. The name Augustine has its origins in the Latin word *augere*, which means "to increase," and has been historically used as an honorific. The Augustinians are a Catholic monastic order, named for Saint Augustine, or Augustine of Hippo, an early Christian philosopher and scholar who was one of the key figures in developing the doctrine of "original sin." He believed that Adam's guilt is inherited by all human beings, who lack a moral compass until accepting God's divine grace. Within a scientific context, he is considered to be an early proponent of evolutionary theory, centuries before scientific enlightenment, positing that the story of Creation as detailed

in Genesis could be interpreted as God sowing seeds that could develop and adapt, rather than God literally bringing the world into existence in a single go.

- Tessa taunts Damon over the phone, providing hints that she bound the Other Side to something immortal that Silas can't destroy. Damon snaps back, "What — his favorite childhood sled?" in a reference to "Rosebud," the dying word of Charles Foster Kane, the titular newspaper magnate in Orson Welles' classic 1941 American drama *Citizen Kane*. The mystery of what "Rosebud" means provides the narrative drive of the film; the audience ultimately learns it's the name of Kane's childhood sled and is a metaphor for the only time in his life he was truly happy. So Damon's not far off the mark: it's safe to wager that Amara also represents the happiest moment of Silas's long, miserable life.
- A clear sign Elena and Damon spend a lot of time together: she references one of his most often-cited movies, *Fatal Attraction*. It is the third name-check of the 1987 Michael Douglas/Glenn Close film. Damon has likened sire-bond Charlotte ("We'll Always Have Bourbon Street," 4.08) and Meredith Fell ("The Ties That Bind," 3.12) to the "bunny boiler" character, and Elena adds Tessa to that list.
- The credits refer to one of the Travelers in the Jersey warehouse as Kristof, the name of the Traveler who called Gregor/Matt on the phone in Matt's video footage.

THE RULES Wes says that the rate of cellular growth is "phenomenal" in vampire blood. In the aftermath of being drained of her Cure-laced blood and left for dead, Katherine is showing signs of decay: her hair grays and her tooth falls out. Super-witch Silas is able to light fire from his fingertips, do a barrier spell powered by the sun, and open drapes from a distance. He doesn't appear to still have his psychic super powers though. Immortal Amara is the Anchor used to bind Tessa's spell to create the Other Side; presumably, if Amara dies, the Other Side is destroyed.

PREVIOUSLY ON *THE VAMPIRE DIARIES* Silas reminds them about the remote island and creepy hallucinations but who could forget season four's trip to Silas Island depicted in "Into the Wild" (4.13) and "Down the Rabbit Hole" (4.14)?

Tessa busts out the phrase "between us girls," but she only demonstrates

© Tina Gill/PRPhotos

that it requires a certain sibilant delivery best left to the Original hybrid, who memorably asked Elena, while draining her of blood, to decide between Stefan and Damon, "Just between us girls, who would you have picked?" ("Before Sunset," 3.21). Oh *Klaus*.

Amnesiac Stefan cooks for Tessa, just as he did for Elena in "You're Undead to Me" (1.05).

The Travelers fry Damon in the sunshine by deactivating his daylight ring, a trick first seen when the Bennett witch spirits pulled it on him in "Know Thy Enemy" (2.17).

Tessa's memory mind-whammy on Stefan is illustrated with clips from "Blood Brothers" (1.20) — of Giuseppe's death, of Stefan tempting Damon to turn — and from the pilot episode (1.01) of fresh-faced Elena Gilbert.

OFF CAMERA Canadian actor Shaun Sipos returned to The CW for the third time here, previously playing David Breck on the 2009 *Melrose Place* reboot and Eric Daniels, the teacher who has an inappropriate relationship with Lux, on *Life Unexpected*. He's also had guest starring roles on *Smallville* (when The CW was still The WB), *ER*, and *CSI: Miami*. He's no stranger to genre film or sinister college experiences, with parts in *Final Destination 2* (2003), *The Skulls III* (2004), *The Grudge 2* (2006), *Lost Boys: The Tribe* (2008), and *Texas Chainsaw 3D* (2013). "We knew we wanted someone with a tortured past who Elena could bond with," says Caroline Dries of Sipos's casting. "We looked at a lot of actors but Shaun had that wounded puppy thing we liked."

"[Aaron] is a very broken human being," Sipos told *TV Guide*. "He's a good guy, he's just . . . really trying to find his way." Nina Dobrev added that Elena is drawn to Aaron. "When she meets Aaron . . . they bond over a similar life and past and the grief and death they both had."

"Rebecca does an amazing job with VFX," says Holly Brix of Rebecca Sonnenshine's work in this episode to realize the sequence in which Amara comes to life. "The dailies had a statue of Amara that a) wobbled and b) didn't look like Nina at all. Enter Sonnenshine and an army of geniuses in post, and by the time the episode aired, the Amara statue looked incredible. But that's all Rebecca, she kept pushing for something great." Says Caroline Dries, "Nina spent like six to eight hours getting her face molded for the statue of Amara. She had to breath out of tiny holes. We ended up only using the statue in wides and Entity FX supplied the rest for us, doing an amazing effects job."

"As for what I wished I wrote, there's a line in 'Handle with Care' — Tessa says, 'I got Elena inside, how much smarter could a duck be?' That made me laugh every single time I saw it. I still laugh. It's the best line."

— Rebecca Sonnenshine

FOGGY MOMENTS Jer is really in control of his hunter instincts to spend hours in a car with the man he's supernaturally programmed to kill and only call him a "dick." Silas's psychic powers (when he had them) were incredibly powerful, so how is it that he didn't get the "what" when he got the "where" of the Anchor?

Two thousand years ago, in Ancient Greece, the Travelers spoke English. Didn't seem so weird in the flashback when Qetsiyah was narrating from the present, but seeing Amara and Silas chatting in English here is a little odd. Even more odd: Silas refers to Qetsiyah as "Tessa" when he's explaining to Amara what's happened, and Amara, who has been inert for two millennia, totally knows who Silas is talking about.

How did Jeremy and Damon beat Elena and Stefan home? They had to get back from New Jersey.

QUESTIONS

- Since Qetisyah snuck through to the Land of the Living while Bonnie was distracted trying to resurrect Jeremy, didn't Bonnie's death really pay for two lives, not just Jer's? If Nature demands a balance, how was Qetsiyah's resurrection accounted for? Did some poor chump in Mystic Falls drop dead *Pushing Daisies*–style?
- Who is the Augustine vampire who killed Megan? It can't be Jesse, since he was a regular ol' human back then. It must be someone who has been invited into Whitmore House, since Megan was killed indoors and then thrown out the window. What is the point of the Augustine secret society? Does it have anything to do with St. Augustine? Are they anti-vampire or pro or some twisted third option?

"[There's] no dictionary of *TVD* languages — usually we'll just ask Missy [Woodward, season five's researcher] to translate something into Latin (if it's spirit magic) or Czech (if it's Traveler magic), and then we change the words a little to make them sound witchy. It's very technical, clearly. We decided to use Czech because we hadn't done it before, and also because we thought it would be sexy to have Matt meet a hot girl in Prague in the summer before 5.01. So when that story started to emerge, we realized Eastern European witches could be cool. In terms of words, the biggest witch word of the season was *Vyjít*, which means 'Come forth,' and every actor pronounced it differently, which was pretty funny."

— Caroline Dries

- Tessa doesn't answer Elena's question about *how* she came back to life — she just tells her when. Esther was also able to sneak through a hole in the veil using some witchy juju. Is that an option for Bonnie?
- What is happening to Katherine? Can Dr. Wes help her? Are Caroline and Elena in danger of being exposed as vampires again, since Katherine outed herself as Elena's doppelgänger?
- Where is Silas, and is he in the same state as Katherine is — graying hair and teeth falling out?
- Did Damon and Jeremy drive Silas's car back to Mystic Falls?
- Is Amara just a little bit crazy from being stuck in her own head for 2,000 years, or is she talking to someone when she mutters, "It's not up to you" and "Leave me alone"? Someone on the Other Side?
- Why don't the Travelers want Silas dead yet? Did they want his blood to cure Amara, and will they now be ready to see him dead? In "True Lies," Gregor says the Travelers want Silas back in his tomb — not dead. What exactly is their agenda, and why are they so anti-immortality, anyway?
- Tessa narrates Stefan's past as she returns his memories — has she been watching him from the Other Side since the mid-1800s? How will Stefan deal with the memory wallop Tessa unleashed on him?

Amara: I've been in hell for 2,000 years.
Damon: What's another five minutes?
Amara: Let me die.

5.07 Death and the Maiden

Original air date November 14, 2013
Written by Rebecca Sonnenshine **Directed by** Leslie Libman
Edited by Tony Solomons **Cinematography by** Darren Genet
Guest cast Autumn Dial (Doppelgänger Acting Double), Elizabeth Faith Ludlow (Girl), Brady McInnes (Guy)
Previously on *The Vampire Diaries* Paul Wesley

Doppelgängers assemble.

For an episode with some heavy storylines and a high death count, "Death and the Maiden" is a heck of a lot of fun, thanks to bonus Ninas and Pauls, more Katherine and Caroline moments, and the triumphant last moments of two bitter-to-the-end badasses.

If there's a thin line between love and hate, Tessa has spent two millennia balancing on it, protest as she may that she no longer loves Silas. Her ability to "let go, move on" (as Lexi advised Stefan in the season four finale) is less than zero, but she more than makes up for that lack with her snark, her ferocity, and her dedication to triumphing over Silas and Amara, and by extension the doppelgänger-loving universe that she believes conspires against her interests. Faced with the pain of Silas and Amara's betrayal all those centuries ago, Tessa turned to bloody vengeance and never looked back. Her suffering at their hands was delivered many-fold upon them: for 2,000 years, Silas was trapped in a tomb, starving save for drips of blood, while Amara (getting the short end of the stick) was encased in stone, trapped, and subjected to the pain of every dying supernatural creature. (From that perspective, Stefan's three months of drowning does sorta pale.)

Tessa's hate-love hasn't faded a bit — after hearing of Silas and Amara's likely happy ending, she says she wants to shoot fireballs at him and then drown him in acid — and the love between Silas and Amara is just as enduring. While Silas has some choice words about love in the amazingly blasé and violent cold open, he truly does "love love" and wants Amara to be free from her suffering. Their goodbye was legitimately moving, despite the fact that Silas has proved time and again that he is willing to be dastardly in pursuit of his own death. Actually, perhaps it's *because* of how awful he can be — killing the mayor and then making a knock-knock joke about it shortly thereafter — that seeing Silas and Amara say goodbye, eyes full of tears, her pleading for him to slit her throat, is such a powerful moment. (As well as a testament to the acting prowess of Nina Dobrev and Paul Wesley that the Amara-Silas romance feels so different from that of Elena-Stefan or Katherine-Stefan.) Whether or not the universe wants them together forever in their every incarnation, free will be damned, what is certain is that their love survived a trial no other has faced. Amara apologizes to Silas, saying she can't live any longer though she still loves him, and it's one of the few "sorry"s in an episode full of them that is met with understanding and acceptance. Amara's earlier apology to Tessa seems to fall on deaf ears: Tessa has a plan, she has forever, and forgiveness is not a part of it. How do you respond when loved ones fail you? Tessa chose to start a war, one she is determined to win at any cost, and in her dying moments she feels she has won it.

Stefan, on the other hand, doesn't have to chase down apologies; Elena is one doppelgänger who can't wait to get her guilt sorted out. From the beginning of the season, and despite her happiness with Damon, Elena has missed having Stefan in her life — that emptiness has evolved from constant low-grade concern at his absence, into panic to find him, into desperation to make him remember their bond. Before he tells her his memories are back, that he is once more a part of their shared history, Elena wants to try the old "start fresh" option again, introducing herself to him, bright-eyed and chipper, cup of black coffee in hand. And by episode's end, it's evident that Elena's need for Stefan to be okay — to reassure her that after killing Silas he is 100 percent peachy-keen again — is fueled by her need for a clear conscience. If Stefan is fine, if he's himself again, then everything is right in the Elena Gilbert–centric universe. She can be in love with Damon, Bonnie is alive, her brother is alive, their enemy is vanquished, and there's a shiny eternity ahead of her. But moored by guilt, she can't yet move on or let go of the past, much like Stefan can't.

While she was happy with Damon this summer, Stefan was dying again and again, on the brink of losing his mind and his humanity. It's an edge he

Writer Rebecca Sonnenshine on "Death and the Maiden"

As soon as Amara was on the table as a character, we knew we *had* to get [the three doppelgängers] all in the same room at the same time. It was too good of a visual to squander! The most important element was making sure each character looked physically different enough to stand out in a wide three shot. But that never ended up being a problem — Nina could sell those three different characters in the same outfit, as far as I'm concerned. She worked really hard to give each one of them a distinctive speech pattern, body language, attitude. She worked really hard in that episode! The shooting of the scene didn't actually involve a lot of CGI trickery. The director used really elegant practical techniques to make it look authentic. She did such a great job.

In "Death and the Maiden," there's a scene where Amara bites into her own wrist, because it's the only way she can think of to kill herself. Everyone on the crew was extremely grossed out by it. They looked at me and said, "That is *so* disgusting." I had to laugh, because this is a show where we pull people's heads off, rip hearts out, set them on fire. A lot of gross stuff — and yet *this* is the thing that really gets to people. Probably because it's so visceral and real. I was very proud to gross everyone out.

Because we'd been talking about Silas and Amara since season four, my favorite moment [of season five] was in "Death and the Maiden" when Amara tells Silas she loves him but needs him to kill her. And villainous Silas hesitates, because he loves her so much. For me, it just paid off a lot of threads and was a truly emotional moment. Not everyone loves stories that don't involve our leads, but I think it worked because Paul and Nina made you believe they were these entirely other characters.

stills finds himself on, smashing glasses, refusing to buy into Elena's hopeful plan, and going rogue by nabbing Amara and killing Silas. But burying Silas doesn't resolve his psychological trauma; Stefan is still haunted by memories of being trapped in the safe, of the pain and fear of repeated death, of the isolation. As Silas says to him, being in the safe is easy in comparison to the emotional aftermath: realizing you were forgotten by the two people you love most in the world. And while that's not fair to Damon or Elena — they didn't *forget* about him, they just didn't clue into the fact that something was horribly wrong — the net result is the same. Stefan's touchstone when he wants to hold on to his sanity has been Elena, imagining her urging him to hold on to his humanity, but the real Elena demands of him a quick recovery from a traumatic event *and* from the memory slam that Tessa unleashed on him — primarily for her own peace of mind.

"Getting over it" proves to be harder for Stefan than he imagined, and it's plum impossible for Tessa who claims not to be "wired" that way. While Silas mock-pities her for her 2,000-year-old obsession with a love that was not returned — for living without real love — she dies, at her own hand, feeling bitterly triumphant. She *won*. Tessa thinks of love, and life, as something you can "win," and Stefan frames his relationship with Silas in the same terms: he is adamant that he can't let Silas "win." But what victory do they have? Tessa is stuck on the Other Side with Silas, who hates her, and she'll be there for only as long as Bonnie remains the Anchor. It seems unlikely that Tessa has separated Silas and Amara *forever*. So has she simply wasted her own life, hurt others, and killed herself? In Tessa's case, perhaps it would have been better never to have loved at all, than to have loved and lost.

With Silas, Tessa, and Amara killed off in one bloody episode, we also reach a tentative end to another kind of long-lost love story, one between daughter and mother (not between a woman with perfect hair and her stylist). Nadia confronts Katherine about her avoidance strategy; after sharing a moment and forming the beginning of a bond in "Monster's Ball," Katherine went AWOL and Nadia is *not* cool with that. But what Mama Katherine won't tell her scary vampire daughter is that she is literally falling apart. Her efforts to find a solution — medical, magical, vampiric — all fail. She is dying. After surviving for 500 years, Katherine has finally encountered an enemy she can't outwit. Time has caught up to her and just might be the end of her. By pushing Nadia away, she could be thinking of her daughter's best interests: better not to develop a relationship only to die on the poor girl.

While we'll all miss the Katherine-Caroline college roomie experience, brilliant as they were together, the witch whose bed Katherine was bunking in is finally back on this side of the life-afterlife divide. Thanks in great part to the Gilbert kids' unwavering faith that some way, somehow they would bring back Bonnie, and the rest due to Bonnie's very clever plan to do an Anchor swap, Bonnie Bennett is alive again. The moment of Jeremy finally touching Bonnie and of the three girls embracing was a beautiful reunion . . . followed naturally by dire consequence. This is *The Vampire Diaries*, after all, where nothing good ever happens without Nature, or the universe, or the writers' room, balancing it out with something *horrible*. And so Bonnie Bennett faces an eternity of pain: the toll due for her return is payable in agony, as each supernatural creature passes through her from the Land of the Living to the Other Side. A shoddy deal for someone who has always put the well-being of her friends above her own. How will Bonnie manage this twist?

COMPELLING MOMENT Three Ninas plus one hardcore witch equals one stunning display of *TVD* magic.

CIRCLE OF KNOWLEDGE

- No Matt or Tyler in this episode.
- "Death and the maiden" is a motif under the wider umbrella of the *danse macabre*, or dance of death, an allegorical illustration of death as inevitable and universal, rooted in classical mythology and at its height of popularity during the Renaissance. "Death and the maiden" depictions are interpreted as connecting sexuality with death and highlight the fact that even beauty will one day rot, like all other life. The "maidens" are sometimes shown as whole-heartedly embracing or being comforted by Death, and other times Death is forcing them, weeping, into their own graves. Amara, desperate for relief, meets Death with open arms.
- Silas says Tessa turned Amara to stone "Medusa style," a reference to the most legendary Gorgon in Greek mythology. Medusa was one of three Gorgon sisters, monsters who had hideous faces and venomous snakes in place of hair. If men looked directly into Medusa's eyes, they were turned to stone.
- Damon says Amara is crazy like "those deserted island guys that talk to volleyballs," referring to Tom Hanks's character Chuck Noland in *Cast Away* (2000). Stranded on a remote island for four years, Noland strikes up a friendship with a volleyball he finds from his plane crash.
- Nadia tells Katherine "he's just not that into you," in reference to the "self-improvement" book for single women titled *He's Just Not That Into You* by Greg Behrendt and Liz Tuccillo, so popular it reached the Bulgarian-orphan-vampire readership. The book, which advises women that if a man doesn't make an effort to pursue them, "he's just not that into you," was inspired by an episode of the HBO dramedy series *Sex and the City*.
- Tessa calls Amara "the face that launched a thousand doppelgängers," in a reference to Greek mythology's Helen of Troy, the legendary beauty whom English playwright Christopher Marlowe famously described as

Darren Genet on Shooting the Triple-Gänger Scene

You'd be surprised how much of that was actually achieved practically, like through the use of body doubles and photo doubles. I think we only had one or two visual effects shots in there, and it's just a wide when they're all three in there. Everything else we used camera trickery. So if you're [looking] over one person to the other, or we have three people in the frame, that's the only time you ever really need Nina in there. You just have to figure out when you see her face and who she is at that moment. So we would basically do the same sequence of shots and then keep changing Nina out to the other person and then whipping around. And then every time you're looking at her, you're actually looking at the back of someone else's head. So you can use body doubles for that. It's pretty old technology for that stuff; it's just about making sure it feels like it's her.

We had the circle track that we were spinning around the table, which meant we were always on someone's back. So at that point when Nina was one character, we would just have two other actors in the frame that were dressed as her but we didn't really see their faces because you're focusing on Nina. So a lot of that sequence was done that way, and when you cut it together it all just looks like it's Nina.

Sometimes the visual effects shots take you out of it, because it's one of the few times the camera isn't moving a lot, because it just makes it a lot more difficult when you move the camera. So you try to limit those effects shots, because they're really expensive and because they stand out in the sequences — if you have split screens and things like that, they are a static shot; they need to be. You try to do as much practically as you can, and sometimes it's just as simple as directing a stand-in in Nina's clothes.

We use fire a lot on the show — actual fire. We use actual flamebars for lighting, because we do a lot of work when the power is out and there's just a fireplace on, or there's lighting with candles, or if we're out in the forest and there's a campfire. I find that the best way to show light coming from a fire is to actually just use fire as a light source, versus trying to use lights to try and make them look like a flickering fire. There's just something really organic about using fire. We have the effects guys bring out little propane flamebars, and we put them where the lights would go, out of the frame. That stuff is always really cool and interesting and strong visually. It does have such a specific feeling. I think that [triple-gänger] scene was mostly lit by fire.

having "the face that launched a thousand ships" in *The Tragicall History of the Life and Death of Doctor Faustus*. Heralded as the cause of the Trojan War, however indirectly, Helen, like Amara, is central to an epic love story marred by betrayal and bloodshed.

- Tessa calls Elena and Amara Tweedle-dee and Tweedle-dum after the twins of an English nursery rhyme, later made iconic in Lewis Carroll's *Through the Looking-Glass*. The comparison is not a flattering one, implying that Elena and Amara look and act exactly the same and Tessa holds them both in equal contempt.
- The symbol that forms on the grimoire is a triquetra, an old symbol with pagan origins symbolizing the tying together of three elements (e.g., in Christianity, the holy trinity). Here Amara and her two doppelgängers are bound with the triquetra and with blood to fuel the Anchor-swap spell.
- Just like the rest of us, Elena can't resist a well-timed Monty Python joke, insisting "it's a flesh wound" when she finds Tessa in the Salvatore library with a fireplace poker still lodged in her shoulder. The Black Knight had *much* worse in *Monty Python and the Holy Grail*, Tessa — like, missing-all-your-limbs worse.

THE RULES Not only is Katherine aging rapidly and having blood-clotting issues (Dr. Maxfield guesses she has a few months left) but, having taken the Cure, she cannot be healed by vampire blood — she spits up Caroline's. Amara also spits up vampire blood (Damon's) because she also consumed the Cure (in the form of Silas's blood).

Tessa uses the blood of three doppelgängers to fuel her spell to "Anchor swap" Amara for Bonnie, and she uses Bonnie's grimoire as talisman. The blood forms a triquetra and sets itself aflame in the final stages of the spell. The Anchor bridges the world of the living and the Other Side as a kind of "toll booth." Every supernatural creature who dies must pass through the Anchor to get to the Other Side; that process — which only requires a single touch — is excruciatingly painful for the Anchor. The Anchor "feels" the death. (No wonder Amara was so ready to die: 2,000 years of ceaseless torment.) After Silas dies, Amara screams in pain when (presumably) he passes through her to the Other Side; we see the same reaction from Bonnie when Tessa passes through her. The Anchor can see those on the Other Side, as well as the living, which explains how Amara learned English (and all manner of other things — but still hadn't heard of a grimoire).

OFF CAMERA *TVD* fun fact! Doppelgänger acting double Autumn Dial played Tina Fell in "Miss Mystic Falls" (1.19).

Reveals writer Holly Brix, "Originally, episode 5.06, 'Handle with Care,' went all the way through Bonnie becoming the new Anchor. It also had hunters and all sorts of other stuff that got cut because it was just too much for one episode. We split it into two episodes to give it some breathing room. But that meant that 5.06 and 5.07 both got written super fast. I'm so impressed with how well it turned out." As for the triple-gängers in "Death and the Maiden," Holly Brix has nothing but praise for the series' lead actress. "Nina is amazing. Hands down. And this season showed her acting chops like no other. Story-wise, we knew Amara had been the Anchor for 2,000 years, calcified in stone, unable to move, and having the deaths of every supernatural creature pass through her on their way to the Other Side. We leaned into the idea that anyone in those circumstances would be batshit crazy. But Nina brought a sweet energy to Amara — something that captured that essence of a simple handmaiden from long ago who fell in love and now has been in a waking hell for 2,000 years. I really loved her performance of Amara and selfishly wanted the character to stay around longer."

"One of the best shots of the series was the triple-gänger," says Caroline Dries, "and originally this notion never existed. We had planned to kill Amara in 5.06."

One of editor Tony Solomons' favorite music moments is in the cold open of this episode: "Our director, Leslie Libman, had done an incredible job with the scene involving Paul Wesley playing Silas [at the bus stop]. The unique setting is what inspired me to find a sound that was timeless, kind of like this desolate location. The mood was melancholy and dangerous at the same time. So I settled on a rare track, 'You' by The Aquatones. It had the perfect timeless quality while adding a haunting vibe with lyrics that complemented the character Silas's dialogue."

Rebecca Sonnenshine singles out Janina's character as a favorite of the season five newbies: "Tessa was really fun to write for, especially in 'Death and the Maiden.' She was so snarky and vulnerable and angry."

FOGGY MOMENTS Why didn't any of the dead supernatural folks who have spoken to Jeremy, Elena, and company while they were visiting as ghosts (or on Drop the Veil days) ever mention that they had to "pass through" a Petrova doppelgänger? Neither Bonnie nor Jeremy remembers passing

"There are so many challenges editing *The Vampire Diaries* (loads of footage, music, song choices, etc.), but for me the biggest one is making sure the story beats are clear to the audience and that the actor performances help push the narrative along. As the editor, I've read the script, I've watched the episode over and over, I know what's going to happen from one scene to the next, and I know what mythology is in play. But I have to make sure to remember this is all new to the audience and they don't know what's coming. They might not remember what happened two acts ago that's now necessary to recall. So I need to make sure important beats are clear and they land properly for the audience to register."

— Marc Pollon

through Amara, but does that mean *no one* remembers? Do they forget the experience once they're on the Other Side? Are they mystically bound to keep the secret?

How did Katherine get back to Whitmore? When she enters the room, Caroline looks a little surprised to see her, not like they shared a ride back to campus, which is (supposedly) a few hours away from Mystic Falls.

QUESTIONS

- Is Amara-level crazy in store for Bonnie if she continues to be the Anchor?
- Where do *human* doppelgängers end up when they die? Are they supernatural enough to end up on the Other Side, like vamps, witches, and weres?
- Will Nadia really leave for Prague? What about Gregor/Matt?
- What will Katherine do with her next (last?) few months?
- How will Stefan get over his debilitating PTSD?
- What happened to Tessa's Chinese food?

Stefan: Hey. You're Katherine Pierce. Suck it up.

5.08 *Dead Man on Campus*

Original air date November 21, 2013
Written by Brian Young and Neil Reynolds **Directed by** Rob Hardy
Edited by Marc Pollon **Cinematography by** Michael Karasick
Guest cast Rebecca Koon (Old Woman)
Previously on *The Vampire Diaries* Paul Wesley

At Whitmore, Elena and Caroline throw a Welcome Back from the Dead party for Bonnie that ends . . . with death. Stefan takes his post-traumatic Silas disorder to the Grill, where Katherine is drowning her fear of mortality in booze.

Speaking from 500 years of experience, Katherine tells an agitated Stefan that he only has two options: he can face his problem now, or he can run from it. But if he runs, at some point, that problem is going to catch up with him. Clearly not okay, Stefan has been trying to just quietly go about his nightmarish business of living — one minute enjoying sitting by the fire in Damon's favorite reading chair, the next minute struggling for breath as he relives the endless drowning of the summer. He brushes off Damon's attempt to reach out to him and rejects Elena's invitation to the college party — he's frankly a bit of a bummer while the girls are in celebration mode.

Bonnie is alive, and she's on campus, and the friends are doing what they do best — hilariously ribbing her about sneaking away to make out with Jeremy and throwing her a proper college dorm party full of strangers and Jell-O shots. (Jeremy seems to have his priorities in order — sex with Bonnie trumps attending high school.) The episode takes time out to enjoy the fun of the three best friends together at last as college gals, before Katherine's motherly advice that you can only run from your problems for so long catches up to them there too. Bonnie must perform her duties as the Anchor to the Other Side whether she's strolling across campus or about to get down with her muscle-bound teenage boyfriend. Caroline and Elena take on the responsibility of being guides to new vampire Jesse after he escapes the evil clutches of Dr. Wes, but they don't seem to grasp the gravity of the situation. After preventing him from killing his roomie, Aaron, they give Jesse a Vampire 101 crash course, declaring that being a vampire is *awesome*. But, well, it's also awful. The girls' confidence in their ability to keep a brand-new

© Andrew Evans/PRPhotos

vampire under control at a party full of blood-filled temptations (a.k.a. college students) proves disastrous — but thanks to the Augustine twist, it's disastrous in an unexpected way. Jesse is more of a threat to vampires than to humans.

Dr. Wes says the Augustine Society has a mission to protect humanity from vampires, and their R&D department of one has finally created a vampire that feeds on other vampires. A "monster" so voracious in its hunger it will never be sated, the only option is to stop it with a stake in the back. It's a sad fate for the kind-hearted and handsome Jesse (and for Caroline, whose luck in the love department is getting really cruddy), and his short time as a vampire is reminiscent of Vicki Donovan's. As Jesse is about to touch Bonnie and go on to the Other Side, he says to her, "I don't want this," just as Vicki did to Stefan. While Damon was responsible for Vicki's afterlife (he turned her out of pure boredom) and Stefan for her final death (staking her to protect Elena from attack), there's a similar chain of responsibility with Jesse and his own bloody end. As Damon injects various communicable and deadly diseases into Wes's bloodstream, he chastises the not-so-good doctor for turning an innocent kid into a vampire, giving Jesse no choice in the matter — no waiver to sign, no recompense . . . no future. And Damon and Elena are responsible for Jesse's death too: Elena for delivering the blow, and Damon for convincing her that there was no other choice. And that choice — to stake Jesse, to consider *that* the only choice — brings forth from Caroline more harsh words for Elena, in a great portrayal of the less often depicted side of friendship. A true friend doesn't just do Jell-O shots with you and make kissy faces when you go off to mack on your boyfriend. They give you the harsh truth, their adversarial opinions; they judge you and your actions because they know who you truly are and who you're capable of being. Caroline forces Elena to acknowledge the darkness Damon brings into her life.

Back in Mystic Falls, the booze is also flowing freely. From Katherine's intoxicated attempt to ward off her death-sentence blues to Stefan's boredom punctuated by traumatizing flashbacks, the two are in parallel states of psychological hell. Katherine may be a lightweight when it comes to her alcohol tolerance now, but she's dead right: she knows how to help Stefan, and she knows what ails him. He is without purpose — Silas dead, Elena off at college with his brother on call, even former nemesis Klaus is gone. All Stefan has is time to ruminate, to relive, to suffer again the pain of being locked in that safe drowning. The distraction of the Gregor mystery abates Stefan's psychological trauma briefly, but afterward there's a wonderfully filmed moment that places us inside Stefan's mental state — he stumbles from the bar, bumping into people, smashing the glass in his hand, the image drifting in and out of focus as Stefan is overwhelmed and soon gasping for air. Katherine's way of bringing him back to himself, of giving him control, is one that only a friend (or, you know, ex-girlfriend turned pseudo stalker) could come up with: knowing that he kept a list of names in his Chicago apartment as a way to remember, a choking Katherine asks Stefan to recite his kills from the beginning. She brings him back to himself, allowing him to regain control. It is a moment of kinship between the two, and one that is beautifully mirrored when Katherine needs a friend to smarten her up just a little later.

Count on Queen Katherine to choose a dramatic and unambiguously symbolic exit: atop the clock tower, unable to escape her one enemy, *time*, Katherine decides there is a third option. No more running, no facing her problems. She can kill herself. End the fight and no longer have to remember all the horrible things that have happened to her and that she has inflicted on others. Thankfully, she has motherly concern enough to write a note for Nadia, which Stefan finds. In a line that should be embroidered on pillows, emblazoned on motivational posters, and said like a mantra whenever you get the blues, Stefan reminds Katherine of who she is — and tells her to suck it up. Her layered reaction to his pithy pep talk, building gradually to a shadow of a smirk, is such a precise piece of acting from Ms. Dobrev, who keeps raising her own benchmark for excellence. Katherine may believe that the universe has all its eggs in the Elena basket when it comes to Stefan, but there is a connection and friendship — not to mention past love and passion — between this set of doppelgängers that should never be discounted. Especially since it makes for epic television.

COMPELLING MOMENT The total twist of Damon's secret past as an Augustine vampire.

CIRCLE OF KNOWLEDGE

- No Tyler in this episode.
- This episode's "Previously On" is the first this season where Stefan's voice-over narration doesn't start with "Love brought me to Mystic Falls" but jumps right into the recap of pertinent events.

Writer Neil Reynolds on "Dead Man on Campus"

Brian Young deserves the lion's share of the credit for the tone on this episode; he had a vision from the beginning. As a group we knew that this episode needed to feel like a new chapter; Silas was finally dead and the focus turned back toward campus and the Augustine mystery. We also only had one episode to set up Damon's connection to the Augustines, so the pace was tight. So, amidst all the dark stuff, we had a good old-fashioned party, which helped keep the episode buoyant. Also, when Damon tortures somebody, he has *fun* doing it.

It's always fun to write for a new voice on the show, and particularly fun to dip back into my college years. The challenge with these new faces is that they were all designed to flesh out the Augustine chapter, so they're burdened with teeing up mythology and plot elements on top of establishing their own characters. I think "Dead Man on Campus" balanced these elements well, giving a Jesse/Caroline romance a real shot before he died, activating Jesse's ripper virus, getting a heart-to-heart between Aaron and Elena, and even getting a little glimpse of Dr. Wes's twisted psychology as Damon interrogated him.

Katherine's suicide attempt was, more than any other event, the genesis of the episode, and if I recall, Brian pitched it from the beginning. While the girls are trying to get another fresh start at college, Katherine and Stefan are both dealing with trauma — Stefan realizing that his PTSD problems run deeper than Silas, Katherine from the revelation that she's rapidly aging. The line "You're Katherine Pierce. Suck it up" came organically out of one of the many revisions; we had originally imagined that Stefan would talk Katherine out of her downward spiral, then realized that Stefan *knows* Katherine well enough to understand that tough love is the best way to get through to her.

- *Dead Man on Campus* is a 1998 American comedy starring Tom Everett Scott and Mark-Paul Gosselaar as college students in search of a depressed roommate whom they can push over the edge to suicide. The plot draws on the urban legend that a college will grant any student whose roommate commits suicide a 4.0 grade point average for the semester as compensation for the shock. Dating back to the '70s, the myth has also provided the plot basis for the movie *Dead Man's Curve* (1998) as well as episodes of *Law & Order: Criminal Intent* and *CSI: New York* in spite of it being categorically false; no United States college has any such policy.

- "What dorm has a fireplace?" Nice one, Bon. You've been keeping up on the fandom's tweets as well as Elena and Caroline's plot lines from the Other Side.
- PTSD, or post-traumatic stress disorder, is a condition that can develop in the aftermath of trauma, be it actual physical harm or psychological shock. The disorder is most common in war veterans and victims of natural or transportation disasters, rape, abuse or other physical assault, and kidnapping. People who suffer from PTSD can experience vivid, recurring flashbacks to the traumatic event; nightmares; feelings of shame, guilt, and depression; and can be easily startled. Stefan's PTSD manifests in flashbacks to drowning over and over, and he tries to hide his suffering from Damon, Elena, Caroline, and even Katherine.
- Stefan recites his first kills: Giuseppe Salvatore ("Blood Brothers," 1.20), Thomas and Honoria Fell ("The Dinner Party," 2.15), and a few other founding family members murdered offscreen — Marianne Lockwood, Christopher Gilbert, and Margaret Forbes.
- Damon injects Wes with a smorgasbord of ultra-nasty viruses that the doctor has in his lab: necrotizing fasciitis is flesh-eating bacteria, rabies is a virus that causes inflammation of the brain, and Ebola causes fever, pain in the muscles, head, and throat, then intense vomiting, diarrhea, impaired kidney and liver function, and in the most severe cases, internal and external bleeding. Basically, it's a super-fun time, so we *totally* get why Damon ducked out of the party.
- Damon calls Dr. Maxfield on his "Mengele-level crap" that he's spouting about the "greater good" that he alleges justifies his experiments on Jesse and other vampires. Nazi SS officer and physician Josef Mengele (1911–1979) performed horrific and unscientific experiments on prisoners at Auschwitz during World War II, in addition to sending countless people he deemed unfit for such experiments to the gas chamber. The indefensible idea that there is either a scientific goal or a "greater good" to be reached through systemic torture, inhumanity, and murder is echoed in Augustine's treatment of Jesse and its other subjects, one of whom was Damon, now back incarcerated by the Augustines.
- "Out of morbid curiosity, which one of you is younger?" Oh Stefan. According to Caroline Dries, while Katherine has been alive longer and is older in years-lived, Nadia was older than Katherine was when she

became a vampire. So in a way, they're both the younger one — surely a pleasing answer for the Petrova women.

- The year that Damon carved into the Augustine cell wall — 1953 — was when "Uncle" Joseph Salvatore, who ran the boarding house, was killed (on June 12th); his murder was attributed to an animal attack, one of four that plagued Mystic Falls that year. Both Salvatore brothers were in Mystic Falls then. Elena learned about this 1953 Salvatore situation from Tiki's granddad in "You're Undead to Me" (1.05). If you've been wondering what Tiki's granddad has been up to since season one (of course you have), head to Twitter and follow @TikisGrandad.

THE RULES As the Anchor to the Other Side, Bonnie did not regain her witch powers when she was made corporeal in the Land of the Living. Elena describes her as "technically still a ghost." This fits into the previously established mythology of no dual citizenship: you can't be both a witch and something else supernatural (like a vampire). Other supernatural creatures retained their powers when they were made mortal again: both Esther and Tessa were witches when they came back from the Other Side, and Jeremy returned from death a hunter. Since Bonnie is still a ghost and native to the Other Side, presumably she won't age or die. But she can get a haircut.

The only way to "truly" kill a passenger is to bring the passenger forth and then stab the host with a very special Traveler knife, one that Katherine is now in possession of. She describes the Travelers as a faction of witches "big on" spirit possession.

By transfusing Jesse's blood with "Augustine blood," Dr. Wes was able to turn him into a special kind of vampire, one that feeds on the blood of other vampires, has superior strength, redder eyes, and a growlier voice. (That last bit might have been specific to Jesse; time will tell.) In his transition, Jesse would have remembered what Caroline compelled him to forget, so he calls her when he's freaking out because he knows she knows about vampires.

Dorm rooms are not subject to the threshold rule: Elena waltzes right into Jesse's.

PREVIOUSLY ON *THE VAMPIRE DIARIES* Bonnie jokes with Jer about having sex in Damon's bathtub; Elena and Caroline got into an argument last season after Caroline commented about all the floozies who've been with Damon in that very tub ("We'll Always Have Bourbon Street," 4.08).

> "This is a crazy show where impossible things happen, yet it always needs to have a genuine emotional core. So you can't exactly use your own life experiences to generate plot — I mean, I've never met a vampire — but you can draw from your emotional experiences to infuse the characters with a sense of reality. Luckily, those experiences usually get so twisted around and engraved into a wild supernatural plot, no one is ever going to recognize themselves in your stories (like . . . friends or exes or parents)."
>
> — Rebecca Sonnenshine

Caroline asks if Elena wants to be the one to teach Jesse about compulsion, just as Caroline helped Elena learn about it in "Memorial" (4.02).

OFF CAMERA "It was immensely gratifying to see a stunt as big as Katherine's jump from the clock-tower executed," says writer Neil Reynolds of being on set during filming of this episode. "And then to be immediately followed by a lovely, intimate moment between her and Stefan."

For editor Marc Pollon, this episode was the most challenging of the season: "That was an episode where the first cut was quite long and it took a while to get it to time. It also had issues with trying to figure out the proper pacing early on. There were a lot of scenes that were inherently slow, and when played all together made the episode seem a bit sluggish. So finding that balance of faster pace and letting the right moments and emotions land was hard." One particularly challenging sequence was the reveal of Damon's past with the Augustines, which Pollon worked on with Julie, Caroline, and Brian Young. "We wanted to make a more lasting impact on the show's ending, by giving the audience something to think about heading into the next week. The footage used was from 5.09 and I wanted to use one- to two-frame flashes of memory shots played off of Damon registering the conversation, to try and get across the idea that all this information we're now finding out about is part of Damon's past — and his past is really horrific. Originally, the ending was simply shot as Damon wakes up in a jail cell, realizes he's trapped, then screams. We felt the memory flashes greatly enhanced the original footage and, as an audience, we are now truly scared for Damon."

FOGGY MOMENTS Wes says it's been 14 days since Jesse transitioned — a strange time marker that means that the girls don't throw Bonnie's welcome-home party until 10 days after she arrives, and Matt just watches that video of Gregor possessing him over and over without doing anything about it.

Jesse was a student in the microbiology class that Elena and Caroline enrolled in and also Wes's lab assistant, not a TA as Elena refers to him.

Though Elena uses vamp speed to grab a weapon to kill Jesse, she human-speed runs down the hallway toward Damon and Jesse, even though time is of the essence.

QUESTIONS

- Why did Wes experiment on Jesse for 14 days before giving him the Augustine blood? Have other vampires been successfully turned into vamp-blood drinkers, or is Wes's "genius" advancing the program? Is there any connection to Mikael, a vampire who deliberately fed on vampires? How was Elena's father involved in this back in the day?
- Do you think the girls have really great fake IDs, or did they compel the liquor store cashier into selling them all that booze?
- When Bonnie talks to the Old Dead Witch at the party, do the people around her just see her standing by herself muttering? Sad.
- How much does Aaron really know? Does he believe that his parents were killed by a bear?
- Katherine reveals that her father (Nadia's grandfather) was a Traveler. Was her mother one as well?
- Why do the Travelers want Katherine dead, and if that knife is "the only way to truly kill a passenger," where did it come from?
- How much of his days spent as a vampire lab rat did Damon remember before he started getting those PTSD-like flashbacks? He says a couple of things to Wes that indicate a familiarity with mad-scientist types. Does he remember the Augustine program? How did he escape back then? How will he escape this time?

Joseph: Well, there's always time to be a better man.
Damon: Not sure I've got one of those in me.

5.09 *The Cell*

Original air date December 5, 2013
Written by Melinda Hsu Taylor **Directed by** Chris Grismer
Edited by Joel T. Pashby **Cinematography by** Darren Genet
Guest cast Judd Lormand (Joseph Salvatore), Jason MacDonald (Grayson Gilbert), Trevor St. John (Dr. Whitmore)
Previously on *The Vampire Diaries* Paul Wesley

Held captive, Damon reveals to Elena his past with the Augustines. Caroline goes along with Katherine's risky but ultimately effective plan to rid Stefan of his PTSD.

As it turns out, there's nothing quite like shared confinement to forge relationships — be it bonds of friendship, as in the case of Damon and Enzo, or blazing passion as demonstrated by Stefan and Katherine. So much sizzle. In the flashback, Enzo tells Damon he should live not in the present moment but for the future in order to survive imprisonment and torture, but "The Cell" also opens up all that has been long locked away. Damon's secret past is closely guarded both for noble reasons (he didn't want Stefan to feel guilty about *not* rescuing him) and for dastardly ones (his bloody revenge mission), but Elena wants the whole story. She wants the truth, no matter what it reveals about Damon's character, just as Aaron Whitmore — having fallen into the rabbit hole — now wants answers, to know the secrets that have been kept from him his whole life. When fundamental truths long withheld are revealed, it's a gamechanger. Aaron starts his day depressed about his dead roommate and makes that fatal mistake of saying the bad day can't get any worse. (Oh Aaron, it always can when you're around Elena Gilbert and company.) By day's end, he's become a gun-toting Whitmore who believes in vampires and wants his own counter revenge for the murder of his family.

So full of secrets, that Damon Salvatore, and in "The Cell" we learn alongside Elena about his torturous time spent locked in the basement of Whitmore House, subjected to cruel experimentation in the name of "science." The rapid-fire cuts of Damon strapped to a gurney, being medically tortured, are gruesome and jarring, and evocatively contrasted with the slower-paced, sepia-toned, Patsy Cline–soundtracked moments between

Enzo and Damon in their neighboring cells. Already a longtime inmate, Enzo teaches Damon how to stay sane: he keeps up the conversation, asks him about past loves, shares with him his strategy for survival — plot creative revenge — and on at least one instance takes Damon's turn in the torture chamber. Never has Damon Salvatore looked so scared or lost as when we see him pacing his cell in horror, listening to Enzo's screams from the nearby lab.

In the opening scene, Joseph Salvatore, a man about to betray his own kin for some cash, tells Damon there's time to be a better man — and Damon's reply is skeptical, displaying an attitude about his potential for goodness that he seems to have since held on to. The end-of-episode reveal is that Damon has carried out his bitter revenge plan — killing off all but one Whitmore in every generation so the family line lives on and keeping up the killing even after he'd had the transformative experience of meeting, falling in love with, and being with Elena. The struggle at Damon's core proves to be the same as it's been since season one: is he a monster or a man? When the escape plan went afoul back in the '50s, Damon chose to save himself and leave his friend behind in what he *thought* was a hopeless situation (to paraphrase Caroline's comment about Elena thinking she *had* to kill Jesse), and he turned off his humanity in order to do that to a friend who was relying on him. Damon dims his humanity switch more often than Elena realizes — he's been lying to her (and misleading the rest of them), keeping his Whitmore murders quiet. He killed Aaron's Aunt Sara and then went home to his happy and oblivious girlfriend. Elena used to demand of Damon that he "be a better man," but lately that argument seemed like it was long behind them. Elena now finds out it isn't: he's still a killer, he's still keeping secrets, he isn't as reformed as he's been pretending to be. While Dr. Whitmore deserved punishment for his crimes, does his clueless great-grandson deserve it? Clearly, Damon has a PTSD issue, like his little brother does, which helps to explain but not excuse the choices he's made since 1958 when he escaped captivity.

While Damon reveals to Elena that he's been secretly villainous, Katherine and her backup, Caroline, force Stefan into choosing between being a ripper and reclaiming his hero throne. From top to bottom, this was an epically watchable story: Katherine's half-assed attempt at journaling; her ongoing not-friends-but-pretty-friendly relationship with Caroline's; Katherine's "So, have you guys . . . ?" question and both Caroline's and Katherine's responses, while Stefan suffocates in a locked safe between them. And of course, the main event: Katherine's wily plan to get Stefan to face his real trauma, Elena choosing Damon over him in "Graduation." She's a pretty insightful gal, that Katherine Pierce, and she sees that Stefan has been avoiding his emotional pain by focusing on the three months he spent repeatedly drowning. Because of Katherine's innate belief in Stefan as hero, and her proximity to death, Katherine happily hops into the safe with a panicking vampire to help him push past his PTSD, to regain control of himself, and to do so in tight quarters. The air has always been charged between Katherine and Stefan — remember in "The Return" when she insisted that his hate was only the beginning of their next chapter of their love story, not its end? — and after their connection in the previous episode and now in this one, Stefan finally embraces it. Despite Katherine's physical vulnerability, and the emotional vulnerability of putting the moves on an ex who's made it very clear in the past he's no longer interested, Ms. Pierce is brave and bold in all ways — even if she doesn't always know what she's doing — and she approaches Stefan by the fireplace in the hopes that that look they exchanged over Caroline's shoulder really was what it felt like. The song choice, the crackling fireplace, the smooching! Hats off to the writers for carefully paving a long path to this moment, which plays as believable and perfectly timed and is as much of a welcome surprise to the audience as it seems to be to the characters.

COMPELLING MOMENT Stefan and Katherine. In the safe. By the fireplace.

CIRCLE OF KNOWLEDGE

- No Matt, Jeremy, Bonnie, or Tyler in this episode.
- This episode's "Previously On" is the first of season five to ditch Stefan's voice-over narration altogether, opting for the old-fashioned clip collection we all know and love.
- *The Cell* (2000) is a "psychological thriller" that stars Jennifer Lopez as a child psychiatrist who can enter the mind-scape of her comatose patients. FBI Agent Vince Vaughn needs help finding the last victim of a serial killer (Vincent D'Onofrio) who's fallen into a schizophrenic virus-fueled coma (if that's a thing). Like the Augustine Society, *The Cell*'s serial killer keeps his victims in a (wait for it) cell, where they receive just enough sustenance to stay alive, but they are also tortured and then wind up dead and mutilated. When J-Lo gets inside the mind palace of the killer, she is determined to save the little innocent boy that he once

Writer Melinda Hsu Taylor on "The Cell"

On the Augustines and Enzo: The Augustine storyline was something that was already in existence by the time I joined the show at the start of season five. They had started a couple of weeks before I came on staff, because I was still in the interview and contract negotiation process while they were starting the boot camp. Every season, we do a boot camp at the end of the year to talk about the season to come. So when I got into the room, they had been at it for two or three weeks, talking about the Augustines and Elena going to college and discovering things about her family. And there would be a connection to Damon's past and maybe he had been a prisoner of these people, and maybe there was some other prisoner who he had had some kind of significant friendship with. That's about as much as I think we had in week three. And from there, it just evolved.

Enzo had a couple of different forms along the way — there was talk about making Enzo a woman at one point; there was talk about making him a little bit younger and more innocent and that was the version that I had in my head for a long time when I was working on ["The Cell"]. And then when we started the casting process, when Michael Malarkey was auditioning, it was completely different from how I had envisioned the character, so it took me a minute to get on board with that version of Enzo. But then as soon as I did, I've been, like, 110 percent Enzo ever since, Michael Malarkey version.

On the backstory: The backstory that I had in my mind for him — and which I told Michael — was that he was a solider in World War II fighting in Italy, because the Allied Forces there had field hospitals that were sometimes staffed by American doctors, and that's where Dr. Whitmore caught up with him — or came across him. We haven't ever said onscreen exactly how Dr. Whitmore found him and [laughs] that's probably not going to be central to any story moving forward. But the idea was Enzo was on the battlefield, he was injured in, like, an explosion that killed everyone else, and there's Dr. Whitmore poking around for survivors, and Enzo comes back to life, and Dr. Whitmore's like, Oh my god. This guy is different from the others.

I think that [Enzo] was the first vampire [Dr. Whitmore] had in those close quarters. I think Whitmore knew about vampires, because it had been something kind of handed down from the founders' days. If you notice in the flashback scene, where he's getting someone from the cocktail party to give her hand to demonstrate the healing power of vampire blood, he calls her Mrs. Fell, which was an intentional Easter egg. I always figured that some of the founding families were in Whitmore College way back in the day, and the lore had been passed down. So I don't think it was his first time seeing and talking to a vampire, but it was the first time he had his very own pet vampire to experiment with.

On Katherine attempting to journal: I forget whose idea it was to have her write in the diary at the beginning of 5.09. It wasn't my idea, or maybe it was — honestly I don't remember [laughs]. But it quickly became apparent that she should not take it seriously, which is so Katherine. Holly Brix wrote the line, "Mortal coil, blah, blah, blah" and that was so delightful. You ask writers for help or ideas or they pitch something to you and you're like, Oh my god I'm totally using that. So Holly Brix, big shout-out for the diary entry. On a team there are people who have strengths in different areas, and one strength that Holly definitely has is the darkly quippy lines and the sort of out-there moments, which is so great.

On Stefan and Katherine in the safe: [That] was really a lot of fun to write. So many of these moments come out of the writers' room and I can't point to the moment in the conversation in the room where we all said, Oh let's put them in the safe together. But it was definitely out of a conversation. It was not something where I just sat in my office and my own brain popped up with this idea, "You know I think they should be in the safe and I think it should go something like this." It's very collaborative in the writers' room, and I work with a great, great group of people.

But we were talking about: how can we get Stefan past his PTSD? What sort of situation can we put him in that would allow him to be a hero, save somebody, and yet not downplay how traumatized he must be? For a long time, it was going to be Caroline who got him over his PTSD and then we thought more toward: we want to advance the Katherine-Stefan romance . . . they had this moment of intense vulnerability and connection together, and in a very Katherine-like way she picks this really awful sort of therapy. It's so extreme and so, like, *deal with it.* There's no coming back from this.

I really enjoyed that about Katherine — she's all in, no matter what she does. It's nothing like, "Oh well if this doesn't work, I have a plan B"; in this situation, there's no plan B. And it wasn't a cerebral decision. She's very impulsive, which I like a lot about her. And it was very manipulative, which is very Katherine [laughs]. Something that Stefan didn't have a lot of say in, which is very Katherine. But it was also something that allowed her to get what she wanted — very Katherine. And it was sexy as hell, the two of them in that safe. They have such great chemistry, Paul and Nina — it's a lot of fun to be a part of any kind of story with those two as Stefan and Katherine, because it's just very natural. So [the scene] came out of conversations about the character of Katherine and what would she do to fix him. But she also wants to help him in a very genuine way.

was — not unlike our Ms. Gilbert always seeing the nugget of purity and goodness inside the hunky murderous exterior of the vampires she loves.

- Caroline's textbook *Clinical and Practical Guide to Conquering Fear* is a prop, but prolonged exposure therapy is a real treatment for PTSD that involves confronting rather than avoiding the triggers associated with the trauma. What Caroline and Katherine do to Stefan is called in vivo exposure — exposing Stefan to the actual location of his trauma (the safe). Rather than opting for the gradual leveling-up technique, from comfortable to more extreme as the PTSD sufferer adjusts, which is the usual procedure in immersion therapy, Katherine opts for the quick and reckless option, locking herself in the safe with Stefan, which is surprisingly effective — and super sexy.
- What Enzo calls "scissor, paper, stone" is the game more familiar to North Americans as "rock, paper, scissors," which spread through the West from Asia in the late 1920s. Obscure *TVD* fun fact: director Jesse Warn ("Original Sin") wrote and directed a film released in certain territories under the title *Scissor, Paper, Stone*, and elsewhere as *Nemesis Game*.
- The photo Elena sees of her father at Whitmore House says "50th Anniversary Celebration." Assuming that photo was taken sometime in the 1990s, when Elena was a child and her father was likely involved with the Augustines, Whitmore House and the Augustine Society were founded in the 1940s, shortly after Dr. Whitmore returned from the war with Enzo in tow.
- Aaron's parents were murdered at the Anna Ruby Campground; Anna Ruby Falls is a real place in Helen, Georgia, within Unicoi State Park. Funny then that the medical examiner's file below the gruesome crime scene photos is from Oklahoma City, Oklahoma.
- The song Enzo is singing at the end, when Elena wakes up strapped to a gurney next to him, is Patsy Cline's "Walkin' After Midnight."

HISTORY LESSON Damon tells Elena that Dr. Whitmore captured Enzo on a European battlefield during World War II (1939–1945), where Whitmore was a doctor in a field hospital and Enzo was a soldier. Whitmore discovered Enzo was a vampire, drugged and subdued him, and then shipped him to the United States in a coffin at some time in 1943, over a year after the United States entered the war following the Japanese attack on Pearl Harbor in December 1941.

© Glenn Francis/PRPhotos.com

"From the beginning, balancing characters and cast schedules impacts who can appear in a given episode, which in turn focuses the scope of the stories we tell on a per-episode basis. But once we know who's in an episode, we break story without worrying too much about logistics, finding the best, most truthful version of the story before censoring ourselves. Then as we outline and move into script, the logistics become an equal player in the writing. Big action, VFX, or crowd-heavy set-pieces shrink in scope, locations change to fit the shooting schedule, and a hundred micro-tweaks are made to slim down the budget. Usually the audience is none the wiser, and our producers and production team are phenomenal at their jobs, consistently delivering cinema-quality scenes under very tight restrictions."

— Neil Reynolds

PREVIOUSLY ON *THE VAMPIRE DIARIES* In the flashback, Damon mentions that the last time he saw Stefan was in New Orleans during World War II ("We'll Always Have Bourbon Street," 4.08).

Elena came face-to-face with her father's anti-vampire stance in "Crying Wolf" (2.14) when she discovered a cache of vampire-killing weapons at the lakehouse.

OFF CAMERA Damon's former Augustine cellmate Enzo is played by London-based actor and musician Michael Malarkey. Born in Beirut, Lebanon, and raised in Ohio, Malarkey studied at the London Academy of Music and Dramatic Art and has had select roles in a few shorts and in dramatic, historical reenactments on *Dark Matters: Twisted but True* and *Curiosity*, as well as Irish TV series *Raw*. He has a previous connection with The CW, having been cast as Prince Maxon in the network's unaired pilot for *The Selection*, based on the young adult novel by Kiera Cass.

In a video interview with *OK! Magazine*, Malarkey recounted filming one of his favorite scenes from this episode, which he compared to working on a short film: "I'm in a cage, and Damon decides he can't help me, so he decides to leave. And they used real fire there, so it's like *blazing*, and having to act on those heightened levels of, you know, *'Don't leave me!'* alongside flames burning around you — that's a challenge." Most of Malarkey's early scenes on the show were with Ian Somerhalder, whom he describes as great to work with. "We have a great working chemistry together."

"I love flashbacks," says Melinda Hsu Taylor, whose episodes this season all included some flashback action. "At first it was just kind of happenstance. We knew that episode 5.03 would be a flashback episode and episode 5.09 we kind of knew would be a flashback episode, and it just happens that I was assigned to both of those the way that the rotation shook out."

FOGGY MOMENTS There are some nice 1950s musical touchstones in this episode, but the timeline is a little wonky on some selections. Patsy Cline's "Walkin' After Midnight" was released in February 1957, but the song plays prior to the 1957 New Year's party. "A Girl Like You" was also released in 1957, making it an unlikely track to play at a "Happy 1957!" party.

In neighboring cells, Enzo and Damon play scissor, paper, stone to decide who will drink the other's rations, but they don't look at each other's hands as they're playing . . . and yet they still know who won.

Was Dr. Whitmore too cocky or a little bit stupid? While he has a vervain watch on — which a vampire could easily snatch off — he doesn't ingest vervain; Damon freely feeds on him after he escapes his chains. Ditto for the guests at the New Year's Eve parties: when treating captive vampires like party favors, best to dose your houseguests with vervain in the champagne for their own protection.

QUESTIONS

- Thanks to Tiki's granddad (and Elena's research skills from season one), we know that Stefan did arrive in Mystic Falls in June 1953, presumably in response to Joseph's telegram summoning him. Did the Whitmore society not know that there were two Salvatore vampires?
- Damon flips off his emotion switch in order to leave Enzo to die in the fire. Does he live emotion-free from New Year's, 1958, all the way until Lexi meets up with him in 1977 ("Because the Night," 4.17)? When did he turn his emotions back on?
- Once the dust settles and the crisis is over, how will Elena react to Damon's revelations that he's been killing Whitmores in a cruel and unusual fashion for the past 60 years?

- Will Caroline tell Elena about the Katherine-Stefan mouth noises she overheard?
- How did Enzo survive the fire?

Enzo (to Damon): You were the most important person in my life and you ruined me, but that's just who you are. That's who you'll always be . . . a monster.

5.10 *Fifty Shades of Grayson*

Original air date December 12, 2013
Written by Caroline Dries **Directed by** Kellie Cyrus
Edited by Tony Solomons **Cinematography by** Michael Karasick
Guest cast Jason MacDonald (Dr. Grayson Gilbert), Kayla Madison (Little Elena)
Previously on *The Vampire Diaries* Paul Wesley

Captured by Dr. Maxfield, Elena learns more about her father, while Damon battles a handsome blast from his past. Nadia comes up with a plan to extend Katherine's life.

"Fifty Shades of Grayson" may only reveal, say, two shades of Grayson in actuality, but there is a multitude of character gradation on display elsewhere in an episode that explores what kind of monstrousness we can turn a blind eye to, what we can face and forgive, and what remains irredeemable and unforgiveable.

The Augustine Society is the epitome of science gone wrong. Here we see delusions of decency, thinly veiled cruelty, torture, and true monstrousness. And though Wes had managed to distract Aaron in the previous episode with an avalanche of life-changing information about his family and about vampires, here Aaron sees Wes's true colors — he is Aaron's guardian but he leaves him for dead, more interested in his ill-designed rabid-vampire masterplan than in doing the decent thing. While Aaron Whitmore responds to the betrayal by giving Wes a good wallop when given the chance, Elena treads a very different path as she finds out about her father's secret history. In brief flashbacks to childhood, Elena remembers being in the basement of Grayson

Gilbert's medical practice (long before it was burnt to hell in the season one finale) and hearing the sounds of what she now knows were vampires being zapped and prodded, cut open and tested upon. Little Elena was perfectly cast and *adorable*, but her simple, childlike acceptance of those she loves still clings to her now, a naivety-turned-deliberate-ignorance that allows Elena to love a chronic murderer.

Damon is right: Elena makes excuses for those she loves — for her father and for Damon now, for Stefan in the past. While there are extenuating circumstances for Ms. Gilbert, living as she does in the center of a maelstrom of supernatural shenanigans that invariably turn violent, Damon's main point holds true. Brushing away the unspeakable acts of others will change — *has* changed — Elena into a person more capable of doing those things herself. (See: Jesse.) The tension between who Elena once was and who she's become has been building this season, but solely in connection to her codependent relationship with Damon. The air is let out of the balloon here in terms of the Grayson Gilbert mystery: it has little to do with Elena as an individual, or with a revelatory backstory about her father. Grayson had previously been revealed as being anti-vampire, owning a cache of weapons and being a member of the Founders' Council. That he actively tortured vampires in the name of "developing" a cure-all is ridiculously weak as far as excuses for bad behavior go: vampire blood *is already a cure-all*, which Elena well knows. What did he want — FDA approval? Ultimately the Gilbert connection to the Augustines is used solely to bring conflict to the romantic relationship in Elena's life — the increasingly narrow focus of her character's emotional arcs. As Damon says as he ramps up into his breakup speech, she reads 100 pages of horror in her father's journal and finds the one sweet and heroic part where he saved the life of a little girl with a heart problem. Elena pushes away the thought that, if alive today, her father would capture and torture her, because in his eyes she is a monster, not a person. Instead of changing her opinion of her father, she burns his diary, a feeble attempt to erase the knowledge she's gained from it.

Elena's willful blindness is enough to spur Damon into action. He refuses to accept her excuses for his behavior, to allow her to change into someone who understands his sins and still loves him, someone who brushes off his choice to methodically kill an entire family and not change course, despite his seeming progression to the not-so-dark side over the course of the series. And in the same spirit, he refuses to change (or believes he cannot change) who he is, which puts them at an impasse. Damon's charged reunion

> "I think Damon has always tried to protect Elena, and in this season, the universe is conspiring to convince Damon that he needs to protect Elena from *himself*. The Augustine chapter is a literal take on ghosts from Damon's past — particularly his baggage with Enzo. Any time Elena gets caught up in the collateral damage of Damon's actions, even ones that happened six decades ago, Damon's guilt overwhelms him, and he pushes the ones he loves away for fear of history repeating."
>
> — Neil Reynolds

with Enzo primes him for this later encounter with Elena. He sees in Enzo's fate what could happen to Elena — he might betray her, harm her, change her into a revenge-seeking monster. Enzo doesn't give Damon forgiveness for leaving him to die with the Augustines, and Damon doesn't want it. Forgiveness won't change Damon. And Enzo, visibly hurt by the betrayal and the abandonment, can't grant him absolution even if he wanted to.

The Elena-Damon storyline mixed heart and horror, but Katherine Pierce, after her hookup with Stefan, brings the heart to the comedy. In all its human charm — the shock of gray hair, the zero-percent-cool morning-after dash out of Stefan's bed, her desire to get "hot" again — her renewed drive to live stems from her hope that Stefan will be able to forgive her, and *love* her. She wants from Stefan what Elena so willingly gives to Damon. But he can't forgive and forget. There's enough nuance and history here for us to see it from both sides and feel for each character. Though Stefan won't give her the redemption or the love she craves, he does reach out to her at the end of the episode, in a small heartbreaking moment, holding her hand and speaking volumes without saying a word.

To add more pathos: enter Nadia. Her earnest belief, followed swiftly by palpable disappointment, that her mother might want redemption and to build a life with *her* goes a long way to shade in a character who is relatively new to this storyworld. Her scene with Matt Donovan resonates — both know the sharp pain of a mother's absence and selfishness, and the impossibility of giving up hope that one day, maybe, the imagined relationship will be realized. It's bittersweet to watch Katherine yearning for love and redemption from Stefan only to be blind to, or seemingly uninterested in, her daughter's yearning . . . Until of course the cliffhanger of an ending — Nadia returning, Katherine plotting, and that takes-a-licking-and-keeps-on-ticking heart of hers giving out, just in time for the series' big 100th episode. Will Katherine find a way to survive it?

COMPELLING MOMENT Damon's intense breakup speech to Elena gave us both sides of his complex character — his refusal to give up the devil inside, but the selfless instincts of a man who loves Elena, desperately.

CIRCLE OF KNOWLEDGE

- No Bonnie, Jeremy, Caroline, or Tyler in this episode.
- E.L. James' erotic novel *Fifty Shades of Grey* is referenced for the second time in the series, though this time the show riffs on the book's title

The *TVD* gang at PaleyFest 2014 © Crissy Calhoun

Kellie Cyrus on Her Various *TVD* Jobs

Script coordinator: Their job is overall continuity. Not only with making sure wardrobe matches, etc., but making sure the actors' actions match as well [from take to take]. They are the eyes and ears for the editors. A good script supervisor will work closely with the director in keeping track of coverage and eyelines and show continuity. There are a lot of VFX and stunts that make this show more complicated than many other shows. Also, the challenges of shooting in Georgia with the unpredictable weather.

Her current position: My job now is to be the on set producer. In case the director or the actors have any questions or concerns about the scenes we are shooting. I guess you could say I'm the eyes and ears for the writers, who are in L.A. Basically, I'm just there to help however I'm needed.

As a director: I like to work very closely with [the writers]. I'm probably more literal to the script than most directors, which I think comes from my script supervisor background. . . . Big stunt scenes are the most challenging for me, so it's nice to be able to have the opportunity to get to shoot them. But I prefer the character stuff. One of my favorite scenes was with Nina as Katherine and Elena in the diner of episode 4.18 ["American Gothic"]. I had a lot of faves in that episode.

rather than its content. (We still know what you've been reading, Stefan "Red Room of Pain" Salvatore.)

- Subject 83182, a.k.a. Elena, manages to still be conscious after having 4.1 pints of blood drained, while 12144 (a.k.a. "Full Name Lorenzo" Enzo) passed out after 2.9 pints. Considering that the average male has a pint more than the average female (10–11, versus 9–10), Elena would make a champ blood donor.
- Katherine says she's 538 years old, and she's right! In *TVD*land, it's only 2011, and her math is correct.
- When Stefan calls Wes to let him know he and Damon have Aaron, the doctor threatens Elena's cerebral cortex — the outermost layer of brain tissue related to memory, thought, language, consciousness, and the senses of sight, sound, and touch.
- After Enzo hurls Damon out the classroom window and onto a car, Enzo clinically details the damage the landing might have done to Damon's clavicle (collarbone), lumbar (lower spine), and thoracic vertebrae (the middle part of the spine). He's spent a *lot* of time with doctors.

- Wes explains that the compound he intends to inject Elena with has effects that are comparable to "Pavlov's dog," or the classical conditioning technique of Russian physiologist Ivan Pavlov (1849–1936), who conditioned dogs to reflexively salivate when they heard a buzzer by repeatedly sounding that noise when they were presented with food. Pavlov found the dogs would still salivate when they heard the noise, even in the absence of food. It is also the conditioning method *The Vampire Diaries* production team uses to provoke instantaneous tears when the audience hears a Birdy song.
- Grayson's diary reveals that many years ago, he cured Megan of her congenital heart defect — a deformity of the heart's structure that can affect blood flow and the heart's rhythm. While many congenital heart defects don't require treatment, complex cases can require surgery or, as in Megan's case, medications like vampire blood.

THE RULES To ensure Enzo comes back to Torture HQ, Dr. Wes injects him with something that will desiccate him if he doesn't return to the lab for the antidote.

Being a Traveler is genetic, like being a witch or a would-be werewolf. Katherine's father was a (nonpracticing) Traveler, therefore Katherine is a Traveler too and should be able to train and hone her magic skills.

Wes says that, thanks to his compound, he conditioned Jesse to salivate at the smell of vampire blood; if he's being literal, then vampire blood smells different from human blood.

PREVIOUSLY ON *THE VAMPIRE DIARIES* Damon's disgust when he finds out someone has slept with Katherine is, and will always be, a delight. His reaction to her telling him she and Stefan spent the night together recalls "American Gothic" when the Elijah bomb dropped.

Elena's drained of crazy amounts of blood, but this ain't her first rodeo: Klaus took as much as he could from the poor girl in "Before Sunset" (3.21) when he wanted hybrid-making blood.

Matt relates to Nadia's absentee-mother issues, thanks to his experiences with Kelly Donovan; when she bowled into town in "A Few Good Men" (1.15), Matt did just what he describes here — fixed her some food, happy to have her home.

"The mythology is just so dense. And not just the supernatural stuff. But the character mythologies, who these characters are and what they've done and said, go back for such a long time. Like history-spanning backstories. This is great because you get such incredible episodes like 3.03 ["The End of the Affair"], and you get to see Paul Wesley in the 1920s. Or Damon in the 1940s. Luckily for us, the oldest characters on our show took off for New Orleans. But then you've got the backstories just within the chronology of the show. Who has slept with who? Who has been invited into where? Where is that damn Traveler knife? How many times has Matt died with the Gilbert ring on? When has Caroline's hair looked the best? (The answer is: always.) Stuff like that."

— Matthew D'Ambrosio

OFF CAMERA Director Kellie Cyrus says Kayla Madison "was the only choice for me" to play Elena as a child, even though the production was hoping to find a local actor for the part. "There was nobody as good as her to play young Elena." She also credits Ian Somerhalder and Michael Malarkey's great working chemistry in capturing Damon and Enzo's epic fight and the intense emotions that follow. "I came on set for the first time Michael was in a scene and I remember Ian telling me how great he was. They enjoy working together, and it shows."

FOGGY MOMENTS Where did Katherine get the money to pay Matt to be her trainer? She had spent her last 20 bucks on breakfast back in "Death and the Maiden" and hasn't been gainfully employed since. A little Salvatore house thievery?

Why was Megan's corpse sent flying out an upper-story window if the vampire-holding cells are in the basement of Whitmore House? Was that their attempt to make it look like a suicide? (Weak, Dr. Wes.) How did Enzo get free to attack her and chase her, as heard in the phone call she makes to Elena in "I Know What You Did Last Summer"? Was Wes chasing her and then Megan leaned her neck right into Enzo's cell? Probably that.

Sure, Enzo's been imprisoned for about 70 years, but he is really chatty for a guy with a fast-acting poison coursing through his veins. Why tell us the big long story we just saw in the previous episode, complete with a reprise of the flashbacks from said previous episode?

Did Wes know Dr. Gilbert personally, or not? In conversation in "True Lies," Wes says he only knew his work, but in "The Cell" Elena tells Damon that Wes knew her father (based on no conversation we hear to that effect), and here she asks Wes when he met Grayson. Wes's answer doesn't indicate that they ever *actually* met. Is Elena a bad listener and a bit loopy here from blood loss?

Why did Matt refer to his mother in the past tense?

QUESTIONS

- Katherine says her father forbade "us" from practicing Traveler magic, calling it the devil's work. Does the "us" refer to Katherine and her sibling? Perhaps the girl in the death tableau from "Katerina" (2.09) is her sister?
- What will Aaron do with the serum that can turn a regular vampire into a rabid vampire-eating vampire? Why did he pick it up?
- Now that Damon has dumped Elena, will Jeremy still live at the Salvatore mansion? Will Elena still hang there when she's in Mystic Falls, which is, like, every day?
- Will Katherine Pierce, survivor of five centuries, live beyond *TVD*'s 100th episode?

Stefan (to Katherine): None of this is your fault.

5.11 500 Years of Solitude

Original air date January 23, 2014
Written by Julie Plec and Caroline Dries **Directed by** Chris Grismer
Edited by Marc Pollon **Cinematography by** Darren Genet
Special appearances by David Anders (John Gilbert), Sara Canning (Jenna Sommers), Matt Davis (Alaric Saltzman), Kayla Ewell (Vicki Donovan), Daniel Gillies (Elijah Mikaelson), Claire Holt (Rebekah Mikaelson), Bianca Lawson (Emily Bennett), Joseph Morgan (Klaus Mikaelson)
Guest cast Madison Connolly (Sister Petrova), Hayley Guard (Doppelgänger Double), Josué Gutierrez (Ivan), Alyssa Lewis (Traveler #1), Monica Louwerens (Doctor), Austin Maxwell (Traveler #2), Oleg Sapoundjiev (Papa Petrova), Sia Sapoundjieva (Mama Petrova), Taylor Treadwell (Mia)
Previously on *The Vampire Diaries* Paul Wesley

Katherine Pierce is on her deathbed.

Thanks to the writing power duo of Julie Plec and Caroline Dries, this 100th episode milestone marks a nostalgic time to be a *TVD* viewer, with memories and manipulations, scandalous sex, and a chance to see so many of the dearly departed — all while pushing the season forward to its next logical doppelgänger twist.

We've had episodes like "Ghost World" where dead-and-gone characters return to find a little peace, but this episode found a new way to bring back old favorites without it feeling forced or like fan service (which it was, and thank you). By centering on the one and only Miss Katherine Pierce, lying on her deathbed, Petrova fire slowly sputtering out, "500 Years of Solitude" gave us a look back at the 99 episodes that led to here, since so many major plot lines have either been a direct result of Katherine's actions or inspired by those in pursuit of her. (Hey, Klaus.)

The gang — minus Stefan — chooses to celebrate a villain's downfall, and they knock back shots of bourbon with a lively recollection of all the terrible things Katherine is responsible for. Or not so terrible, in the case of Caroline: "She did kill me — though I'm weirdly better off." Damon takes this little drinking game to the next level, using his ability to manipulate a weaker mind to push the memories that Katherine is reliving from bad to truly terrible as a way of punishing her in her final, defenseless moments. Damon's a funny guy when it comes to personal responsibility: last episode in the breakup speech (which Caroline memorized), he refused Elena's excuses for his behavior. Back in season one, he told Stefan that he alone was responsible for his actions ("I own them. They belong to me."). But now in the wake of his decision to break up with Elena — a very boozy wake, granted — he pins everything on his other doppelgänger ex, echoing Enzo's accusation of him in "Fifty Shades," saying, "She ruined me." He sees Katherine as the root cause of all of his own evil-doings, and wise Sheriff Forbes points out that he still allows Katherine to exert too much determination over who he is. He's standing over her deathbed, pillow in hand ready to smother her. The only living-and-present Mystic Falls parent's advice? Prove her wrong.

Katherine believes she deserves all the things the gang is saying about her (not that she can hear them, she has the hearing of a *very* old lady). Unlike Damon in this episode, she accepts responsibility for what she is, but importantly, brilliantly, in the end, she doesn't change her M.O. She is still Katherine Pierce, a survivor, a fighter. She cares about Nadia and won't accept her offer to be her host body, but she will take over her doppelgänger, who's just forgiven her for her past sins. The character of Katherine has always resisted the simple classifications of purely evil or solely selfish. She loves her daughter, she loves Stefan (and for that weird, brief blip, Elijah). But she's also guilty of that laundry list of wrongs. She's simultaneously complex and crafty yet relatably clear in her motivation. It's a combination that makes her choices seem unpredictable but, once revealed, they feel inevitable and entirely logical.

Fresh from experiencing what a good pal Ms. Pierce can be (plus that hot hookup), Stefan gives the gang the much-needed alternative perspective on Katherine. Yes, she's responsible for all manner of terrible things, but she began as an innocent. Shunned by her family. Chased for ritual blood sacrifice by the most powerful supernatural creature on earth. Stefan doesn't defend Katherine's worst actions or excuse them, as Elena is wont to do with Damon. Instead, he stands for compassion and respect in (what promised to be) her final moments. And Elena, though reserving the right to hate Katherine, forgives her. Elena doesn't want to let go of her own humanity — her capacity for forgiveness, empathy, or kindness — because she has been subjected to similarly traumatic forces as Katherine experienced back in

Julie Plec on Her Road to 100

It probably meant more [to me] than it needed to. When I first moved [to L.A.] and started taking an interest in TV in general, I would read the trades every day and I remember seeing all the celebrations of the 100th episodes of shows. There'd be people buying ads in the trades and there'd be pictures of the big party and the cake. Within the industry, it's such a milestone and has so much meaning. They used to say that until you get to 100, you'll never get syndicated, so that was always the big get back in the day — when there actually was syndication. Now it's become a much more metaphoric celebration. [Making it to 100] just doesn't happen very often.

When we first started this show, Kevin and I were like, "Well, this could be the one that just kills the vampire genre forever and won't that be embarrassing. Won't that be embarrassing that we were the ones that did it." We had such non-expectations, because we really didn't know if the audience appetite would be strong enough. So then when it was a hit, we were like, "Okay, that's cool. This feels good. It's a hit and we're okay with it being a hit, because we're working so hard and we really are doing everything we can to make it *great*." And so that was the first two seasons — we're just trying to make a spectacular series here that people can be really proud of.

Then, when Kevin moved on in the third season, for me, it became *oh god, I have to not screw up this whole show*. It's no longer Kevin and Julie, it's just Julie, and so I need to make sure this season doesn't take a hit, that by the end of season three we haven't lost 90 percent of our viewers and everyone can look to me and say, "Well, you ruined it!" So that's what kind of kept me going emotionally during season three, just this desire to make it stand out and to make it sing and to not screw it up.

That got us to season four, which got us to: Okay, we're finally in the Elena-is-a-vampire season. We had that to work with, which gave us so much opportunity that we finally hit our stride and felt like we know what we're doing. It went from being the hardest, most dysfunctional, soul-crushing process for three years to suddenly becoming an actual, functional machine. Between building up to graduation, all the Elena vampire stuff, and "Who's gonna get the Cure?" we just had story spine. We had a production team working well, we had a good team in place that had been with us now for three years and everyone was hitting their groove. The success of that season was that we finally felt like we weren't one step away from chaos every minute. Scripts were delivered on time.

I think that's what people *don't* realize is that making 22 episodes of television a year is probably both creatively and physically the hardest job in town. I mean, when you *care*. When you care, when you pay attention to every detail, when you're part of every choice, when you make sure every word is a good word. For the crew, it's 12- to 15-hour days, nine, 10 months out of a year; for an actor, it's 22 episodes of character work and relentless, nonstop, no-break work. And for showrunners, it's upwards of a thousand pages of delivery, [and you can] multiply that times three with the amount of pages you throw out or rewrite. So you're putting together 3,000 pages of material, hundreds and hundreds of minutes of editing, prepping, and shooting and all that at the same time — it is *so awful*!

So the only thing that brings you joy is the content; pride in content, pride in the process — when the process evens out, it's *thrilling*. And then, of course, success, or at least appreciation from the audience. And then your relationships with the people that you work with. When all of those are firing, when you *love* the people that you work with, and you go home at night and you think, "Aw, I miss those guys," that takes a couple of years to find that on a show.

When your process runs smoothly and people are on time and on schedule, and people aren't working until six o'clock in the morning, you feel *good* about that. When the show is still creatively strong and people still like it and get all worked up about it . . . they're still *passionate*.

Now we're four years deep, right? So season five was like, okay we kept our strength creatively and we love our team and each other, our process is running well, we had a good year of story, so now season five, we get to say we made 100 episodes of television. And it doesn't suck yet! And anybody can bitch about the sire bond, or Delena versus Stelena, or singular moments over the course of the series, and they can have their complaints — like this year, the Travelers — whatever it is somebody wants to take umbrage with creatively.

But I still believe, if you look at the series as a whole, it has never sucked. And I can't really name a lot of TV shows that have gotten this far that have never sucked. So to get to 100 and feel like we still like each other, the scripts are still on time, the machine is running smoothly, people still love the show, we're still getting the same attention that we got in season one, if not more so — and sometimes negative attention — but it just felt like such an accomplishment, and one that we might never have again. Because who knows if I will ever have that accomplishment again. I might get another 100 episodes again on another show, but it might suck for half of them. I might never get a show past season one, ever again. So it was that sense of *This is a big moment and I'm gonna freakin' enjoy it.*

the day. Like the doppelgänger before her, Elena knows she has to be careful of who she might become in her vampire's eternity.

In her last moments, Katherine revisits those great early traumas: her baby being taken from her, her family massacred by Klaus. Damon plays on Katherine's worst fears, telling her that her entire family's death was her fault. But he's not "adding it up right." It's not true that no one cares about her, that she doesn't deserve to be loved — Damon is working out his own demons with Katherine's mind, his actions revealing more about his own character than hers. When Stefan messes with Katherine's mind, he does so with the opposite intention — to give her peace. For Katherine, that means erasing the horror of her murdered family and returning her infant daughter to her. Katherine's reaction as she looks at baby Nadia's crib is proof positive of her capacity to love, of her need for a little humanity in her final moments, just like anyone else.

Stefan's do-goodery doesn't begin and end with Katherine though: he gives both Elena and Damon pep talks, urging them not to give up on their relationship. It can't be easy to tell the woman you love to go ahead and be with your brother, but Stefan pulls off this selfless moment. It's that same spirit that made Damon push Elena away in the first place: his belief that he is no better than Katherine, that Elena would be better off without him. Just like Katherine, Damon deserves to be loved, and both Stefan and Elena seem determined to stick with him through his selfless, self-destructive moments.

Of course, the final selfish action of Katherine Pierce hugely complicates this love quadrilateral: if Katherine has control of Elena's body, then it doesn't matter what Elena wants. Katherine's in the driver's seat with a particular fondness for the younger Salvatore that dates back further than we thought. Katherine reveals to Damon that she felt the doppelgänger draw when she glimpsed Stefan by the side of the road in 1864. Was it fate that brought them together? Is there really a "prophecy" that all the knockoffs of Silas and Amara are meant to be? Is there more scandalous sex to be had in the future?

It will be hard to top this episode's throwdown in the woods for its sheer OMG-it's-finally-happening twist. The Klaus-Caroline banter, always amazing, is perhaps at its best here, and beyond the passion and shirt-ripping and post-coital leaf stuck in Caroline's hair, there's a beautiful symmetry (to borrow a Klausism) in the two couples: the sparks between good-girl Caroline and evil-one Klaus and the recent screen-scorching connection between Stefan and Katherine. The darkest part of Caroline cares for Klaus in spite of all he's done.

As for the parade of fallen friends seen again briefly, this show once again manages to bring back characters in a way that feels right — not a cheap trick — and that's no easy feat. An appropriately nostalgic and celebratory episode for *The Vampire Diaries*' 100th episode, "500 Years of Solitude" gives us everything that's great about this show in its 42 minutes. And that's something worth toasting with the top-shelf bourbon.

COMPELLING MOMENT In an episode with 100 moments to choose from, Aunt Jenna making a brief and stabby appearance was an unexpected delight. (Thanks, Damon.)

CIRCLE OF KNOWLEDGE

- Not only are all the current season's cast members in the episode, but "500 Years of Solitude" features appearances by all series regulars from the show's five seasons, including fallen characters Vicki Donovan, Jenna Sommers, Alaric Saltzman, and the former Big Bad who's moved on to the Big Easy, Klaus Mikaelson.
- "500 Years of Solitude" riffs on Colombian Nobel Laureate Gabriel García Márquez's 1967 novel *One Hundred Years of Solitude*. The magic realist story is set in the utopian village of Macondo where multiple generations of the Buendía family bear the same name and similar traits, akin to successive doppelgängers. The novel also includes ghosts from the past who return to visit the living, and the concepts of selfishness and

"There was one episode that Chris Grismer directed ["500 Years of Solitude"] with the Travelers and the interior of this creepy house. The idea was that there were these holes in the walls and the boards and to bring these shots of light in, but none of them could actually touch our heroes because their rings weren't working and it would've burned them. So that was really fun and we ended up getting this really gothic and interesting lighting there, like shots of light coming in where it's super-dark, and these [Travelers] that appear out of nowhere."

— Darren Genet

TVD Turns 100

Julie Plec: Programming-wise, it was not the best episode [timing] — it's like the first one back after the break or something, there's no fanfare, no buildup — but we wanted to do something special for the 100th and the death, or so we thought, of Katherine was that for us. And we were super-excited about it. There was talk that Kevin and I might write it; Caroline and I ended up writing it, but I knew I wanted to be a part of it, no matter how much chaos was happening over at *The Originals*. And for a long time, it was actually going to be the death of Katherine. That was the episode. And we knew we wanted to bring back as many faces as we could and have some fun with the flashbacks and hallucinations and stuff like that.

Caroline Dries: When we created the passenger idea, the room joked that if Katherine had any brains, she would hop into Elena. But we laughed it off and said forget it because we knew she was meant to die. Well, one morning Brian and I were Instant Messaging each other over breakfast, since we're always talking to each other about work because that's what cool people do, and we were like, it's a bummer we're killing our coolest character. And at the exact same time we both typed something like "what if she does hop inside Elena?? What if we lose Elena for a chunk of episodes and have Katherine pretend to be Elena?" and we were like *we have to do this*. I was so excited about it that I was actually nervous pitching it to Julie in between seeing actors at a casting session that day. And she lit up and liked it a lot. You have to realize, for us to commit to that was very risky-sounding at the time. Looking back at the choice, I actually have anxiety wondering what we would have done if we hadn't done that. It provided so much great story. We were so thankful Nina was brilliant, because the entire plot rested on her shoulders.

Julie Plec: Caroline, about a quarter of the way through the season, walked into my office and she said, "We just thought of something you're either going to love or going to hate." And I was like, "And what might that be?" And she pitched me the whole "Katherine at the last minute passengers Elena," and it would give us a nice big twist at the end, it would give us a good storyline for Stefan in the middle of the season, and I was like, "That's kinda got the ring of Kevin Williamson genius to it." It wasn't the original intention; it became the story once we were breaking the season and wanted to have a nice run following the [100th] episode that would take us into that . . . there's always that mid-season chunk, from episode 12 to 17, that we call our "mid-chapter," that can kind of make you or break you in a lot of ways. You always want to find a good hook for it, because if you don't have a good hook for that middle chapter, you can flounder. And so that gave us the hook that we really needed and we had a lot of fun with it.

Caroline Dries: Julie and I sat at this lunch place by her apartment in Atlanta and ate sandwiches and discussed things that the writers' room in L.A. had been breaking out. We knew we wanted to see the [guest stars] who ended up onscreen. We knew we wanted Katherine to be bedridden and then lurch up and take over Elena's body. And we knew that when we incorporate flashbacks into an episode, we don't have a ton of room for other hijinks. So we wanted to keep it character-based and do our best to give everyone their moment in a 44-minute show. I really enjoyed the process of writing. I think what happened is that we went back to her apartment, she sat at her counter and I sat at her dining room table and we wrote in silence, occasionally emailing each other our pages. Originally the plan was to get all the way [to the moment with Damon that ends "The Devil Inside"], but we figured out early on we were going to run out of space. And as it often does, a simple beat like that can be turned into a whole new episode's plot. By around 1 a.m., we had finished the entire script, which floored me. I think she was surprised too, but there is a certain ease about writing character bits versus plot twists that makes writing so incredibly enjoyable. I was dead, of course. Julie, however, asked me to drop her off at the bar where the rest of the crew was gathered. It was hilarious to me that she had energy for anything else. We had planned on a Wes element of 5.11 that would have incorporated what the Travelers were up to with the blood they took from Stefan and Elena, but we lost it because we decided it didn't matter in the scope of the 100th episode. I'm glad we did. It was simply to answer a potential question and I didn't want to use up space on it.
Julie Plec: [Director] Chris [Grismer] came to us in season three and his first episode was "The End of the Affair" [3.03], which was one of our best episodes ever, and he just kind of hit it out of the park and is so dialed in to the show and the aesthetic of the show. You can always tell when he directs because it just looks *good*. He's a brilliant artist and he really shoots these shows well. I thought he did such a beautiful job on "Graduation" [4.23], and so it was important for us — for the 100th, especially — that Chris do it. Had Marcos [Siega] been available, maybe we would have made an exception, but he wasn't, so . . . Chris has done the most and been in the directing family for quite some time.
Darren Genet: [Hitting 100 episodes is] a great landmark and congratulations to all those guys who've been there since day one. For me, it wasn't as much of an end-of-the-marathon [moment] as for some of the other guys. I got there in the middle of the fourth season. But even as long as I've been there, I'd been there a year at that point, it was really fun to share that with them and especially to see some of the actors who came back to do that. It just gives you a really good time to reflect on the show, from what I've

done to what's happened since the first episode. It's a *huge* accomplishment in television, to be able to get 100 episodes, and to be able to share that was a real honor. And also to be able to shoot it with Chris. Chris and I work so well together, so it was a real pleasure, and it was just really fun, and it was a good script and it all kind of came together. We were super happy to do it — and on to 200! This show is a force to be reckoned with.

Caroline Dries: As we were working toward the 100th ep (which happened to fall in the middle of the season), I was so focused on keeping the train on the tracks the best I could — breaking stories, getting scripts written and rewritten, etc. — that I didn't go into the break of the 100th ep with that much sentimentality. I didn't even think I was going to be a part of it, which is why I decided to write the episode before it. I figured Kevin and Julie wanted to do it, so I was ready to help them break it and then step back. But Kevin was in New York on *The Following* and Julie asked me to cowrite it with her, so I was incredibly flattered. Then once we started talking about everything we wanted to happen and who we wanted to bring back for cameos, it started to sink in how important this was. There was a day on set where we had that string of old friends return — Jenna, John, and Elijah. It was the day before the 100th ep party and we were making it a light day so we could get out early to go to a bar (this is not rare that we go to a bar, but incredibly rare we don't shoot for at least 12 hours), and there was this vibe on set that felt so much like a gathering of loved ones. Studio people were there. Julie was there. A lot of the former actors. It was really nice.

Marc Pollon: Working on the 100th episode was quite an honor, but there was so much more to be proud of [besides just the milestone]. I think so many aspects of the filmmaking process all came together to make it a truly great episode. Julie and Caroline's script was so awesome. Director Chris Grismer and DP Darren Genet's footage was shot so beautifully, especially the flashbacks of Katherine's past. Nina's acting was perfect and heart-breaking as both Katherine and Elena. I love all the songs and, of course, the ending!

Kellie Cyrus: It was epic.

Michael Allowitz: Not many shows make it that far. It was an honor for us all to have been part of it.

Rebecca Sonnenshine: I think I tweeted something — that we'd told 300 episodes worth of story in 100 episodes. We really do just churn through story, so 100 episodes is quite an achievement.

Joshua Butler: *The Vampire Diaries* is an incredible phenomenon, capturing both the hearts of its viewers and the adoring attention of pop culture these past few years. Talk about the right show at the right time! That said, I am also in awe of Julie Plec, Kevin Williamson, Caroline Dries, and all of

the writers who have created so many wonderful stories within the world of *TVD*. Creating 100 hours of television — roughly 4,200 minutes of actual content — and still remaining popular and relevant, that is a truly jaw-dropping achievement in my mind.
Paul Wesley: To be honest, the 100th ep was just another ep. I don't really know what it all means. It's sort of like birthdays. They are silly. But on a grand scale, I'm proud of the longevity and viewership we have retained over the years. A rarity in television.

solitude are explored in opposition to solidarity and love. It's a fitting title choice for *TVD*'s 100th episode.

- Bonnie sees Katherine appear in the Salvatore library and Damon quips, "Ding dong, does that mean the witch is dead?" But unlike the Wicked Witch of the East, crushed to death under Dorothy Gale's house in the 1939 film adaptation of L. Frank Baum's *The Wonderful Wizard of Oz*, Katherine is able to will herself back to life and into her body before the Mystic Falls gang can sing the merry Munchkin song "Ding! Dong! The Witch Is Dead" in celebration.

HISTORY LESSON The cover story Katherine dreams up in the coach with Emily Bennett — that she lost her family in the fires in Atlanta, which we first heard about in "Children of the Damned" (1.13) — refers to the Atlanta Campaign of the Civil War in the summer of 1864. Atlanta was occupied by Union troops at the beginning of September and fires consumed the city as it was evacuated. Take note, history majors: the lady responsible for Atlanta burning is actually the one and only Miss Katherine Pierce.

THE RULES The Travelers are able to prevent Elena's and Stefan's cuts from healing until they are done collecting their blood.

Katherine doesn't want more sedatives, saying when she is weak, Damon can get in her head. But as a human, she's an easy mark for a vampire like Damon to manipulate. Katherine's real reason for not wanting to be overly sedated is that she needs to be awake in order to do the passenger spell on Elena.

Bonnie thinks Katherine will pass to the Other Side, despite her human status because she's both doppelgänger and Traveler; when Katherine briefly appears in front of her, that proves true.

PREVIOUSLY ON *THE VAMPIRE DIARIES* Katherine returns in her mind to the two key traumatic moments in her life, both shown in "Katerina" (2.09) — her baby being stolen from her and discovering her family has been slaughtered.

Elena wants to stay in bed in the wake of the Damon breakup, just as she retreated under the covers in "162 Candles" (1.08).

The gang gathers to recap all the bad that Katherine ever did: in "Fool Me Once" (1.14), Damon discovered Katherine was *not* in the tomb, and Bonnie blames Grams's death in the wake of the tomb spell on Katherine too. Katherine pretended to be Elena, and Damon smooched her in "Founder's Day" (1.22). She fed Jeremy to Silas in "Down the Rabbit Hole" (4.14) and crashed his car and left him for dead ("I Know What You Did Last Summer"). In a huge leap of logic, Matt and Damon blame Vicki's death in "Haunted" (1.07) on Katherine — and by extension, anyone turned and/or killed by Damon and Stefan? Also Katherine's fault. Sure, boys.

After Elena recaps sins against Aunt Jenna and Uncle John, Damon recreates those memories for Katherine: a hallucination of Aunt Jenna appears wearing the same olive-green silk shirt she had on in "Plan B" (2.06) when Katherine compelled her to stab herself, and an imaginary Uncle John cuts off Katherine's fingers with a riff on her famous Hello, Goodbye line from "Founder's Day." Caroline mentions that Tyler's werewolf curse was triggered by Katherine in "Masquerade" (2.07) when she compelled Matt and Sarah to provoke Tyler to the point of murder. Klaus's crimes — and Esther's — are also pinned on Katherine since he followed her to Mystic Falls: Jenna's death in the sacrifice ("The Sun Also Rises," 2.21) and Alaric's death after Esther turned him into a super-vamp ("The Departed," 3.22). Katherine killed Caroline in "The Return" (2.01), smothering her with a pillow, just as Damon is about to do to Katherine before Liz stops him.

Here Damon provides nightmares for dying Katherine, and Stefan gives her pleasant dreams, but in "The Descent" (2.12), Damon gave Rose a peaceful dream to end her long vampire life.

The 1864 flashback of Katherine and Emily Bennett in their carriage predates the ones previously seen in "Lost Girls" (1.06) of Katherine arriving at the Salvatore house.

OFF CAMERA This 100th episode is the only one this season that Julie Plec has a cowriting credit on. Candice Accola appears in the music video for the first song featured in this episode; in the clip for "Love Don't Die," her fiancé, Joe King of The Fray, starts a bar fight in her honor and then they smooch.

For editor Marc Pollon, Katherine's wake "was a scene that was really fun to cut, fine tune, and is one of my favorite scenes this season. The idea behind the wake scene was that Damon, Jeremy, and Matt are finally able to celebrate the news of Katherine's imminent demise. What better way than remembering all the terrible things she had done to them chased down by bourbon shots! It was intended to be fast paced and fun, until Elena and the girls come to put a stop to it. It took awhile to put together and get the right looks, performances, quick pacing, and timing of all the pouring and

Julie Plec on Klaus and Caroline

Joseph [Morgan] said to me, "Don't you think [their sex scene in 5.11] is going to fuel the fire more than putting it out?" And I said, "No, I think it's nice closure." And now he gets to be right, which is upsetting, but for me — look, I'm a TV fan. I watch television and I have relationships that I like and when those relationships move on . . . you get over it and you let the next relationship come by. Buffy and Angel, they were on two completely separate shows and I ended up rooting for her and Spike more, when all is said and done, than I did for them, because I moved on and I found something new to get excited about. So the idea of holding on to a relationship that isn't part of the show anymore is just so interesting to me.

If Caroline was a wallflower on *The Vampire Diaries* and would fit into the world of *The Originals*, and it was a seamless shift to make, then of course we would keep exploring the relationship, but she *cannot* leave that show. She is the only one of her tone that exists on that show and she's so special and she's a centerpiece of that show. Just to service a relationship desire, there's no way. For me, what we were trying to do [in "500 Years"] is basically say, look, this relationship is and was important to us too, and she never got to express her feelings; it was always done in mystery and looks, and you weren't really sure where she stood. And where she stands is that she thinks he's a despicable human being and yet they've had some pretty magical experiences together and she's wildly attracted to him and there are parts of her that care about him — not enough to go running off into the sunset because he still killed a lot of people that she cared about. There's always that balance.

Truthfully, the hardest thing in the shipper universe is balancing people's desires for characters to be together and our own moral standards of why. Even Damon and Elena is hard because of all the things that he did and has continued to do over the series — first and foremost being killing her brother. It's *hard* to get behind it sometimes, which is why you had to wait 'til she was a vampire for us to really allow it, because then you're not in control of your own emotions, and then all your deepest desires can take over your rational thought. And then it can become true love. But it's tough. It's tough to balance. And Klaus and Caroline is that thing — Caroline's a good girl, Klaus is a bad boy, she made him want to be good, but he still was a bad boy, so you want him to get what he wants because it's satisfying, and you want her to give in to her deepest desires, because it's thrilling, but it's hard to be like, *Oh and then they lived happily ever after.* Sorry, Aunt Jenna.

Honestly, what was fun about the crossover in the 100th episode was to let Caroline deliver on her very conflicted feelings for Klaus, and Klaus had to come back because the whole premise of his character is that he chased Katherine for 500 years. We had to service that and service Caroline's character and then she grew from that and she had a lot of things she had to work through as a result of her actions and it was fun, and it was a great scene, and it was really thrilling to see those two characters come together.

drinking. Ian was really terrific. Regarding the song, I had heard Jagwa Ma's 'Come Save Me' earlier and had it in mind for a while. The song cutting out when Elena tells Jeremy, 'You're cut off' was editor Tony Solomons' idea. It worked great. Having that silent moment makes the Damon/Elena face-off tenser than if the song had continued throughout the scene. It is, after all, the first time they've seen each other since breaking up. Then when she decides to join in and the music kicks back in, it's priceless!"

FOGGY MOMENTS Funny that none of the vampires hear the two bottles of bourbon smash in the cellar when Nadia attacks Matt. Or hear her moving the giant heavy safe from wherever they've stashed it. She must've moved pretty quickly to attack Matt, move the safe, bury it somewhere, and return to the library before the gang notices Matt hasn't returned with more bourbon.

After establishing their connection in "Katerina" and a romance in

"American Gothic" (4.18), why didn't Elijah come along with Klaus and Rebekah to bid farewell to Katherine?

In the end credits, doppelgänger is misspelled.

QUESTIONS

- What do the Travelers want with a bucket each of Stefan's and Elena's blood?
- Will Nadia get from Matt that ever-so-important Traveler knife that has the power to expel a passenger?
- When did Katherine and Nadia make the plan for Katherine to be a passenger in Elena's body?
- How long before everyone figures out that Elena is not Elena?
- Will Tyler stay in Mystic Falls?
- Will Katherine get rid of that pink streak in Elena's hair?

Katherine: Seriously, I have never met a group of needier people.

5.12 The Devil Inside

Original air date January 30, 2014
Written by Brett Matthews and Sonny Postiglione
Directed by Kellie Cyrus
Edited by Joel T. Pashby **Cinematography by** Michael Karasick
Guest cast Taylor Treadwell (Mia)
Previously on *The Vampire Diaries* Paul Wesley

Matt and Tyler throw a party, and Katherine stirs up trouble as Elena.

Relationship drama can have deadly consequences on a vampire show, and in "The Devil Inside" Katherine Pierce does what she does best: she goes after what she wants and raises some hell on her way there. The Katherine-bodyjacking-Elena plot line takes its next inevitable step, with dutiful daughter Nadia securing a way for her mother to take control of Elena — for Katherine to be pilot, not passenger.

In past seasons, the writers have gained a lot of mileage out of the delight of seeing one doppelgänger impersonate the other, and here the gag goes further. As Nadia says to Katherine, she isn't pretending to be Elena, she *is* Elena. There's no end to the ruse — by episode's end, Katherine's corpse has been torched — and her top-notch Elena impersonation is put to the test. While Nadia is concerned about her mother tripping up on the details of Elena's life, Katherine is more confident, and bolder, in her knowledge of Elena, her life, and her loved ones. She calls on a compelled Matt to be her informant in a comedic BFF consultation about wardrobe and hair. From taking out the trash to "accidentally" spilling Caroline's Klaus-hookup secret within earshot of Tyler, Katherine manages to simultaneously impersonate and mock Elena, giving the audience relief from and perspective on a character who can be all the things Katherine has accused her of being (self-righteous, the world's most boring vampire . . .). But Elena is also the center of the show, the girl who has fought for love and to live, despite all the horror thrown her way, and here during those brief moments she has control of her own body, she fights to escape what she immediately recognizes as a Katherine Pierce hijack. Though Elena briefly fools Nadia and Mia in order to escape, she is ultimately not as ruthless as her doppelgänger — she doesn't kill Mia or Nadia; she runs, and she loses the battle for dominance.

In Damon's arms for just a moment before she's gone, Elena doesn't get the chance to even hint at what's going on, and the raucous fun of seeing Katherine as Elena takes a turn. With Damon blazing up Elena's phone all day trying to get back together, and Katherine plotting to end things between Damon and Elena for good, the scene is set with the two characters in charged opposition. Katherine uses all she knows about Damon: his weaknesses, his dark desires, and his past attempts to be a better man in the pursuit of Elena Gilbert. And she uses her intimate knowledge of her doppelgänger — information more vital than who Elena likes better, Bonnie or Caroline — to shape a breakup speech that is painful in its believability. The reason Katherine's words have such a powerful effect on Damon is because in many ways they are true, though Elena herself would never speak them. The struggle between Damon and Elena has always been about change: whether he could change himself to "deserve" her, or whether she could change herself to accept him as he is. Katherine pushes Damon's buttons, telling him that he is who he is, someone Elena could never change, not in any permanent or meaningful way — which is precisely Damon's fear and was his rationale for breaking up with Elena in "Fifty Shades of Grayson."

Even when Damon is being the "good" version of himself, he's still murderous, as Elena learned in "The Cell." He didn't give up his Whitmore revenge scheme; he killed innocent people for the sins of their fathers. But when Enzo shows up with Aaron Whitmore in a body bag, Damon tries again to resist his monstrous instincts. While Elena's devil is literally inside her thanks to Katherine's spirit possession trick, Damon's devil takes on the alluring form of Enzo. Enzo goads Damon into being who he is at heart — a revenge-seeking, murderous vampire; a man who too often follows his first instinct, which is to kill. Katherine's razor-sharp breakup with Damon is enough to make him give in to that devil, and instead of letting Aaron Whitmore drive north 'til he hits ice, Damon teaches Enzo the very first trick Katherine taught him in a nice callback to the first kill Damon made in the pilot. As he was back then, Damon now is not remotely conflicted about whether he's a monster or a man: he embraces his desire to kill, believing (at least for the moment) that his victims deserved their gruesome deaths, and that his mission to be "better" to earn Elena's love was a wasted effort. Damon tears into Aaron Whitmore, smirking, blood dripping, embracing the darkness in him, cut off from his reasons to abstain. While Damon has lost a girlfriend, he's up a best friend, and Enzo is proving to be as loyal as the rest of the Mystic Falls gang.

While Matt is forced into best friend duty for "Elena," he willingly plays that role for his lost and purposeless best friend. Tyler is spiraling even before the big reveal at the party, and Matt tries to pull him out of his isolation and boozing with . . . more boozing. The party is nothing but a band-aid solution for Tyler, something to get him off the couch and into the shower, but by its end, he is even more purposeless. Tyler has always had a powerful rage, and after hearing that the woman he loves slept with the man he hates, he turns on Caroline in a truly dark way. Since one tiny bite from Tyler is a death sentence for Caroline, when he bares his teeth at her, it's not mere aggression, it's a death threat. Just as Damon is in crisis, unmoored without Elena, so is Tyler. His revenge mission on *The Originals* a failure, Tyler has nothing left — no family, no job or school to go to, no girlfriend — all he has is Matt. His own stalwart best friend is there for him, as Enzo is there for Damon. And thankfully, since Bonnie's out of town and Elena's possessed by her evil twin, Caroline has a shoulder to lean on in Stefan. Possessing a kind of cool calm ever since Katherine cured him of his PTSD symptoms, Stefan has spent the last couple of episodes just *being there* for people: for Katherine, for Elena, for his brother, and for Caroline here in her post-Klaus fallout. Their friendship was a true surprise back in season two, and it is wonderful to see them enduring so much insanity. Stefan, of course, understands the dark side in Caroline because he shares her inclination too. Every single one of them has that devil inside. Not only does Stefan pop Tyler in the face for the hybrid-bite threat to Caroline, he gives Caroline what she needs most: some perspective, some company, and some empathy. The road ahead for Stefan will no doubt be bumpy. His goal to reunite Damon and Elena for the good of his brother — he believes Damon is a better person with her than without — is in direct opposition to Katherine's goal. While Tyler waffles about what to do with the eternity that lies ahead of him, Katherine, in the guise of Elena, knows precisely what she wants: a home, her daughter, and Stefan.

COMPELLING MOMENT From Elena's run across the lawn into Damon's arms to the Katherine smirk that ended the scene, the Damon and "Elena" breakup scene was messy, complicated, layered perfection.

CIRCLE OF KNOWLEDGE

- No Bonnie or Jeremy; they're off visiting Bonnie's grumpy vampire mother.
- "Devil Inside" is a 1988 single by Australian band INXS from the album *Kick*, and it is also the title of a 2012 horror film about demon possession and exorcism.
- Matt reminds "Elena" that he doesn't drink vervain, just in case one of his vampire pals needs his blood. Now that, Matty Pants, is the sweetest.
- Nadia quizzes Katherine on Elena fun facts and stumps her on where Stefan and Elena first kissed: outside the Salvatore mansion back on the night of the comet (1.02).
- Interestingly, both Nadia and Enzo wear daylight rings, and no explanation has been provided about their source, while over on sister show *The Originals*, most vampires do not have daylight rings and it's a big old deal to acquire one.

© Emiley Schweich/PRPhotos

THE RULES Mia says that Travelers don't have access to "traditional magic" so they improvise. To give Katherine "permanent" control of Elena's body, Mia requires some of Elena's blood. She makes an incision in Katherine's corpse's gut, chants, throws what appears to be salt on the wound, and then Katherine's body ignites in flames. When Katherine can feel Elena's consciousness start to return, she hears a disconcerting whispering; when Elena feels Katherine about to take hold of her mind for good, she gets flashes of Katherine's memories from key moments in her life.

PREVIOUSLY ON *THE VAMPIRE DIARIES* This episode has the first Lockwood mansion party since season three ("Our Town," 3.11).

Elena dyed a streak in her hair in "Because the Night" (4.17), and here Katherine finally gets it gone.

Damon puts Katherine's corpse "where she was always meant to be," a.k.a. the tomb underneath the old church ("Fool Me Once," 1.14). She was also imprisoned in the tomb at the end of "Masquerade" (2.07), for a little poetic justice.

Guess that time that Klaus made out with Caroline while in the shape of Tyler ("Growing Pains," 4.01) pales in comparison, eh Tyler?

As Katherine gains control of Elena's consciousness, Elena sees flashes from Katherine's life from "Katerina" (2.09), "Klaus" (2.19), "The Return" (2.01), "Lost Girls" (1.06), "Down the Rabbit Hole" (4.14), and "Graduation" (4.23).

Stefan jokingly calls Caroline "shallow," but in "162 Candles" (1.08) Damon called Caroline shallow in earnest, and she took the insult to heart, telling Matt that she was as shallow as a kiddie pool.

Now with Enzo at his side, Damon reprises his favorite lie-in-the-road trick and references his existential crisis conversation from "The Descent" (2.12); to answer Aaron's question, yes, Damon *did* kill the innocent woman he told about his conflicted feelings regarding killing innocent strangers.

OFF CAMERA Brett Matthews enjoyed writing this episode's sixth act (the last chunk of the episode, following the final commercial break), with "the emotions of all those stories crashing together, and in particular Damon's monologue before killing Aaron Whitmore." As for the scene where Elena is overwhelmed by Katherine's memories as she runs, he says, "It's like a mix tape of a band's greatest hits, so we were all tossing moments around in the

Meanwhile in New Orleans . . .

Tyler: Klaus put me through hell in New Orleans, Matt. He crushed me. And just when I thought it was over, that he couldn't destroy anything else, or do anything worse . . .

After choosing revenge instead of Caroline in "Monster's Ball," Tyler heads to New Orleans in pursuit of Klaus. In *The Originals'* episode "Bloodletting" (1.07), he kidnaps Hayley, his former werewolf ally who is now pregnant with Klaus's child, and takes her to the bayou to test a theory: that the blood of her unborn baby is capable of creating hybrids. Tyler can't outright kill Klaus, an Original, but he seems intent on harming Hayley and the baby, especially when his theory turns out to be correct. He turns one of the Louisianan werewolves into a hybrid by injecting him with blood from Hayley's womb.

The episode culminates in a knock-'em-down, drag-'em-out brawl between Tyler and Klaus in the bayou. Klaus eventually overcomes Tyler but, realizing his protégé has a death wish, spares Tyler's life and compels him to live with the knowledge that he means nothing to Klaus.

Afterward, Tyler goes straight to Klaus's French Quarter nemesis Marcel and offers to help him and Rebekah take out Klaus. But Rebekah has other plans for Tyler and, before the vampires execute their ill-fated plan to capture Klaus in "The River in Reverse" (1.08), Rebekah snaps Tyler's neck and tosses him into Marcel's "garden" — an underground crypt full of imprisoned and desiccating vampires. The plan to take out Klaus fails and an uncertain truce is established in the Quarter; Rebekah brings Tyler back to Mystic Falls in "500 Years of Solitude," the same episode in which Caroline and Klaus finally give in to their long-simmering sexual tension — thus fulfilling the "anything worse."

room. And they're all in there. Editorial did a really nice job pulling that sequence together."

One particularly delightful bit of *TVD* trivia from this episode: the ugly shirt Matt Donovan sports at the party, most clearly seen in his conversation with Tyler at episode's end, was ordered "burned, buried, and exorcised" by Julie Plec due to its absolute hideousness. Matthews and Neil Reynolds framed it and gave it to her as a Christmas present.

FOGGY MOMENTS Under compulsion, Matt tells Katherine that Elena's birthday is June 22, but in "The Birthday" (3.01) Elena celebrates her 18th one week before the start of the school semester, making it late August or early September.

> "I think it can be really hard [to write one character as another character] . . . but it's a hell of a lot easier when it's Katherine. The character is so great because you just always know where she stands, and Nina really enjoys playing her and digs so deep when she does that it just takes it over the top and makes it memorable."
>
> — Brett Matthews

Let's assume that when Damon overpowers Nadia after she attacks him at the Salvatore house, her heart's just not in the fight. Since she's the older vampire by a few hundred years, she's the stronger one.

Damon compelled Aaron to drive north and not stop until he hit ice — should Aaron even be capable of stopping the car when he sees a man lying in the road?

After Damon kills Aaron Whitmore, Enzo says to Damon, "Now that's the Damon Salvatore I remember." But when he knew Damon, Damon was in lockup, not a rampaging vampire, and from what we saw in "The Cell" Damon wasn't in braggadocio mode either — he was shell shocked.

QUESTIONS

- Does Katherine really have *permanent* control of Elena's body?
- Will Bonnie notice that Katherine hasn't yet passed through to the Other Side, but only appeared for a brief moment in "500 Years of Solitude"?
- Why can't Travelers access traditional magic?
- How dark will Damon go on this post-breakup bender?
- Is this the actual, forever end of the Caroline-Tyler relationship?

Stefan: C'mon, Damon. You're better than this.
Damon: On the contrary, brother. I'm better like *this.*

5.13 *Total Eclipse of the Heart*

Original air date February 6, 2014
Written by Rebecca Sonnenshine and Holly Brix
Directed by Darren Genet
Edited by Tony Solomons **Cinematography by** Michael Karasick
Guest cast Christopher Marrone (Joey)
Previously on *The Vampire Diaries* Ian Somerhalder

Damon and his murder buddy, Enzo, have no qualms about ruining the gang's time at the Whitmore College Bitter Ball in order to find their next victim.

Way back in "Original Sin," Damon said to Elena, "You are my life," and here, mere weeks later in TV time, Damon is proving just how much he meant it with his spiraling misbehavior, which Stefan predicted and which Enzo embraces. There's a world of difference between making a fresh start and straying so far from the kind of person you once were as to make the return path near impossible. "Total Eclipse of the Heart" throws the gang together at the appropriately titled Bitter Ball on college campus to see how far they will go under duress and stress — and we get to see just how dedicated an "Elena" Katherine is.

Though they have *very* different approaches, both Caroline and Damon want to make clean, no-looking-back, burn-the-bridges breaks from their past relationships. Caroline's method — shredding photos along with a fan-favorite, irreplaceable horse drawing — is a little less dark than Damon's, which involves murder, more murder, and attempted murder on a little brother who's seen way more than his fair share of being murdered. In the wake of the Klaus Encounter Revelation (thanks, Katherine), Caroline is burning from Tyler's scorn and she wants nothing to do with either of her former suitors. Her reaction is as typically Caroline as Damon's is typically Damon. She is all pep about a new start — motivational-poster truisms, cleansing symbolic acts, and a well-decorated dance. And Damon puts just as much verve and enthusiasm into his new plan: he and Enzo are having a *good time*, as the empty bottles, broken glass, and crashed-and-bloody car indicate at the top of the episode. As Stefan theorizes to Caroline at the Bitter Ball,

Damon seems to enjoy his darkness, enjoys being this Damon, and — from an audience perspective — it makes for *excellent* entertainment. When Damon delights in doing bad, he's his quippiest, smirkiest, and evilest self. The guy that Elena, once upon a time, hated. The guy that Stefan worked his darndest to get rid of. Stefan seems to have his older brother's psychological profile all figured out, but the question remains: what, if anything, can he and his friends do about it?

Stefan's first attempt to get rid of bad-influence Enzo is a total failure. He delivers a rousing "get out of town" speech, complete with physically threatening Enzo with the shovel Enzo had been using to bury a recent kill in the woods (which must be littered with shallow graves by this point). But Enzo reminds Stefan of the hell he's just escaped. You can't scare a man who has no fear, and after decades upon decades of being tortured by the Augustines, Enzo has no fear. He has only a delight in dastardly deeds, and a desire to escape with Damon for adventure far from the doldrums of Mystic Falls. There's nothing Stefan can threaten Enzo with, not even the finality of death; Enzo is dedicated to achieving vengeance against Whitmore and to sticking by Damon's side. He proves his loyalty most at the end of the episode when their revenge scheme leads them into a sticky situation with some Travelers: Damon, mouth bloody, eyes rabid, infected with the vampire-eating virus. And yet Enzo is decidedly blasé about the troublesome turn — yes, a cannibalistic vampire for a best friend *might* be a problem. While an antidote is in existence somewhere, the question that lies before Damon and Enzo now is how to get it, or how to make Wes make some more, before Damon ends up killing everyone he's ever loved, and then some.

Though Stefan unwittingly tells Katherine, not Elena, about how and why his tune has changed in regard to the Damon-Elena pairing, it's still a milestone on his road to finding peace in the aftermath of Elena choosing his brother over him. In "Graduation," Stefan generously told his big bro that he was "not not happy" for him, and now that the Silas-safe-PTSD situation, along with the emotional trauma it masked, has been resolved, Stefan is no longer a bitter ex. He admits that he's stopped wishing for Damon to do something unforgiveable to drive Elena out of his arms. Instead, Stefan wants Elena and Damon together, because he believes their relationship makes Damon a better person. Where does that leave Elena? Katherine's argument for why she (meaning Elena) doesn't want to return to Damon is, of course, entirely self-serving and done to manipulate a situation to her

"Julie and Caroline are so good at seeing the big picture and knowing how to get the most out of a scene and cutting what's not necessary. When many episodes start out five, 10, or more minutes too long, the editing process in every episode's evolution involves cutting down certain scenes to their most important bare-bones information, either to save them from a total cut or to just make it altogether better. In our show, since there usually is a lot of information revealed, being concise and on point is best."

— Marc Pollon

advantage, but she's not *wrong*. In fact, her argument for staying away from Damon, for rejecting codependence, is sound-minded and harkens back to the Elena of yore — a girl who would put morality, honesty, and the well-being of her loved ones ahead of her passion.

Every moment she keeps up this ruse, Katherine has to ask herself: what would Elena do? With Matty Blue Eyes' help with the details ("Who the hell is Enzo?"), Katherine manages to play out a complicated day — navigating BFF relationships, the Stefan Mission, a kidnapped kid brother and some *eww*-worthy mouth-to-mouth resuscitation, as well an ex-boyfriend gone serial killer — in a believably Elena Gilbert way. Even when Elena's life is a shambles, it's entertaining (if a bit exasperating) to Katherine Pierce. The hard parts — the breakup with Damon, Jeremy nearly dying — don't matter to Katherine; she is all eye-rolls and smirks. And the part that does matter to her — getting close to Stefan — is going as well as can be hoped for. With so many winks to the camera, letting the audience in on Katherine's reactions while keeping the other characters in the dark, Katherine's manipulative wiles are in action like we've never before seen them, and she does manage to get close to Stefan both physically and emotionally.

But a good thing can never last forever, and now that Matt knows the secret, Tyler has his suspicions about Nadia, and Caroline keeps on staring at "Elena" being "so available" to Stefan, how much longer can Katherine keep up the act? Luckily for her, a cannibalistic Damon might make a useful distraction from her identity crisis.

© Andrew Evans/PRPhotos

COMPELLING MOMENT Stefan and Enzo facing off over Damon, with a particular shout-out to the shovel that Enzo fearlessly takes hold of. You'll have to try harder than that to scare an Augustine victim, Stefan.

CIRCLE OF KNOWLEDGE

- "Total Eclipse of the Heart" is the fourth *Vampire Diaries* episode to be named after a 1980s song; this time it's the 1983 hit power ballad written by American songwriter Jim Steinman and performed by Welsh singer Bonnie Tyler. According to Steinman, he wrote the song as he was working on a Nosferatu musical, and the original title was "Vampires in Love." (Previous '80s song–inspired titles: "The Devil Inside," "A View to a Kill," and "Pictures of You.")
- The college chums attend sociology class in the same lecture hall as Wes's bio class was held, and Whitmore College has already fixed up the seats Enzo tore out in "Fifty Shades of Grayson."
- Bonnie's middle name is Sheila (thanks, KP!), named after Sheila "Grams" Bennett.
- Enzo wants to go to Cape Horn, located on Hornos Island off southern Chile in South America. From the 18th century into the early 20th century, Cape Horn was a notable point along clipper trading routes, particularly for ships sailing between Australia and England, and known for its potentially hazardous conditions, including horrible storms, rogue waves, strong winds, and icebergs.
- New witch Liv Parker is concerned about going all "Carrie" and burning the school down; in Stephen King's first published novel, title character Carrie — "a girl with a frightening power" — is telekinetic, abused by her mother, and terribly bullied at school. Bad combo. After the most famous and cruelest prom prank, Carrie loses control of her powers as she's consumed with rage, and the high school ends up going kablooey.

THE RULES Hybrids pee.

PREVIOUSLY ON *THE VAMPIRE DIARIES* Tyler, Matt, and Nadia reminisce about maternal bad behavior. Katherine compelled an entire town for friendship (and so that she'd be hidden and safe, but *details*) in "American Gothic" (4.18). Tyler made out with Kelly Donovan, Matt's mom, at the Founders' Day kick-off party in "Under Control" (1.18).

R.I.P., horse drawing! In "Dangerous Liaisons" (3.14), Klaus took his wooing of Caroline to the next level with the sketch of her and a horse, here shredded.

Bonnie teaches Liv how to do a locator spell under Gilbert-in-danger circumstances, just as she learned about it from Stefan in another crisis situation, when Elena was AWOL with Damon in "Bloodlines" (1.11).

OFF CAMERA Head Traveler Sloan is played by Caitlin McHugh, a Wilhelmina model who has had small roles on TV shows like *Rescue Me*, *Law & Order: Special Victims Unit*, and *Castle*.

Fan reaction was definitely kept in mind when it came to the Moment of Shredding, says Holly Brix. "Caroline and Klaus had this hot, impulsive sex in 5.11. But he's got his own life (and his own show) and she's got her path to walk and they're not going to be able to go any further with their feelings right now. So we wanted a way to definitively put a pin in that relationship for the immediate future. Caroline shredding his picture was her way of moving on from all her past relationships." As the writer responsible for that drawing in "Dangerous Liaisons," Rebecca Sonnenshine agrees: "I was very excited to have Caroline shred it up. Caroline Forbes is done with Klaus and she wants to prove it to herself by destroying that lingering reminder of her tender feelings toward him — I think a physical representation of her emotional desire to end things will go a long way in closing that door for her."

Keeping Katherine, Elena, and Katherine-as-Elena distinct was up to Nina to pull off. "Most of that was in the performance," says Brix. "If you read the lines as written, there's nothing that gives it away. I feel like Nina had a hard line to walk and pulled it off brilliantly." But the writers did consciously work to keep the audience in the loop. "Luckily, Katherine had Nadia to talk to as her mean old self, so she could really let loose in those phone calls in all her Katherine glory," explains Sonnenshine. "Otherwise, she was supposed to be pretending to be Elena, so she had to reel it in. But we contrived lots of moments where she turned away from the other characters and gave us a window into Katherine's mind. Or when we could see her face in a mirror and other characters couldn't. It was definitely one of the most blocking-heavy scripts we've done — we had to think a lot about how the scenes were staged in the script process to get those little moments."

Director Darren Genet on "Total Eclipse of the Heart"

On shifting from cinematographer to director: I don't think you can ever take the cinematographer hat off, which I think is a *good* thing. It's just good to have someone like Mike [Karasick] there that I trust, and we know each other so well and we've built this [season's] look together in a way. So I can feel like that side of my brain doesn't overpower the other side. I'm very specific about how I want it to look, but I don't have to get caught up in the technicality of how to get it there. So there's one less thing to worry about; but there's a million *other* things to worry about. It's probably the hardest I've worked in a long time. But I thought it went very well and it just felt very natural to be [directing], because as the cinematographer you're one degree removed from that.

One of the funny things the first couple of days is that I just caught myself always wanting to check in with someone before I made a decision. As the cinematographer, you can only take your choices so far, because the director ultimately makes the final decision on something. So I would say, "Oh yeah, this is a great idea! We should check — oh, wait a second, I don't need to check with anyone, I'm the — okay, let's just do that!" That was kind of fun, and it also just streamlines the whole process. In that sense, it was really creatively rewarding.

On working with the actors: Nina was really good in that episode; that was so much about her showing and hiding and being two people and playing a role and all of these things. Real subtle stuff that we could play with. Every time she would look into a mirror or turned her back on the person she was talking to, she could let a little bit of Katherine out. So that was fun to navigate with her, and she really ran with that. And also taking Ian, being darker than he's normally because he was on a downward spiral and it culminated with my episode, when he was turning into a ripper for a very short moment. So that was fun — helping guide him into a place where it's a little darker than he's been used to doing on the show. And then we had some really fun stuff with Olga and Zach and Trevino in the bar, which was really good stuff and I thought we got really great performances. And maybe that's because I know those guys so well, we have such a good relationship, and they may have been rooting for me a little bit — they could sort of bring it, they felt a bit responsible to help me. Which was great. It was all pretty seamless.

On his directorial debut: It's always difficult to do something for the first time, especially directing, because there are just so many questions that come at you in any given moment, in a day. But my philosophy on that was: just know the story and the script better than anyone else on the set, and be prepared to answer any question anyone has. That was my main goal and I just worked as hard as I could to learn the script in and out, and know it, and have lots of different theories about each choice the actor would make, and then be able to talk about it with them and collaborate with them. It was really about all those things I learned in film school and have been watching and learning — shooting all the time, just breaking down the script, breaking down the scene, and being able to express that and make quick choices. Which is a big part of what I do anyway. But it was fun, because it was a lot more creative in a weird way than when I've been shooting. Because shooting does become a bit technical. You have to figure out where the lights go, you have to figure out where the camera goes. But directing was a bit more like a pure, creative art form, which is really fun, and I hope to continue to do that.

On editing and the final product: I wasn't able to physically be in the [editing] room, which is always a disadvantage because you can sort of experiment when you're in there. So what would happen is I would get a cut via email and I'd watch it and send them notes, and then another cut would come. You have four days to do all this, so you really only get three or four cracks at it. Luckily, I had a great editor [Tony Solomons] and we saw eye to eye on most things. There are a couple things that I just played with, but you also have to realize that you're the first cut and then it's gonna change after you've got your hands on it. So you just try to put your best foot forward in that sense. But I think it would be really great to, at some point, do an episode and then be able to be there in the room, because then you can really play with things and play with music and you can do all these things; I feel I didn't really get a lot of time to get into the minor details of things.

But, that said, I was super happy with the episode and my cut. And they didn't actually change very much after I cut it so I felt like we did a good job first time around. And it was mostly on the page; you know, it's good when you're in a place in the editing room where you have everything and you're not wishing you had done things differently [in production]. There wasn't a lot of that, where we felt like we didn't have something and would have to reshoot something or we got it wrong. It was just playing around with tone and the order of things and music and stuff like that. Once we turned it in, the network didn't have any notes, so they didn't make any changes. So that was a good confidence boost, to know that we were all on the same page.

And god bless Julie for the opportunity and for just being really collaborative the whole way, so I wasn't just trying to figure it out on my own. By the time we did shoot and get into the editing room, any issue that would've been there had already been discussed at length. It was so collaborative that there were no surprises in the editing room, which is nice.

On directing in season six: Yeah! I'm gonna do one at least next year and then hopefully continue to just keep doing more and more. I mean, I love what I do, but I feel like all this shooting I've done has made me a better director than someone else who's just starting, and then any directing I do will just make me a better cameraman. It's a really good symbiotic relationship, those two jobs. Some people have a difficult time going back to the thing they're doing after they've directed, because they've tasted . . . whatever it is, the gold? And then it's hard to fall back into a lesser position. But I don't feel that way. I feel like knowing what it feels like to direct and what's important to the director makes me a better cameraman, so it's all great. It's a great learning process.

As for Damon, one of Brix's favorite characters to write for, and his rampage with Enzo in this episode, the writer has mixed feelings. "There are times when personally I feel like it's going too far, like Damon being party to [almost] killing Jeremy to find Dr. Wes's location. But I'm not the only voice in the room and ultimately, there's a bigger collective compass that points the direction. Left to my own devices, I might have played it softer, but I think I would've been wrong because it made for some great television and really launched Damon and Elena's next chapter." While Enzo enjoys his newfound freedom and their violent spree, Sonnenshine notes that Damon is meant to be more conflicted by the havoc they're wreaking. "In one draft, Damon killed Diane Freeman (head of campus security), but then we felt that was going too far for Damon, so we had Enzo do it." But she loves exploring Damon's darker side. "We always refer to Damon as a 'ruiner' — he sees trouble coming and he lashes out to avoid feeling his own disappointments," she says. "So 'Total Eclipse' was fun, because Damon was lashing out. He was hurting, he was conflicted about what he was doing, he was pushing everyone away and wondering if they would ever accept him back."

Who is Matthew D'Ambrosio's favorite new character of season five? "Diane Freeman. Head of campus security. Kidding. Obviously Enzo." R.I.P. Diane!

FOGGY MOMENTS Enzo and Damon say the vervain is out of Diane Freeman's system, but it's been less than a day since she's been captured: they murder Aaron Whitmore, get hammered, and then kidnap her from her office and put her in the Salvatore holding cell. Vervain usually takes a few days to leave a person's system, unless it's sped along by a lot of blood-letting, which doesn't appear to be the case here.

Why do Bonnie, Caroline, and Elena have a bulletin board full of tacky campus flyers inside their dorm room? Caroline would *not* let that happen.

Jeremy is still a hunter, gifted with strength and a burning urge to kill vampires. Why doesn't he fight Damon and Enzo? He is both supernaturally inclined and physically trained to go into fighter-mode when vampires are around, and yet he goes without protest.

When will Bonnie realize that Katherine didn't pass through to the Other Side? It made sense for her not to realize *instantly*, since we've seen dead supernaturals take their time before passing through. But now enough time has passed that it is more of a convenient plot oversight than a believable mistake on Bonnie's part.

Why doesn't Matt tell Tyler the truth about Katherine and Nadia and leave with him, instead of doing what Nadia told him to do and getting into her car? He's on vervain, so he does it of his own free will.

How did Katherine know that Aaron was the owner of Whitmore House? When she was at Whitmore House, she was human and didn't need an invite to walk inside (that was the whole point of her going there) — and Aaron didn't tell her. Did she ask Matt Donovan in an offscreen conversation for details on Elena's college friend about whom he likely knows nothing?

QUESTIONS

- What did Stefan study when he "did the college thing" in the past? Brooding 101 and a third-year course in martyred patience?
- Sloan asks Dr. Wes for help analyzing some blood — shall we assume that it's the two buckets of doppelgänger blood the Travelers collected in "500 Years of Solitude"?
- What would Stefan's answer be to faux-Elena's question: does he like who she is, or does he miss who she was? Inquiring minds, Stefan!
- Does Tyler believe Matt's story about why Nadia was compelling him for information?
- Caroline had her eye on Stefan and "Elena" all Bitter Ball — does she have her suspicions about Elena being Elena or is she concerned about a potentially disastrous rebound situation? Or . . . is she into Stefan?
- What kind of Carrie-esque havoc has Liv unleashed in the past?

Enzo: That's what you do, isn't it? There's a problem, you run.
You did it to me, you did it to your girl.
Damon: Because when I stay, I destroy things.
Enzo: We're not all as fragile as you think we are.
[They kiss.][1]

5.14 *No Exit*

Original air date February 27, 2014
Written by Brian Young **Directed by** Michael Allowitz
Edited by Marc Pollon **Cinematography by** Michael Karasick
Guest cast Cedric L. Hatcher (Traveler #2), Ryan Kessler (John), Alyssa Lewis (Traveler #1)
Previously on *The Vampire Diaries* Paul Wesley

Infected with the ripper virus, Damon finds himself trapped in a farmhouse with Enzo. Katherine takes her Elena shenanigans too far.

"No Exit" pulls off the great narrative trick of trapping its characters in impossible situations, whether orchestrated or enforced, in order to trigger breakthroughs, and the *TVD* writers can sure come up with some delightfully tricky situations. And here, as with most trouble in the lives of the Salvatore brothers for the past 150-odd years, all roads lead back to Katherine Pierce.

Though by act six the jig is up, Katherine Pierce has made the most of her time masquerading as Elena. As with any big bold lie, eventually the truth will out. In Katherine's case, it's not her intimate knowledge of history that outs her as an imposter, or her seduction techniques, but her greed. She wants it all, and "all" seems to begin and end with Stefan. What she fails to recognize is that even when the brothers Salvatore are at odds, they are still *brothers* bound together for eternity. No doppelgänger can truly come between them. Katherine underestimates the bond the brothers share, while overestimating Stefan's willingness to do *anything* for Elena, and her miscalculation is, in its essence, what outs her as not-Elena.

---

[1] Did this not happen onscreen? Huh. Seems like it should've.

No matter what his brother does, Stefan will never give up on Damon. And it seems that Damon has another stalwart man at his side now too, in Enzo. While Enzo steadfastly refuses to leave Damon behind (. . . until he does), Stefan won't give up on his brother, and even Tyler and Caroline will put their bitterness aside to reunite ever so briefly to help Matt when he's in trouble. You just don't abandon your friends in the *TVD*verse. But that's exactly how Katherine has survived for so long — she is selfish. Nadia feels every word that Matt has to say about his own deadbeat mom who he just can't help loving, despite the fact Kelly Donovan never put anyone, not even her lonely son, ahead of her own self-interest. No one has stronger impulses in that way than Katherine Pierce, and though Nadia knows intellectually that her mother is not maternal, she still feels deeply hurt by the realization that she is less important to Katherine than Stefan is. That Nadia gets a fatal werewolf bite because of her mother's scheming is the salt in the wound.

Katherine's good mood and feeling of victory are shortlived in "No Exit." She's had her carefully orchestrated "moment" with Stefan and believes she's proved herself willing to die to save Damon; in fact she's done the opposite — she's pushed Nadia, Stefan, and Damon away and has been way too un-Elena-y to fly under the radar any longer. With the clue of Matt's "help K" text, Stefan and Caroline finally figure out why Elena is being *so strange*.

Katherine may not yet realize her scam has crumbled, but Damon is very aware that his chickens have come home to roost. With Enzo by his side, he begins the episode with a not-terrible game plan: go on the lam, turning humans into vampires and feeding on *them* instead of on his brother, ex-girlfriend, or best mate. And, loyal to the last, Enzo proves to be a stand-up friend in "No Exit," making sure that Damon is not alone, despite the danger Enzo faces in being best buds with a guy programmed to eat him. What Enzo does that's so very alien to our other *TVD*ers is stay calm and keep his head screwed on straight: he's seen worse, he knows they'll figure it out — even after Wes and the Travelers magically cage them together. There's a maturity to Enzo's character that seems built on his soldier-who's-seen-battle backstory, and his lack of angst is refreshing in contrast to the others.

For an episode full of rallying by friends and loved ones no matter the circumstance, "No Exit" also reminds us that there are some things that can never be forgiven or forgotten. While Katherine's rationale for "giving up" on Damon is ultimately as carefully plotted as Stefan's car's breakdown, there's nothing more raw and honest than the betrayal that Tyler feels with

Melinda Hsu Taylor on Writing with Production Concerns in Mind

More and more as I spend time in Atlanta and stay up really late outside where it's cold and there's mud and bugs [laughs], I think, "This scene will be Interior, Great Room, Salvatore house, and also light outside." I mean, you can do so much when you have a controlled environment and you don't have to worry about what time of day it is, or what the weather is, how cold it is, and you can pack a lot into these scenes. And that's really what people are watching for. As much as you love to have these flashy visuals, it's really the moments between the brothers, or the triangle, or some awesome revelation of mythology that is really quiet and contained. It doesn't need to have a lot of stunt work around it — although I would never give up the stunt work, don't get me wrong.

I think about it all the time when I write, because even in the story break when you're looking at the dry-erase board, you think, Oh my god, this is all outdoors, night. What can we put inside at night? What can we put that's all in the Lockwood house? Can we consolidate the Mystic Grill thing, or consolidate Salvatore house and Lockwood? Because those two sets are right next to each other. It makes a difference. Even the difference between shooting something at Scull bar and the Salvatore house would be a different consideration on the schedule than shooting something at Salvatore house and the Lockwood house, because the whole crew doesn't have to push carts down the driveways just to get to the next stage and set themselves up — craft services, everybody can just stay in the same spot and just walk over.

It's a matter of minutes rather than of a half hour, and at a certain point a half hour is crucial. Because you're going to run out of time and you can't get the last shot. We've got to stop filming because we're turning actors around and they have a schedule or they've got to go or there's overtime or there's daylight [scenes] tomorrow or whatever. There are all these crazy constraints that start to squeeze your time as the day goes on and as the week goes on. And so every minute that you can spare is time and money that you can put on the screen instead.

Caroline. Despite their collaboration to help Matt, they won't be going back to being friends. And Matt and Nadia? It's unlikely we'll see any more canoodling between those two. Though he can clearly relate to her absentee mother issues, Matt tells it to her straight: he hasn't forgiven the wrong she's done him and his friends, and never will. Sometimes, it's not just a matter of time until you get what you want, as Katherine says; it's a matter of time before it all falls to pieces.

COMPELLING MOMENT The Team Salvatore moment in the holding cell, Damon in chains and Stefan telling him, "You're my brother. I'm not going to give up on you, and I never will."

CIRCLE OF KNOWLEDGE

- No Bonnie or Jeremy.
- This episode takes its title from French existentialist Jean-Paul Sartre's 1944 one-act play *No Exit* (titled in French *Huis Clos*). Set in a single room, the play depicts a hellscape in a normal setting, a drawing room, in which three characters are confined. There are no racks, red-hot pokers, or other traditional fire-and-brimstone moments; here "hell is other people," as the famous line from the final act goes. Garcin, Estelle, and Inez are forced to face their true "damned souls" and to either come to terms with their situation or live in willful denial. The three of them are inextricably linked, stuck together with no respite for eternity, driving each other mad. Here's hoping this is *not* a commentary on the three main characters of *TVD*, also bound for eternity . . .
- The book on the end table near Stefan when he's quizzing Katherine-as-Elena for her history test is *Blood Trance,* the second of three novels in the Alex and Maddy Phillips series by American author R.D. Zimmerman. The mysteries center on Maddy Phillips, "the world's foremost forensic hypnotherapist," and her technical writer brother, Alex; the pair works to solve murders. Maddy would've figured out Elena was not Elena a *lot* sooner than the Mystic Falls gang.
- Nadia dines at Covington, Georgia's Town House Café (1145 Washington St. SW) twice in one day.
- The Travelers magically raise the acidity in Enzo's blood to the level of hydrochloric acid, which is what you get from mixing hydrogen chloride (a gas) with water. Also referred to by the alchemical name "spirits of salt," it's a strong corrosive acid that is used in the production of PVC plastic, household cleaners, gelatin and other food additives, as well as in leather processing. It can also remove rust from iron and basically melt human flesh. Enjoy your Jell-O.

HISTORY LESSON In addition to her many other talents, Katherine wields an impressive knowledge of history as Stefan quizzes "Elena" on key dates for an upcoming test, specifically the demise of important empires and dynasties. The Western Roman Empire, established after a series of civil wars ended the Roman Republic in 27 BCE and Augustus became the first emperor, ended in 476 CE when it was sacked by the Goths — an eastern Germanic tribe — over a period of 100 years. The Han dynasty was a Chinese imperial line initiated in 206 BCE; their rule spanned four centuries and ended in 220 CE, when the last Han ruler, Emperor Xian, was forced to abdicate his throne to Cao Pi after more than 30 years of war that ultimately divided the empire into three kingdoms. And while the history books may not agree with Katherine on the end of the Holy Roman Empire in the strictest sense, as 1806 is widely considered to be the official end date, she is correct about the Peace of Westphalia. The Peace, made in 1648, essentially forced the empire to give more power and self-governance to local rulers throughout Europe, which undermined the empire's authority while it gave princes and the Church more control. But, just as Rome wasn't built in a day (thank you, Caroline), great and powerful empires require time to truly crumble.

Katherine may appreciate the finer things in life, but she's less impressed with Stefan's "classic" 1963 Porsche 356b Karmann Coupe after spending several hours folded into it on their "save Damon" road trip. The Wright

"The greatest strength of the series in my opinion is the depth of each episode. Every episode is loaded from top to bottom. There is love, death, supernatural events, and action. They are so well written it is a challenge every time out, one that I love taking on. My favorite part of the process has happened on every episode I have directed. It is a moment that arrives after days of planning and talking and imagining when you finally get to shooting. When you get to a scene you have visualized many times over. Sometimes it goes the way you planned, but sometimes there is a magic moment when you are deep into the scene and watching the monitor and I realize this is going to be even greater than I could have imagined."

— Michael Allowitz

brothers' plane was a classic too, she points out, "but you don't see people still flying around in that thing." American aviation pioneers Orville and Wilbur Wright's 1902 glider is widely considered to be the first airplane. But, in all fairness to Stefan, it was not nearly as sexy as a cherry red Porsche.

THE RULES Infected with the "virus" (which doesn't have any virus-like qualities), Damon needs to feed about every eight hours on a vampire, and when he does, he defaults to ripper mode. He feeds until he kills and does it so violently that his victims' heads tend to pop off. Tyler says to Nadia that a young hybrid beats an old vampire every time. (Except all those times when vampires beat hybrids.)

PREVIOUSLY ON *THE VAMPIRE DIARIES* Stefan's proven his prowess at history: in "Friday Night Bites" (1.03), he and Tanner had a key-dates-in-history showdown in class, which Stefan won.

Tyler reminds Caroline that Matt went away with Rebekah after she'd run his truck off Wickery Bridge, nearly killing Matt and actually killing Elena in "The Departed" (3.22).

Katherine's highly orchestrated motel moment with Stefan finds a parallel to that very earnest and passionate surprise-kiss moment in a motel between Damon and Elena in "Heart of Darkness" (3.19).

After Kelly Donovan came home in "A Few Good Men" (1.15), she showed more interest in chasing men — like Damon Salvatore ("There Goes the Neighborhood," 1.16) — than in parenting Matt.

Katherine-as-Elena urges Damon to fight his desire to feed on her blood, by channeling his deep and abiding love for her, much as real Elena did with Stefan when he was compelled by Klaus to attack her in "The Reckoning" (3.05). Damon was compelled to kill Jeremy in "Catch Me If You Can" (4.11), and Elena urged him, as she had Stefan, to fight the impulse. He couldn't.

OFF CAMERA The episode is in memoriam to Sarah Jones (1986–2014), who was struck and killed by a train while working in unsafe conditions on the set of a film. "Sarah was a truly special person, with an enthusiasm for working in the camera department and an overall life-affirming set presence," says Joshua Butler. "This kind of energy was truly infectious, and I remember many moments when Sarah really kept the cast and crew going through some difficult shooting days with her positivity. The day she died, the *TVD* crew shut down and then took another day off to attend her memorial service. There was a huge feeling of loss for everyone who knew Sarah, and we rallied together to help support the Slates for Sarah campaign, which is currently focused on making our industry a more humane place to work and preventing the type of unsafe work environments that put people in jeopardy."

Alyssa Lewis (a.k.a. Traveler #1) has played Elena's double in doppelgänger scenes in "Monster's Ball" and "Original Sin."

Director Michael Allowitz had a specific film in mind when shooting the scenes of Damon and Enzo trapped together in the farmhouse. "I was always very fond of Ben Kingsley's and Sigourney Weaver's performances in *Death and the Maiden*," he explains, referring to Roman Polanski's 1995 film. "I used that play/film as inspiration to find that feeling. I wanted to give the farmhouse its own trapped-world feel. Mike Karasick and I encouraged each other to find the more extreme angles and make the farmhouse a world to itself."

Cinematographer Michael Karasick's favorite scene of the season to shoot is in this episode: "Katherine is in Elena's body and people don't know it . . . and there's a kissing scene that happens in the motel room. It was a good, romantic, sexual energy to that scene — that was pretty fun."

Caroline Dries "loved crafting Nadia because here was a woman with Katherine's devilish instincts but who is obviously longing to be loved."

FOGGY MOMENTS The police report Stefan gets from Caroline doesn't match the details of the homicides that Damon has been committing. In fact, the "offender name" listed on the police department form is none other than . . . Alaric Saltzman. Looks like a prop was recycled from "1912" (3.16) when Meredith dug up dirt on Alaric's violent past.

QUESTIONS

- Can Damon learn to control the urge to feed on vampires, like Stefan controls his ripper instincts? Or is it a whole different kettle of fish?
- What is the "one last thing" Wes wants with Enzo? Will he stay true to his word and release him afterward?
- What are the Travelers up to? Why are they helping Wes? What the heck happened to those two buckets of doppelgänger blood?
- Can Elena be brought back to her own body?
- Will Nadia survive Tyler's bite?

Katherine: I'm here to see my daughter.

5.15 *Gone Girl*

Original air date March 6, 2014
Written by Melinda Hsu Taylor **Directed by** Lance Anderson
Edited by Joel T. Pashby **Cinematography by** Darren Genet
Guest cast Ashlyn Lopez (Young Nadia)
Previously on *The Vampire Diaries* Nina Dobrev

Katherine stops running.

A stand-out episode of the season, "Gone Girl" manages to give Katherine Pierce an epic send-off as she leaves the mortal coil for good after a season filled with much foreshadowing, fake outs, and last chances before the main event.

We've long known that on *The Vampire Diaries* there is more than one après-death option for supernaturals: there is the Other Side, a kind of supernatural purgatory, and there is "finding peace," which, as we understand it, is wherever Aunt Jenna went and where it seems Anna and Pearl managed to go after "Ghost World." And it's fitting that, just as Katherine chose an option three in "Dead Man on Campus," she discovers an unexpected option three here. In a glorious twist, Katherine puts her hands on Bonnie's shoulders, ready to be sent to the Other Side, and nothing happens. And then? She's dragged away to some sort of hell-like destination. Katherine won't be seeing Bon-Bon on the flip side. She won't be waltzing back into town if there's another disturbance on the Other Side. While it raises a ton of questions about the fates of supernatural characters — who else has been whisked off to darkness, if anyone? who decides where dead folks go? — the unavoidable and most important fact is that Katherine Pierce, a character who has wittingly shaped and reshaped the *TVD* universe over the past five seasons, is dead and gone forever. Caroline says that outsmarting Katherine is next to impossible, but here the Powers That Be pull it off, taking Ms. Pierce by complete surprise as she's dragged off to the underworld. Just as Katherine gets in her last trick on Elena, the writers pressed the big red button on Katherine. They went nuclear.

Season five has been a Katherine fan's dream, watching her journey through the perils and perks of being human, of discovering that her daughter is alive, and of handling the consequences of her former life as a vampire who'd chosen to spend her half millennium with very little respect for others' lives. Katherine Pierce has always been a runner, a survivor, but in the end, she chooses not to run. She chooses to give her daughter the goodbye she deserves, and she stays by Nadia's side, though she doesn't keep her promise to save Nadia's life. Her unwillingness to call Klaus for his magic hybrid blood means she trusts in Wes instead, a miscalculation that costs Nadia her life. Just as Damon showed his compassion back when Rose was dying from a werewolf bite, here Katherine calms her feverish daughter with a vision of their perfect day together. It's one little bit of peace for the both of them, especially affecting after we see Nadia returning to the past in her hallucinations, searching for a mother she only knows as a legendary liar, murderer, and manipulator. Ultimately Katherine is able to prove that, while all that is true, she's more than that — and she gives her daughter a glimpse of the life they could have shared, the life they *both* deserved. That moment in Nadia's dreamscape is not only a gift for Nadia, but it is, poignantly, the only time Katherine ever sees Nadia as a little girl, having lost Nadia as a baby and not seen her again until she was the fierce vampire she had become. Though it was Katherine's actions that led to Nadia's death, she has the ability and grace to give Nadia one final moment of true love, peace, and connection.

As Katherine says goodbye to each character in turn, she reminds them (and us) that without her, they'd be . . . well, dull. Katherine has always been a plot instigator and a character builder, and she is seemingly aware of her importance to the storyworld in this meta-moment goodbye. She kick-started Tyler's and Caroline's best plot arcs, she shaped the Salvatore brothers into the men who adore Elena, and she admired Matty Blue as he should rightly be admired. It's a thing of beauty that it's Stefan who kills her, and Katherine makes a callback to when she returned to Mystic Falls at the beginning of season two, realizing that *this* is the end to their love story. Her willingness to walk into a death trap, and to just make one feeble attempt at escape before accepting her fate, makes even more sense when we learn at the end that she already had Wes's super-virus running through Elena's veins when she made that choice. Katherine Pierce does not go gentle. What is left in her wake is a rabid Elena about to learn about all the terrible things Damon did in his post-breakup freakout.

Even after being told the truth about Katherine's "brilliant" trick, Damon masterfully escapes — easily outwitting Tyler, who is so raw about so many things he makes an easy mark — and brutally kills Dr. Wes. An eye for an eye, as it were. It's a bit of a dunce move for Damon: murdering the one person capable of concocting an antidote, while adding to his list of sins for which he'll have to repent if he hopes to win back Elena. But Damon learned from the best: he follows his passion, like Katherine taught him to, for better or for worse.

And taking a note from Queen Katherine, Caroline decides enough is enough and kicks her guilty conscience to the curb. In a great speech, Caroline demands that Tyler stop his guilt-tripping and harping on her failures already. She's not perfect, it's not a breeze to be a totally-under-control vampire, she made a choice — wrong or so-wrong-it's-right — and she's living with it. Caroline points out the hypocrisy in Tyler's judgment: she has the same overwhelming impulses that he does. He "nipped" Nadia, knowing it would be fatal, and all he gets is a disappointed look from Matt as punishment. On *The Vampire Diaries*, everyone's allowed to make mistakes, Caroline included. As they all strive for redemption, Katherine serves as both a model and a cautionary tale, inspiring in her determination and fearlessness and sobering in her ultimate downfall. She will be missed.

COMPELLING MOMENT That final scene. From the comedic "nothing's happening" to the terror-filled Katherine being dragged down that church aisle, scrambling to avoid her fate — amazing and so unexpected.

CIRCLE OF KNOWLEDGE

- "Gone Girl" is titled after the thriller by American novelist Gillian Flynn, a mainstay on the *New York Times* bestseller list since its release in June 2012, which centers on the troubled marriage of Nick and Amy Dunne and on Amy's disappearance on their fifth wedding anniversary, which casts suspicion on Nick. The book delivers a boatload of unreliable narration and plot twists along the way, while exploring terrible people doing terrible things. The 2014 *Gone Girl* film adaptation, starring Ben Affleck and Rosamund Pike and directed by David Fincher, was in production as *Vampire Diaries* season five aired.

- Liv calls Bonnie "Mr. Miyagi," beloved mentor in the Karate Kid films as portrayed by Pat Morita.
- Borrowing a line from Welsh poet Dylan Thomas's most famous work, "Do not go gentle into that good night," which was written for his dying father, Katherine wasn't "about to go gentle" to her death. *TVD* has used the turn of phrase before in "After School Special" (4.10) and as the title of an episode (3.20).

Creating "Gone Girl"

Melinda Hsu Taylor: A lot of [writers'] room conversations went into the exit of Katherine, and Caroline and Julie were from the very beginning determined and very clear about Katherine leaving the show permanently. There's no question, there's no fuzzy area, there shouldn't be a fan debate; it should be like, She's gone. She's dead and she's not on the Other Side and she's not coming back.

Caroline Dries: My happiest moment in the writers' room [this season] was when Melinda and I were working late and alone. We were banging our heads against the wall, because I'd just dropped a bomb on "Gone Girl" and now we were starting a bit from scratch. I was being hard on everything, and we couldn't figure out what the big twist of the ep was. I was worried about it getting plotty (which takes away from character moments). I didn't want Melinda to get frustrated with me, so I said, "Well, we'll figure it out tomorrow, let's go home." And Melinda instead goes, "Well, this is sort of an asshole move for Stefan, but what if he steals Nadia and makes Katherine choose whether to say goodbye to her daughter or to run?" And I was like, THAT IS GENIUS, THANK YOU. And it made the episode work. It may sound small, but those moments of gold are truly priceless. I was so proud even though it wasn't my idea in the slightest!

Hsu Taylor: The Nadia flashbacks actually started out more as fever dreams, and they were snippets from her past to expand on the character a little bit and to let you know where she was coming from emotionally by the time she was dying. But then as Julie read the early draft of that, she said, "You know I'd really like to make these kind of get to a point that tells a beginning, middle, and end to Nadia's story." Actually the initial flashbacks were very similar; the one that we changed was the one in the hotel in Prague.

I had written a scene that, you know, in my mind still happened in the timeline. It was a scene where Nadia was in a hallway and had just killed a mailman and was at this heroin-chic kind of rock bottom. She had given up on finding Katherine but was still living this Euro-trashy life in Prague, but that day she had found out — she had heard through the vampire grapevine — that Katherine had been spotted in the United States, and so now she was going to get her act together and go after her. It was a little more of a glimpse into the Nadia timeline, and Julie read that, and by then Julie was keen to use the flashbacky dreams and said, "Let's use this last flashback as something that completes the story of Nadia and is not just a little window into a moment that could actually tell the whole piece of the story." So that's how we came up with Nadia and Matt in the hotel.

Dries: I could just see [Katherine's goodbyes] very clearly because, in my opinion, Katherine is the centerpiece of the series. All the drama everyone has gone through links back, somehow, to her. In the 100th ep, our characters talked to and about Katherine a lot. In her final ep, we wanted Katherine to get to say something back. This speech was Katherine having the last word, and the thing is, she was right. That's what I loved about it.

Hsu Taylor: I really like moments that have a shorthand — like a mother tucking a daughter in to bed, everybody understands that, but it's in this very heightened circumstance of a woman with werewolf venom dying on the couch of her captors and they've used her to entrap her mom, who's giving her this supernatural ability to have a peaceful moment of death followed instantly by this other thing that's a setup for the final scene. I like finding small intimate moments like that that tell a story by themselves but also serve in the greater purpose.

I took a particular pleasure as a mom to be able to put it onscreen even in a character as dark and ruthless as Katherine. Because if you ask any mom about the capacity for ruthlessness that they have after they have kids, they say it greatly increased because it's like now you have this person you're responsible for and that you'd do anything [for them]. So that to me is a completely logical continuation of her usual M.O.

It was really a lot of fun to play that at the same time that she's being incredibly selfish and wanting to try to have it all, which is one of her many fatal flaws. That she just can't leave it alone. That she's going to try to get Stefan, she's going to try to fix things without calling Klaus and outing herself. Her downfall has always been she just wants it all. Something's got to give and that's really a lesson that she never learns until the end.

Dries: It was always the plan to have Katherine *not* go to the Other Side. We just loved the imagery of the church and wanted to try something new and fitting. It was important to us to tell the audience, you will not be seeing her again. She's dead.

Hsu Taylor: We talked about some different ways to achieve this in terms of the "Bonnie Other Side" moment and we had this whole sequence put together, once we had the idea of like, "Well she's going to be in a church." And Caroline was very interested in it being a church. Julie was kind of like, "I'm not against the church but it's not where we usually go. Are you guys sure we want to do it?" and Caroline and I are both like *Oh yes yes yes*. We were both raised Catholic and to us, it was a very quick shorthand for "I'm contemplating my life and the hereafter and all my sins." Not that the show's religious and not that we were trying to say something religious, but it's just a shorthand. You're in a church, you're looking at candles, you get sucked into a void — you get it, you know? We really enjoyed writing that scene because it starts out very heartfelt with Bonnie and then it gets to this kind of weird existential place and then it gets to this straight horror visual moment and then poof it's over.

Darren Genet: That sequence is one of my favorites. There's one image at the end of that sequence: it's the last image of that episode which is just this wide shot and it's pulling back from Kat Graham and these big candelabras that are just floating from the ceiling and they're swinging from the wind and there's like wisping smoke coming out of the candles that were blown out from the force of Katherine getting sucked out. I just love that image. In terms of shooting that sequence, we were just trying to keep that as contrast-y and dark and moody as possible, for a number of reasons. We were shooting on a set we didn't want [the audience] to see very much of [*The Originals*' church set], so that was one reason to keep it really dark — but that sequence should be dark.

That's a big, big moment for Katherine's character, it's a big moment in the season, so we wanted to make sure that we really nailed the tone of that and the mood of that. Again, we used very little lighting and a lot of candles in the frame. We just kept it very minimal, and then we had some great stuntwork that Nina did herself, which was really cool — flying her out, so she got to be on a harness and yanked up on a wire, which was fun for her. When an actor gets into the practicality, it's really cool. That's hard to shoot with stunt doubles. She just nailed it. Nina was really great on that day, and Kat was great, and we had a nice set that we could dolly through the pews and get up above.

Lance [Anderson] did a great job directing that [scene]; we work really well together so I feel like whenever we work together we bring each other's game up. That [scene] was a good example of that. And Nina doing such a good job as well. It was bittersweet because I was sad to see Katherine go.

Matthew D'Ambrosio: Hoo boy. What a ride. I remember putting down the script after I read it for the first time and just raising my fist like Judd Nelson at the end of *The Breakfast Club*. The plotting was so tight. Katherine was so f--ed. And Katherine's final moments, staring at everyone and realizing she's

finally lost. I think that's what it is: our characters finally outsmarted the infamous Katherine Pierce. And then that ending. Oh, MAN. We watched the dailies in the writers' room of Katherine's drag into the void and I clapped. Then the writers asked who I was and how I got in the room and security escorted me out of the building. Sent from my prison iPhone.
Julie Plec: It's funny, saying goodbye to a character like Katherine is obviously not an easy decision to make. It was so hard on Nina Dobrev; so every time we play Katherine it's a battle with the studio, with money, with the shooting, with the actress, because it just takes twice as long. So, you know, there's the practical logistics of how often we could use the character. And then I was thinking about it and it's season five, you know? There has not been a massive and significant death that is final in quite a long time, and it feels like whether we go for six, seven, eight, nine, 10 seasons — whatever it is, however many seasons we go for — to profoundly say goodbye to this character as we pass our 100th-episode milestone felt bold; and not necessarily like we were excited to say goodbye to her, because we love her too, but it just felt like it was time to have a good death; a good, big death.
Neil Reynolds: What a perfect send-off, and in many ways, the end of an era.

- According to writer Neil Reynolds, the working title of this episode was "Drag Me to Hell," a reference to the 2009 American horror film directed by Sam "Evil Dead" Raimi, and a parallel many fans drew immediately after the episode aired. In the film, Alison Lohman plays Christine Brown, a loan officer whose boss pressures her to refuse a loan to a gypsy woman, resulting in the woman cursing Christine to an eternity in hell. After a horrifying series of events that lead to Christine believing she has finally outwitted the demon that has been stalking her, she learns that she has made a fatal mistake and unwittingly damned herself, much like Katherine realizes when Stefan calls her to say he has her dying daughter. The final image of the movie is Christine falling onto train tracks where hands thrust up from the ground and drag her, screaming, to hell.
- When Katherine arose from the dead in "Monster's Ball" after Silas drained her of her cure-laced blood, she quipped, "Am I in hell?" and here Damon's last words to her are "See you in hell." Though the final scene takes place in a church, *TVD* has always avoided the explicitly religious references to heaven/hell/higher powers, and it manages to just skirt it

here, with Katherine scoffing at organized religion and Bonnie having no answer to who makes up the rules regarding afterlife destinations.

- The "dragged to hell" shot in this episode is also a tip of the hat to similar horrifying ends in Spanish horror film *REC* (2007) and its American remake *Quarantine* (2008).

THE RULES Nadia experiences the usual werewolf-bite symptoms: hallucinations, sweats, weakness, and a ugly, ugly looking wound. Her weakened state makes her mind more open to Katherine's "perfect day" vision. Caroline calculates (with a calculator) that Damon will be able to survive with four ounces of blood three times a day. Wes isolates the werewolf venom's toxin from Nadia's blood and combines it with the ripper virus to make it "more deadly" for vampires. When Mia did the spell to give Katherine "permanent" control of Elena's body, she didn't destroy Elena's "spirit," she just repressed it. The spell held only until the magical Traveler knife stabbed the host body, expelling passenger Katherine.

PREVIOUSLY ON *THE VAMPIRE DIARIES* In her feverish memories, Nadia refers to a Katherine sighting outside London in 1492, which would be concurrent with the events of "Klaus" (2.19).

In a moment that recalls "The Return" (2.01), Katherine's last words to Stefan, as he stabs her, are "This is how our love story ends"; in the season two premiere, Katherine stabbed Stefan, telling him that that hate was the beginning of a love story, not its end.

OFF CAMERA The church where Katherine hides Nadia might look familiar to *TVD* watchers who also tune into *The Originals* (which should be *all of you*): *The Originals*' set for St. Anne's church doubles for a generic Mystic Falls area church in this episode.

"Gone Girl" is one of Marc Pollon's top two episodes of the season: "The whole combination of an emotional script, the camera lighting and movement, the smoothness of the editing, and especially capped by how Katherine dies in the end was so great!"

FOGGY MOMENTS Stefan tells Damon that Katherine has been in Elena's body for "weeks" but it's actually just been six days by timeline references within the show.

QUESTIONS

- When Bonnie calls Katherine, she tells her that a coven of Russian witches passed through her that morning — was that just a creative lie, or are there some serious supernatural problems over in Russia?
- Will Bonnie get her spa day? Does Jeremy ever go to school, or does he just live on Whitmore Campus now, tagging along with Bon-Bon?
- Katherine asks Bonnie a question that Bonnie doesn't know the answer to: if Bonnie doesn't control who gets to pass through to the Other Side, who or what does?
- How will Damon and Elena kick the ripper virus?

© Blake Tyers/The CW/Landov

Katherine Pierce, Queen of Our Hearts

She may be dead and gone, but the one and only Katherine Pierce will live on in *TVD* infamy forever. We asked some of the *TVD* family to look back at the best there ever was.

What did you think of Katherine's arc in season five?

Melinda Hsu Taylor: I thought it was so fun. This is Caroline and Julie wanting to give the character a great exit and take this idea to the fullest, that she'd become human and was going to die because of it. Because of the mythology, it was going to get us all these great moments of her declining and trying to save her own life and having that last great run, and then actually dying for good, forever, goodbye. It was great fun to be on board for that.

Marc Pollon: I think it was fitting of someone like Katherine. I would expect nothing less than for her to be so desperate to live that she'd conspire to extend her life by jumping into the body of her archenemy, then only to be dragged to "hell" as the ultimate payback.

Paul Wesley: I enjoyed her compassion.

Matthew D'Ambrosio: It hurt my heart, but I think it was time. Katherine's story with Nadia was such a fun period to Katherine's otherwise cut-and-run lifestyle. She reunited with her daughter, she got Stefan to save her life, she came to terms with her own mortality. All before pulling the most Katherine-esque move in history.

Holly Brix: I loved her this season. She had such good story. First, she's a human again. She's vulnerable in a way that she hasn't been vulnerable in 500 years. Then she realizes she's dying and there's nothing she can do about it. Then, as if all of that wasn't enough, she realizes her daughter has come to find her. Amazing. I was so moved by Katherine's final scene: when she, after see-sawing all season, comes to the Salvatore house to see Nadia, knowing that she's not going to leave there alive. I loved that. It was a final moment for her that, in my opinion, redeemed what we all secretly loved about her. There was still a person worth rooting for in there.

Kellie Cyrus: She was my favorite character of the season and my favorite Katherine!

Rebecca Sonnenshine: Amazing! So much fun. She was so good and so bad. The perfect end to her character. She got to do it all. She got to be vulnerable, be contrite, have an emotional reunion with her daughter, make sacrifices, then turn around and do something even *more* horrible.

Neil Reynolds: Her relationship with Nadia broke my heart and humanized Katherine in a way I didn't expect. I think she redeemed herself, in her own

Katherine way, but it was too late to save her daughter, making her own end all the more tragic.
Caroline Dries: I loved it. She started a selfish bitch and Nadia softened her slightly and she nearly found redemption. But it was too late. She is who she is and, like Stefan said in 5.10, 400-plus years is a lot to have to forgive.
Price Peterson, TV.com: While fans will always argue about season five's merits, no sane person could complain about how great Katherine's plot line was. Starting off as basically a hobo, she scraped her way back into her role as HBIC with ingenuity and that same characteristic guile she's always had. But along the way she gained a daughter and some humanity both literal and metaphorical. Season five Katherine was Katherine on steroids and the show will truly not be the same without her.
Robyn Ross, *TV Guide*: At first I was unsure of the decision to make Katherine human, but it added another dimension to the character we hadn't yet seen: vulnerability. Yet even as her humanity and weakness started to show through, and she even sought some redemption, Katherine never lost the selfish and manipulative side that made her who she was. So I was happy that in turning human, she didn't completely change, we just got to see more. It was also fun to watch the dynamic between her and Stefan shift and see the side of him that she sometimes brought out. Although I was sad to see her go, her death made sense in looking at the future of the series and at least she went out with one hell of a bang.
Carrie Raisler, *A.V. Club*: Katherine was hands down my favorite thing about season five. Because she's such a survivor, giving her an arc all about facing her own mortality was a tiny bit of genius (except for the part about her dying, because I can't deal with a world without Katherine Pierce in it). Katherine the human was hilarious and strangely heartfelt, Katherine scheming to take over Elena's life was tremendously satisfying, and the show even managed to soften Katherine in a realistic manner by exploring her relationship with Nadia. There are a few things I would have changed (having her whole goal while in Elena's body be winning over Stefan was a bit dull) but overall I thought Katherine's arc was the season's greatest achievement.
Brett Matthews: I thought we saw more depth from Katherine this season than ever before. She was who she was right to the bitter end, but you understood on a deeper level why she was that way and did the villainous things she did. I loved her beyond words this season.
Michael Allowitz: I miss her and want her back.

What did you think of Katherine's exit in "Gone Girl"?
Paul Wesley: Very well shot. I like the idea of people disappearing into nothingness with no explanation. That's what death is.

Price Peterson: Suitably over the top. While I'm not sure I'm happy with the idea of the show's most dynamic and clever character banished to fate worse than purgatory for her lifetime of self-preservation — certainly other dead vampires had done worse things than her right? — I'm glad her death felt epic. I just wish it wasn't quite so permanent.
Marc Pollon: Being the great antagonist she is, it seems only fitting she should be the first one to be sucked into the Other Side's black hole. And the unexpected manner that it happened made it all the more awesome!
Robyn Ross: While heartbreaking, it was so fitting that in the end Stefan was the one to put the final stake in her. It also brought their relationship full circle after we learned he was actually the first Salvatore brother she met. And I would've expected nothing less than for Katherine to leave a wake of destruction behind.
Neil Reynolds: What did *you* think of it? Where did she go?! What dragged her there?!
Carrie Raisler: I'm sorry, I don't know what you're talking about. Katherine isn't gone. I refuse to accept it.

What is Katherine's hell like?
Melinda Hsu Taylor: To be irrelevant. It would not just be to have an ordinary life because I think she could be happy in an ordinary life where she was in her own little circle, important even as a mom — you're the center of your kid's life so that's being important and very relevant. But to be dime a dozen, nobody notices if you die at your cubicle desk? That would be her hell.
Matthew D'Ambrosio: Listening to Elena, Caroline, and Bonnie talk about mundane details of their day. On a loop. Forever and ever and ever and ever.
Holly Brix: Bitch has done some terrible things. I dunno. Her hell is going to be bad.
Rebecca Sonnenshine: I'm not sure what Katherine's definition of hell would be, but I like to think of it as a big, cold void of nothing.
Neil Reynolds: Trapped in a small room with Elena Gilbert and Damon Salvatore.
Caroline Dries: We touched on it this season with the gray hair and wrinkles — aging is her hell.
Julie Plec: Shoes with no heels, no mascara, no curling iron, and no boys. Although she'd make an excellent lesbian.
Robyn Ross: Since, theoretically, Silas could be up there with her, I picture the two going from having an epic war of words to a just as passionate hookup. From there I see those two ruling the dark side, while keeping an eye on those down below.

Carrie Raisler: I imagine Katherine's hell as being filled with thousands of Elena Gilberts, acting all Elena-like. Can you imagine anything she would think was more horrible?
Price Peterson: Hanging around the same boring basics she'd been dealing with all through her life. Katherine wasn't exactly living a blessed life what with all her boyfriends dumping her for Elena and immortal vampire werewolves trying to murder her for half a millennium. True, she was a bit of a jerk toward the end, but however bad her ultimate hell might be, I hope it's at least exciting enough for Katherine to enjoy herself somewhat. Plus she'd probably be scheming alongside the devil in no time.

What's the best all-time Katherine murder?
Paul Wesley: There's been so many deaths on *TVD* that I'm so confused with who killed who and I honestly don't even remember who she's killed at this point.
Melinda Hsu Taylor: Herself — does that count as a murder? Because it sets the series in motion, first of all, and also it's such a *fuck you* to Klaus.
Price Peterson: Herself! Take that, Klaus.
Rebecca Sonnenshine: While she didn't technically murder Jeremy in that cave, she was completely responsible for his death. Which was one cold move.
Holly Brix: Caroline. I was just so shocked. And it launched Caroline in such a new direction for the whole show.
Neil Reynolds: Caroline Forbes, natch — because, like Caroline said, it ultimately changed Caroline's life for the better.
Caroline Dries: When she killed Caroline with the pillow.
Robyn Ross: Caroline, but only because it led to her becoming a vampire, which turned the character into one of my favorites in the series.
Matthew D'Ambrosio: Poor Aimee Bradley. All she wanted to do was dance at the Lockwoods' masquerade party. Then Katherine broke her neck, paralyzing her. And then she killed her. Not to mention this was *after* Aimee complimented "Elena" on her dress and called her pretty. Poor Aimee Bradley.
Julie Plec: Attempted murder: Uncle John. Actual murder? Girl on dance floor in "Masquerade."
Carrie Raisler: Katherine snapping Aimee's spine in the middle of the dance floor during "Masquerade" is a classic moment, and for good reason. It defines Katherine in one eight-second scene: ruthless, brutal, and willing to do anything to get results.

What is your overall favorite Katherine moment?

Paul Wesley: I did rather enjoy when she pretended to be Elena, and her and Damon kissed on the porch at the end of season one. That was an amazing twist. Bravo to Kevin and Julie.

Melinda Hsu Taylor: One of them would definitely be when she kisses Damon on the porch right before going in to chop off John's fingers. She does such a great like, *Oh. He fell for it.* Like you can see it on her face. It's brilliant. And pretty much anything that she does as a human, that she does that expresses vulnerability or exasperation with the mundane physical aspects of being human. Like she's hungry, she wants sandwiches at the party. Or she's cold and she wants a sweater. Or she's catching a cold and she's mortified. They're so heightened and they're so funny because they come out of her experience and it's just the *indignity* of it. I just loved all of that. It's so fun when you see a supervillain reduced to something very human. That can be a moment of great vulnerability or it's just great relatability.

Matthew D'Ambrosio: This is gonna be sort of sappy, but I loved Katherine learning who Nadia actually was. But that's a one-two punch with Katherine admitting she came back to look for Nadia. That simple moment in the hotel room, Katherine is busying herself doing something, but you can't quite tell what. Katherine asks Nadia where she was in 1498. Nadia says she doesn't know, she was a child. And Katherine admits she had shaken Klaus off long enough to come search for Nadia, but she was gone. She searched everywhere, every village, and never found out what happened to Nadia. Katherine admits it's nice to finally meet her. And then we realize she's been making a cup of tea this whole time, and extends it out to Nadia. Just a tiny, selfless act from Katherine. Nadia cries, I cry, everybody cries.

Holly Brix: In "Handle with Care," Katherine is so desperate to stay alive and procure simple human needs like a shower and food that she sneaks into Elena and Caroline's dorm room to bathe and swipe Elena's meal card. That's all she's angling for. And I love it because it's one of those "oh, how the mighty have fallen moments." When she learns that Caroline is scared of Dr. Wes, Katherine sees an opportunity to get what she wants. She concocts and executes the plan to pass as Elena and sneak into the Augustine mixer. I love her and Caroline teaming up and I love when Katherine steals sandwiches into her purse at the tea party. That's probably my favorite Katherine moment.

Michael Allowitz: In "No Exit," when she lures Stefan into a motel room and gets him to kiss her — in her twisted romantic way. (But I am biased.)

Neil Reynolds: I loved Elena and Rebekah's takedown of her style and mannerisms in the "American Gothic" diner scene. So fun, so meta.

Price Peterson: "Ba-boom."

Caroline Dries: The end of 5.10: she shows up to see Stefan to check in on his feelings about last night, and we see her vulnerability. I loved when they held hands. I loved her realizing that she could have had everything she wanted if she hadn't been such a monster and now it was too late. Second fave moment came in act one of 5.10 when Katherine was escaping Stefan's bed. Nina added the bit where Katherine crashed into the wall, and I loved it. I laughed really hard when I saw that.

Julie Plec: Stefan taking her sad memories away of the death of her parents as she saw a light coming from the crib in the 100th.

Robyn Ross: As much as I love all of her sassy moments, my favorite is from "500 Years of Solitude" when she hallucinates about the day her family was massacred, her daughter taken, and cries with Stefan by her side. In that moment, you see the devastation that, while not necessarily justifiable, set her on the path she'd ultimately go down for the next 500 years.

Carrie Raisler: Turning Caroline into a vampire. I think even Caroline would agree with me here.

What made Katherine such a great character?

Marc Pollon: Nina Dobrev makes Katherine great. For me, what stands out about Katherine as a character was that every time she was on the screen, she owned the scene. She was manipulative, funny, mostly without a conscience, totally self-involved. So. Great.

Paul Wesley: The fact that no matter how benevolent or empathetic she may appear to be in a rare moment, she always gravitates toward deception and maliciousness. This makes her very exciting.

Matthew D'Ambrosio: She's fun. When everyone is plotting and seriously trying to solve a problem, Katherine is there to point out the futility in their actions. Katherine's a voice of reason, saying the things no one else will say at all the wrong moments to say them. She's also a great dresser.

Holly Brix: She's completely selfish. She's always trying to do what's best for her and that makes her drives strong and her motives easy to understand. Great characters are born of clear, strong drives.

Kellie Cyrus: You love to hate her.

Michael Allowitz: Her unstoppable drive.

Joshua Butler: Katherine Pierce is such a great character — especially the way Nina Dobrev portrays her — because she's a true romantic who, over the centuries, has given in to a kind of witty cynicism about the world. The way Katherine fights off sentimentality, and then unwittingly gives into it every now and then, makes her supremely lovable, even if she has done some hateful things.

Rebecca Sonnenshine: She's funny, she's selfish, she's sexy, and she's a survivor. But she's also a romantic — I truly believe she falls in love, hard. She's a villain, but we can so clearly understand why she does the things she does. At her core, she's extremely emotional.
Caroline Dries: She's a bitch who tells people the truth, which often hurts and she doesn't care. She's also, deep down, super trashy even though she seems classy.
Julie Plec: She's everything you love to hate and hate to love. Manipulative, slinky, bossy, bitchy, and yet so wildly emotionally vulnerable that you can't help but feel compassion for her. The ultimate soap opera vixen.
Robyn Ross: The key to an awesome TV villain is someone you want to keep watching despite all the bad things they do. What was great about Katherine is that she was the complete opposite of Elena and that provided a look into the two very different ways each of them could've ended up. But more than that, Katherine was downright fun and her sass and humor livened up the show often at dark moments.
Carrie Raisler: I think Katherine's appeal can be boiled down to her two main qualities: she's a survivor, and she's absolutely unapologetic about that fact. In a show full of vampires who tend to agonize over the morally questionable things they must do to stay alive, Katherine embraces those things without hesitation; if it's to her benefit she'll do it, without reservation. This makes her like a warm summer breeze of amorality drifting in and out of the cold angst that can sometimes take over the rest of Mystic Falls. That she's also essentially the exact opposite of Elena — yet also played to perfection by Nina Dobrev — adds an extra layer of intrigue (a sort of "Wow, all of *that* is in *there*?" thing) and just makes her all the more interesting. Essentially, she's like our heroine, but so much more *fun*.
Melinda Hsu Taylor: I think people love to be bad, or imagine that they could be bad, or that they'd be as awesome as Katherine if they were bad. It's no fun to be good. But it's great to see somebody just tell it like it is. You just wish you had those zingers and could call people on their stuff, and Katherine does it all the time. Which is, I think, a large part of the fun of her. Also that she makes no apologies ever, I think that's very appealing in a character. An unrepentant person is a lot more fun than someone who's angsty all the time — unless they're angsty about something terrible romantic, in which case we love them.
Price Peterson: Katherine was not only hilarious, she was an active character in a show centered around a very passive protagonist. Katherine did some bad things in her lifetime, but they always felt motivated and understandable. Most people will remember Katherine for her villainy, but I will remember her for what a surprisingly good sport she was about getting

involved in the Salvatores' various schemes. It never felt less than thrilling whenever she used her skills for subterfuge in the interest of the common good (like at Klaus's homecoming party) or when she'd have memorable moments of humanity with our heroes (Matt, Jeremy). Also, she turned Stefan, Damon, and Caroline into vampires. This show could literally not exist without Katherine. (Katherine is also Nina Dobrev's best work of her entire career.)
Neil Reynolds: I thought we all agreed it was the hair?

Bonnie: Elena, stop. You're not yourself.
Elena: Oh that's ironic, because I wasn't myself for weeks and yet nobody noticed.
Liv: She's losing it.

5.16 *While You Were Sleeping*

Original air date March 20, 2014
Written by Caroline Dries **Directed by** Pascal Verschooris
Edited by Tony Solomons **Cinematography by** Michael Karasick
Previously on *The Vampire Diaries* Paul Wesley

Trapped in her dorm, Elena slowly goes crazy from the werewolf-ripper virus, and she learns what's been going on in her absence. Caroline and Stefan get embroiled with Enzo and the Travelers.

With Elena magically trapped in the empty dorm, she's left to figure out what happened while she was "sleeping" with only minimal guidance to help her — brief conversations with Stefan, phone calls galore with Damon, Katherine's diary entries, and a feverish imagination. Three weeks of lost time means Elena has missed out on a *lot*, and we see her confront her friends about how they could've let Katherine's ruse go on so long. Though Elena's back in control of her body, she's still adrift — thanks to her isolation, the gaping holes in her memory, and that pesky virus that's slowly driving her crazy and killing her.

Though Elena is feeling estranged, the others prove what they're willing to do to help each other out. Not only does Stefan go through the offscreen rigmarole of replacing Elena's phone (a total drag) he's managing everyone's crises. Damon is in lockdown with two prison guards, Bonnie and Liv are in service, and Caroline on antidote duty. Stefan's even willing to risk losing himself again — subjecting himself to Traveler torture — in order to get the cures for Damon's and Elena's variant viruses. Stefan says to Caroline that he knows she would do the same for him — risk herself and her life — and it's true across the board in this ragtag community. A community that now includes Enzo, who asks if it is really such an anomaly that Damon should have a friend. And when it comes down to brass tacks, Damon has many — Jeremy and Matt take care of him despite the fact that he's shown them extreme violence over the years, and Stefan and Caroline are helping Damon as much as they are helping Elena in finding the antidote. They respect the fact that Damon will tell Elena his list of sins in his own way, in good time.

Damon wants to tell her the truth, and knows he has to, but he just can't bear to tell her over the phone — instead enjoying the flirtation and the comfort of having Elena back and wanting him as much as he wants her. Unfortunately for Ms. Gilbert, Damon's dillydallying leads to her craziest spell since she experienced the Hunter's Curse. (And she's had some crazy spells.) It's a manic episode, and Nina Dobrev plays each moment with great honesty. As with so much of this season in particular, the episode's success hinges on her performance — the whole thing would fall apart if she couldn't pull off her acting feats. As "While You Were Sleeping" progresses, Elena gets sicker and sicker, more and more violent, and less and less willing to believe that she's hearing the full truth from her friends. Damon's reluctance to tell her that he killed Aaron makes her think the worst: that Katherine killed Aaron, that he died thinking Elena was murdering him. Damon busts out of lockup (again) to go to her — both in order to save her from herself, somehow, and to unload his secrets.

Though Elena says she wants to fight for her relationship with Damon — notably before she hears that he is responsible for murdering Wes and Aaron — she's also terrified at losing herself. In her hallucinations, her greatest fears are of being so easily mistaken for the monster that she thinks Katherine was. Her best friends, her brother, her two great loves, none of them noticed that she wasn't herself. In her feverish state, Elena doesn't acknowledge her lack of culpability for the things that *Katherine* did while possessing Elena's body. Even if Katherine *had* killed Aaron while in Elena's body, that wouldn't

> "We have no formula. There is no murder of the week or bad guy of the week kind of model. We're always generating story. Big story out of nothing at all — I always have that old song running through my head, 'making love out of nothing at all.' It doesn't quite make sense, but I do feel like we start each episode break with some gold nuggets and a pile of straw and from there we spin gold."
>
> — Holly Brix

be Elena's fault; it wouldn't be her sin to repent. But in addition to feeling rage toward Katherine, Elena takes on the guilt of her doppelgänger's actions — real and imagined. In the hallucination sequences, she mixes up and uses "she" and "me" interchangeably — how do you separate yourself from an identical twin who took possession of your body and duped everyone you know for three whole weeks?

As Elena loses her grasp on what is real and what is true, she tries to "cleanse" herself of Katherine by torching her stuff, but she can't seem to get back to being Elena — not with the virus ruling over her best intentions. Though Bonnie urges her not to let Katherine win, to fight off the virus, Elena pulls one of the greatest villainous sneak attacks ever on Liv — with a move stolen right from the Klaus Mikaelson playbook. She gives the witch she just met an impossible choice: drop the seal or die. In those moments, she is becoming a person who will do whatever she needs to do, collateral damage be damned: a monster who would hurt, even kill, innocent people. Sound familiar?

There's a parallel between her battle against the virus and the on-again, off-again relationship she has with Damon. In their heated conversation at the end of the episode, she says that in order to be with him, to love him, she has been compromising her morals and beliefs, making excuses for him and for what he's done. Her love for him is turning her into something she didn't used to be, someone that neither one of them is particularly proud of. But despite the fact that both of them say they shouldn't be together, their passion for each other is strong enough to overpower any logical argument. Shirts are ripped, resolve is broken. The control they wield over each other is powerful, and there's no easy answer to their dilemma: being together means that one or the other of them must deny their core instincts.

On the other side of the relationship spectrum, Caroline and Stefan's perfect friendship continues, as they chill with the Travelers at an awesome train-track location whilst wearing beautifully becoming coats. But just as Caroline doesn't want to see Stefan put himself too much at risk to save Damon and Elena, she ends up making a choice analogous to Elena's ethically sketchy choices with Damon. Caroline won't let Sloan destroy Stefan's mind, and so she agrees to commit stone-cold murder with the best murder-buddy in town, *the* Enzo. The Travelers only want one Silas doppelgänger to live in order to complete their Super Top Secret Plan, and Caroline is willing to go with Enzo — whom she doesn't trust — to Atlanta to kill a paramedic with a face like Stefan's. And the echoed "You'd do the same for me" comment rings true: these are friends who prove time and again that there are very few lines they wouldn't cross to protect each other. For better or for worse.

COMPELLING MOMENT Elena's "I'm a monster" freakout with Damon. Nina Dobrev's talent knows no bounds.

CIRCLE OF KNOWLEDGE

- No Tyler in this episode.
- This episode borrows its title from the 1995 movie *While You Were Sleeping* — *TVD*'s Garreth Stover was production designer for the film! — about lonely Lucy (Sandra Bullock) who, through zany rom-com mixups, spends a week pretending to be the fiancée of in-a-coma Peter (Peter Gallagher) and, in the process, falls in love with his family and in love-love with his brother, Jack (Bill Pullman). Fortunately, when Peter wakes from his coma, he doesn't burn anything, threaten anyone, or hallucinate.
- In case you didn't get a chance to read Katherine's diary entry before Elena burnt it, she wrote, "Just the two of us, a cramped hotel room, a steamy shower. I saw the way he looked at me, I knew what he wanted, and . . . well . . . let's just say things are finally starting to go my way."
- Back in season two, it seemed like there needed to be a direct descendant for a doppelgänger to generate again — Katherine had a child, eventually down that bloodline came Elena. But with the Silas and Amara origin story earlier this season, it appears that direct blood descendants

are not required. Neither of those two had children, and yet there have been doppelgängers again and again over the past 2,000 years. The Silas doppelgänger living in Atlanta is not linked via bloodline to Stefan or any previous edition of Silas.

THE RULES Elena suffers from a heady mix of werewolf-venom crazies and the ripper virus: she is starving for vampire blood, she's violent, she's woozy and coughing up blood and having hallucinations galore.

As we already know, the Travelers' magic works differently (and is perhaps weaker?) than traditional witch magic. As Stefan noted, when Qetisyah brain-melded him to Silas, she didn't require his blood, but here it's needed in order for the whole gang of Travelers to connect Stefan to his doppelgänger in Atlanta.

Sloan demands that the Travelers chant louder, in order to give more power to the spell.

Whatever the Travelers want to do with Stefan's and Elena's blood, it won't work until they are the last two remaining doppelgängers — thus the impetus behind the linking spell to find Stefan's twin in Atlanta.

Though judging by her "show-off" abilities at the end of the episode Liv could've set the salt on fire, the fact that Bonnie challenges her with that task might mean that burning salt offers a degree of difficulty to a witch.

PREVIOUSLY ON *THE VAMPIRE DIARIES* To be fair to the dream versions of Jer, Matt, Bon, and Caroline that Elena admonishes in the opening sequence, she *did* dance on a table and booze it up when she had her humanity off in "Bring It On" (4.16).

Enzo doesn't know about werewolves, just as Damon was a non-believer back in season two ("Brave New World," 2.02).

Stefan says he knew it wasn't Elena because Elena wouldn't have kissed him, because she loves Damon; this moment plays as an inverse of "The Return" (2.01) when Elena says of Damon, "He kissed Katherine, not me. I wouldn't do that," because she loved Stefan.

Amnesia Stefan burned his journals in "For Whom the Bell Tolls," like Elena does here.

Ms. Gilbert just might have pyromaniac tendencies: not only does she do a "fire cleanse" here but nearly blew up herself and Damon with a gas

© Andrew Evans/PR Photos

fire in "True Lies" and she burned her whole house down in "Stand By Me" (4.15).

Elena creatively stabs Liv in order to get her way, just as Klaus staked Caroline outside the boundary spell in "Into the Wild" (4.13).

In the scene at the train tracks, Caroline says to Stefan of the Travelers, "I think we can take them"; she's probably right — the last time she wagered that was in "Kill or Be Killed" (2.05) up against werewolf Mason Lockwood, and she did, saving Elena and taking him down.

OFF CAMERA Caroline Dries reveals that during the filming of this episode, "Nina was horribly sick with a cold but the character was going through a werewolf infection so it just made her acting that much more realistic." Damon's comment about the unseasonably cold temperatures was a reference to the frigid conditions under which they were filming in Atlanta. Says Dries, "While we were shooting at the train yard, the temperature dipped down to single digits." Luke only became Liv's brother as Caroline Dries was writing that final scene, and "originally Luke was going to be a potential love interest for Elena but I decided to make him someone Katherine would want to be friends with, and my first thought was: the fun cute gay boy from one of her classes."

Witch Liv Parker is played by Australian actress Penelope Mitchell, best known to American audiences as Letha Godfrey on Netflix's original horror series *Hemlock Grove*. Prior to *Hemlock Grove*, Mitchell had one-off roles on Australian shows *Offspring* and *Rush*, and she was featured on the reality series *Next Stop Hollywood*, which followed six Australian actors who move to Hollywood for pilot season. Of the new characters introduced in season five, Rebecca Sonnenshine enjoys writing Liv. "She's got a sassy streak — but also seems to be able to flirt with anyone, even when she's not trying." Caroline Dries also finds Liv interesting "because she's so weird. There's something dangerous and sexy about her and then moments of kindness and warmth."

FOGGY MOMENTS Jeans and an undershirt do not constitute "half naked," Elena. Nor was Katherine "leading on" Stefan when she had every intention of following through.

What address did Caroline text to Stefan — #1 Old Derelict Train Tracks?

Why would Dr. Wes have made an antidote to the ripper virus if his goal was to eradicate vampires by having them kill each other? Sloan says the Travelers are using Wes's research to make an antidote to the souped-up virus Elena suffers from, and they make a successful one really quickly — how do Travelers have the appropriate science background to whip up antidotes?

Luke says Elena was trying to compel him so he had to get Liv involved, or else he'd have to reveal he knew about vampires and was on vervain. So what was his game plan when Elena was seconds away from snapping his neck and turning him? Was he just going to let it happen?

Garreth Stover on *TVD*'s Production Design

On getting into the business: I started production designing about 24 years ago, after working in the camera department for about two years. Originally I wanted to be a cinematographer, but at some point, in that two-year period, I realized it would take way too long and that hopefully what I really wanted to do was become a director. During my career as a production designer, I have gotten to direct second unit for many directors on feature films with directors such as Jon Turteltaub, Joe Roth, and Steve Carr, to name a few. A year ago, I directed my first episode of *TVD* ["Because the Night," 4.17].

On his job on *TVD*: As the production designer, I am responsible for picking locations with the producer, as well as designing sets. I oversee the decorations for the sets and locations as well. All colors used during an episode are run by me — like wall colors in conjunction with wardrobe and even car colors.

On the process for each episode: Oftentimes I will be given an idea of upcoming sets or script ideas. Usually this is in a conversation with the writer/producers along with the producer, or I might be given a beat sheet. This is done so that the producer and I can understand the scope both design-wise and financially of an upcoming set or location. Sometimes an alternative for the set can be discussed to ease the construction or financial impact. We are usually designing and building at least one or two sets on every episode. It's a hectic schedule and sometimes a big set can overwhelm the construction and paint department, so everything must be considered before we embark on it.

On *TVD*'s look: The aesthetic of the show exists in a modern-day gothic world. Everything is dark, shiny, and earth tone–based. This last season was the first time we have ever introduced white. It was used against black to highlight a specific event. It worked really well and I give Michael Karasick, the cinematographer of the episode, a lot of credit for going along with the idea. Stylistically the show has always remained in its world of dark gothic environments, though as my construction and paint crew have grown and developed into an amazing group of craftspeople, the quality of everything has gone up exponentially. Even the texture of the bricks is amazing. I am the luckiest designer here in Atlanta to be working with such an amazing group of artists. I can actually say the construction department on this show, here in Atlanta, is the best I have ever worked with in my career as a production designer. The set decorating department, led by Karen Bruck with her leadman Troy Borisy, is most accomplished and make my job much easier.

On the magical moments in his job: Okay, this is going to sound silly, but oftentimes while designing a set, things are happening at breakneck speeds. Sets are designed in a matter of hours, and then as the budgets come in, we start to redesign. And then as the sets start to get built, certain items are not available, so things in the set — wallpaper or hardware — have to be repicked and changed. The real magic — and Karen Bruck and I are amazed at how often it happens — is that when we look at the final, completed set, everything looks perfect together, incredibly well coordinated and well designed. It's amazing how things just fall into place and look great, even though the process seemed as though it was unraveling and things were picked in a split second.

QUESTIONS

- Will Damon tell Elena that in addition to killing Aaron and Wes, he also nearly killed Jeremy just to get information?
- Enzo says that "among other things" Wes experimented on him in the time after "No Exit" to develop an antidote to the werewolf-ripper virus. What were those "other things"?
- Why don't the Travelers want Liv to know what they are up to, and how do they know her? What is the endgame for the Travelers? Are they after the same thing as Liv and Luke?
- How is the last remaining pair of doppelgängers special and what will combining their blood do?
- Will Caroline and Enzo actually kill the Atlanta doppelgänger?

Damon: Little tip: if you're gonna show up to kill someone, don't waste time feeling bad about it.

5.17 Rescue Me

Original air date March 27, 2014
Written by Brett Matthews and Neil Reynolds
Directed by Leslie Libman
Edited by Marc Pollon **Cinematography by** Darren Genet
Guest cast Brian LaFontaine (ER Doctor), Dane Northcutt (Teacher), Gena Shaw (Hazel)
Previously on *The Vampire Diaries* Paul Wesley

To save Stefan from the Travelers, Caroline and Enzo head to Atlanta to do some doppelgänger murdering, Elena and Damon try not to have sex at parent-teacher conference day, and Jeremy declares his independence.

Elena and Caroline are forced to confront their boundaries in an episode that relies on fantasy sequences (Elena imagines getting down in the chemistry classroom; Caroline, less sexily, sees Tom choke on a waffle) to explore the questions of What If and What Could Be. While Caroline is in Atlanta on an assassination mission with the can't-help-but-be-charming Enzo, Elena finds herself crawling out of Damon's bed and heading back to Mystic Falls High School, putting on the role of Jeremy's caretaker, something she has not done all season. And big sis is surprised to hear that her kid brother who's almost always had trouble at school is . . . having trouble at school.

The bond between the Salvatore brothers and scenes involving the two are, as always, front and center in season five, but the Gilbert kids have been distant with each other — both emotionally and in terms of plot lines. (Where was Jeremy when Elena was discovering their father's dark past?) As much as Elena's romance with any Salvatore brother is of great concern to everyone involved, this series shines when it highlights other kinds of relationships. In "Rescue Me," Elena reacts to the Jeremy situation only as it relates to *her* — what his troubled state of mind says about her relationship with Damon — rather than rally in support of her brother. In the woodshop (a genius location to stake a vampire or torture a witch), Elena questions Jeremy's judgment — because he cheated on a math test — and it's laughable. She is standing there with her barely reformed serial killer of a lover, torturing a witch. Elena should know firsthand what it's like for her brother to try to be normal amid supernaturally crazy circumstances; she knows what Jeremy has been through and what he has lost. Here's hoping that Elena's decision at the end of the episode, and Damon's respect for it, signals a healthy shift in the character akin to Jer's declaration of independence. While Elena has been in a hot-sex-with-Damon fog, Jeremy has been seeing clearly. And it's long past time for him to start taking action. Though he should probably return Bonnie's phone calls (enough with the secrets, everybody!), Jeremy is ready to solve some supernatural mysteries with Matt and Tyler and to form an alliance with Liv and Luke, secure in the knowledge that their interests can align with his. And front of mind for Little Gilbert? Protecting his sister . . . while minimizing violence.

Writers Brett Matthews and Neil Reynolds on "Rescue Me"

Matthews on Tom Avery: I actually really enjoy writing good guys. So Tom was way more fun than you'd think, especially the way Paul really committed to playing him as a different person. And let us never, ever forget his amazing doppel-hair. Caroline is, of course, the perfect person to put opposite him, and in an episode where she's dealing with her repressed feelings for Stefan, every scene she has with Tom just has that extra, added level.

Reynolds: Poor, poor Tom Avery. Caroline really did sell how good and wholesome Tom was, but the irony is, following our own mythology, Tom's existence as one half of the doppelgänger "pairings" means that he was *probably* meant to fall in love with Elena, his once-human counterpart. We teased some of that energy into early outlines for the episode, even considered bringing Tom and Elena together to see the initial sparks from Tom's POV. But we veered away from that once we realized the story we cared about more was Caroline/Stefan.

Matthews on Caroline and Enzo: Those two characters just worked in this episode, on the page and on set. I dig the funny stuff, I dig the murderous stuff, I dig the tragic stuff. Candice and Michael just got it right from the jump. Their hospital scene is probably my favorite.

Reynolds: The flirtatious energy was fun, and we made a very conscious effort to evoke some of the "Klaroline" energy from previous seasons. But my favorite scenes are the two that brought this team-up to a close: when Enzo kills Tom, and Caroline cuts him down. You can see that Enzo is actually wounded, despite his bravado. And then Caroline's scene with Stefan in the junkyard, which I hope launched a thousand ships.

Reynolds on the "death by doorknob" moment: We needed to sell the idea that the witch Hazel had been keeping Tom Avery off the witch and Traveler radars for months, and presumably also wanted to protect themselves from vampires who might come snooping. The threshold curse would prevent vampires from entering, but of course we needed Enzo and Caroline to get in there. Actually, now that I'm thinking about it, we did want there to be a clear schism between Enzo and Caroline on their doppel-hunt . . . the doorknob murder was an easy way for Enzo to remove an obstacle, without heeding the consequences — which, of course, is the opposite of how Caroline functions.
Matthews: Neil and I pitched it from the very beginning, and that beat never changed. We thought it was maybe a little broad but [Caroline] Dries loved it when she first heard it — she's twisted that way. It's typically Enzo in just the right way. And, as an Easter egg, the actress who plays Hazel and gets killed by the doorknob is my girlfriend. So . . . weird day on set, that one. But getting to work with Gena [Shaw] was so much fun and makes "Rescue Me" very special to me and one I'll always remember.

The battle between doing "whatever it takes" to protect a loved one and holding on to a moral code has been fought in various ways on this series since its beginning, and here we watch Caroline struggle to do right and still do right by Stefan. She rejects Enzo's soldier-at-war analogy, but he does predict her inability to kill. She won't be able to murder Tom Avery, an innocent and affable EMT who looks identical to a person who means the world to her. There's a lot to enjoy in "Rescue Me" — from oversexed Damon and Elena to the boys snarking at the Grill — and the Caroline and Enzo murder team is high on that list. Quippy fight-flirting aside, Enzo gives us an insight into Caroline's friendship with Stefan when he describes who Maggie was to him. Not a woman who made him "want to be a better man" (i.e., the dynamic between Elena and Damon, once upon a time), but one who reminded him that he was good all along.

It's that sentiment that makes the junkyard scene between Caroline and Stefan lying in the derelict van so powerful. She recognizes that he already knew and admired what makes her *her* — he knows what she would never be able to do, not even for a loved one. It's a beautifully filmed scene full of intimacy, heart, and humor — and (for a couple of prisoners trapped by evil wannabe witches) one that is surprisingly angst free. They'll rest, together, and then they'll return to their heroics.

But the calm ends, and the storm rises by episode's end: the Travelers burn themselves alive in order to see their leader Markos resurrected, rising out of the shadow of our long-suffering Anchor to the Other Side, Bonnie Bennett. The troops are ready. Jeremy, his bros, and the wonder twins of Liv and Luke are all prepared to fight for the last living doppelgängers. The end of the season must be nigh.

COMPELLING MOMENT Caroline and Stefan in the junkyard minivan — a beautiful scene.

CIRCLE OF KNOWLEDGE

- "Rescue Me" is a terribly popular choice for a song title, and the name of an FX Network TV series (2004–2011) about firefighters in New York City.
- When we first see Tom Avery, the paramedic, he is using a 10-gauge needle to remove fluid from an accident victim's lung, allowing the lung to expand and improve her breathing.
- Enzo drops loads of religious references in "Rescue Me," calling Caroline an angel of death, referring to them both as angels to Tom, and making a reference to Tom's last supper before he's delivered to the sweet hereafter. To take it further, sacrificing Tom will save and protect others, positioning him as Jesus and setting Enzo up as his betrayer, Judas.
- The two diner scenes in this episode were filmed at the Thumbs Up Diner (573 Edgewood Ave. SE) in Atlanta. Before her death-by-doorknob, Hazel lived on Peachtree Drive, an actual street in Atlanta (though there is no house at her street number). Enzo's joke about all the streets bearing peachy names is decidedly on point.
- Enzo drops an apt reference to Edgar Allan Poe's classic 1843 short story "The Tell-Tale Heart" when he and Caroline hear Tom's heartbeat in the basement. The story is a first-person tale of madness by a nameless, unreliable narrator who has murdered an old man and hidden his dismembered body beneath the floorboards, only to become convinced he can hear the victim's heart still beating as police officers arrive to investigate a scream overheard by a neighbor. The heartbeat in his ears, along

with his own guilt, become so overwhelming that he confesses his crime and reveals where he has hidden the body.

- Damon jokes about Jeremy's affair with Ghost Anna, suggesting he needs a love song and a pottery wheel, which marks his second reference to *Ghost*, the 1990 romance film starring Patrick Swayze and Demi Moore. In "Heart of Darkness" (3.19), Damon called Jeremy "Whoopi," referring to Whoopi Goldberg's character in the film who could communicate with the spirit world.

THE RULES Despite Caroline's fears, Stefan doesn't seem to experience any memory loss from Sloan's relentless doppel-linking, but he is weakened and he blacks out.

Liv does a silencing spell by throwing some table salt into the flame of a candle; we saw a different kind of silencing spell with Esther and her sage back in "Dangerous Liaisons" (3.14).

Liv reminds Jeremy that, as a hunter, his mind can't be controlled by Travelers. She also offers some vague differentiation between Travelers and witches: Travelers are like the "ugly stepsisters" to witches, upset about the witches cursing the land to turn it against them.

Hazel had Tom Avery in some sort of magical/medical coma for four months, thanks to lots of squiggly salt lines, candles, chanting, and witchy-white eyes.

Sloan leads the Travelers in a spell that resurrects Markos: they all chant (of course), drink the doppelgänger blood, and — linked together — burn to death. Then they pass through the Anchor until she is overwhelmed and collapses. Markos emerges from her shadow.

PREVIOUSLY ON *THE VAMPIRE DIARIES* Elena gets a talking-to from a concerned and judgey educator, just like Aunt Jenna (R.I.P.) did back in season one, when she got Tanner'd ("The Night of the Comet," 1.02).

Tyler thinks Liv is "weird hot" and as we learned from Damon in "Children of the Damned" (1.13): "Hot trumps weird."

Caroline snaps Enzo's neck instead of killing innocent Tom, just as Damon snapped Enzo's neck instead of killing innocent Aaron Whitmore in "The Devil Inside." In both cases the solution is only temporary as both Aaron and Tom end up murdered.

In the woodshop, determined to rescue Liv from a murderous Damon,

© Glenn Francis/PRPhotos.com

Jeremy tells him that it wouldn't be the first time Damon killed him if he tried to here. Damon killed Jeremy in "The Return" (2.01), he was compelled to kill him in "Catch Me If You Can" (4.11), and he was aiming to kill him in "Total Eclipse of the Heart."

Jeremy made a similar speech about how far from normal his teen years are in "The New Deal" (3.10). Elena opted to compel and exile him to Denver to protect him, whereas here she respects his choice to get the heck out of the Salvatore mansion.

Caroline says she basically invented the charm-and-distract flirtation tactic, and she's used it to great effect, especially with Klaus in "The Murder of One" (3.18) and "We All Go a Little Mad Sometimes" (4.06).

OFF CAMERA Prior to playing Liv's brother Luke Parker, and *Vampire Diaries*' first gay character who isn't a daughter torturer, North Carolina native Chris Brochu was best known as the arrogant, teen dream Ray Beech, lead singer of the band Mudslide Crush, in Disney's 2011 *Lemonade Mouth*. He's also appeared in other films, such as *Solar Flare* (2008) and *Soul Surfer* (2011) and has guest starred on episodes of *Hannah Montana*, *The Mentalist*, *Melissa & Joey*, and *NCIS: Los Angeles*.

According to cowriter Neil Reynolds, the MMA magazine Caroline picks up in the hospital was a scripted prop. "We pitched it as *Men's Health* or similar, but couldn't get a real magazine cleared," he says. "I believe our props department whipped that one up. We thought it would be funny if Caroline was *so* uninterested in talking to Enzo that she didn't care *what* she read to avoid conversation."

"Rescue Me" features yet another breakfast scene, but when interrogated about the pervasive pro-pancake agenda throughout season five, Caroline Dries plays it cool, claiming it was not intentional. "Our episodes are becoming more and more just one day," she explains. "And they usually start in the morning and end at night. I don't know why this happens but it's sort of the pattern we got into. So it feels natural to start with breakfast. Sometimes, we need characters to meet in places where they're not necessarily in Mystic Falls, but we can't justify taking production on location, so we film in a universal set like our diner. And yes, writers are eating constantly, but if we had a pro-anything agenda you would see our characters eating a lot of cinnamon gummy bears, Trader Joe's salads, and drinking LaCroix instead of bourbon." A likely story.

> "[Filming] 'Rescue Me' was hell because of Snowpocalypse. I know everyone thinks of Atlanta as Hotlanta, but it really gets freezing cold in the winter and the city just got hammered by a winter storm and we were totally shut down. Pascal [Verschooris] and Trish [Stanard] really went above and beyond to do the right thing and make sure our crew was safe at all times. I think I was there for three weeks because of it, and every day seemed colder than the last . . . not that it kept Ian from getting incredibly naked in his first scene of the episode — trust me, I was there. A man could not be more naked."
>
> — Brett Matthews

Neil Reynolds' favorite writing material this season came in "Rescue Me": "Caroline and Enzo's love/hate road trip to find Stefan's last doppelgänger was so much fun to write, although my cowriter Brett Matthews had just as much to do with that." Matthews was partial to "the Stefan-Caroline snuggle scene. That's what we always called it on the [writers'] board."

FOGGY MOMENTS As observed by TV.com's Price Peterson, the background images on Elena's phone are bizarre: stock photos of pastries, a forest, and a woman in an office. WTF.

Hazel is a traditional draws-power-from-Nature witch, and yet — judging by the pile of mail on her porch — she's been stuck in her house chanting for four months in order to keep Tom Avery's location a secret. Were no other witches in the coven willing to help out? Is there no spell that requires less than constant vigilance?

Enzo equates his deal with the Travelers to Caroline's, saying he'll do anything for the people he loves, including cold-blooded murder. But he isn't saving Maggie's life; he's just tracking her down. Why not hire a PI first? Or Bing her? *Then* resort to murder.

Does Elena still not know that Damon nearly killed Jeremy while she was under Katherine's reign? Or is that just one of the many things she's been making excuses for? In "Total Eclipse of the Heart," Bonnie says that Elena would *kill* Damon for hurting Jeremy, and yet . . . nothing comes of it.

Does doppelgänger blood have special preservative properties or did all those poor Travelers, in their dying moments, drink rancid, weeks-old blood from a dirty bucket?

QUESTIONS

- Luke professes to be studying wave mechanics. Are Luke and Liv actually students at Whitmore or are they solely there to monitor the doppelgänger situation? Or both?
- What do the Travelers know about Maggie? How old is she now?
- Why is Damon so convinced that Jeremy is cheating on Bonnie with Liv? Can't two people drink at the Grill together without romancin'?
- Luke asks Bonnie not to be mad at Liv because their "family's kinda messed up." What does he mean by that? And Liv mentions a coven — how many witches are in her coven? Will we meet any more of their witchy friends?
- Do the Travelers still need Elena and Stefan for some nefarious plot, or did they just need them to be the last living doppelgängers so their blood became magical enough to revive Markos?
- Why did they resurrect Markos?

Luke: We need your help. We think the Travelers are about to make their move. Their leader, Markos, is here.
Damon: From where — chant camp?

5.18 *Resident Evil*

Original air date April 17, 2014
Written by Brian Young and Caroline Dries **Directed by** Paul Wesley
Edited by Glenn Garland **Cinematography by** Michael Karasick
Guest cast Cynthia Barrett (Yuppie Mom Traveler), Nick Basta (Deputy Traveler), Nathaniel Buzolic (Kol Mikaelson), Kayla Ewell (Vicki Donovan), Tommy Groth (City Worker Traveler), Jasmine Guy (Grams Bennett), Kenneth Israel (Traveler #1)
Previously on *The Vampire Diaries* Ian Somerhalder

In the wake of the Traveler leader's resurrection, Elena and Stefan experience vivid happily-ever-after visions; the Travelers make a bodysnatching move on Mystic Falls.

If there's one thing we've learned from this show over the past five seasons, it's to never trust a prophecy. The directorial debut of Paul Wesley, this episode not only presents us with the usual complicated *TVD* reality but it shows us the Other Side in flux and a fantasy life that never was. The opening doppel-vision that Stefan and Elena share, thanks to Markos, takes us on a nostalgic journey to an alternate origin story romance, filled with journaling jokes, flirting, and the same instant spark we saw between these two when they bumped into each other in the high school hallway in the pilot episode. Despite the fact that the real-world romance between Stefan and Elena has been officially over since last season, it was moving to see these two back in love — experiencing a highlight reel of perfect moments from a perfect relationship in a house that looks just enough like the Gilbert one as to resonate even more. It's the life that Stefan and Elena never could have had, as Elena puts it. The sequence of fantasies harkens back to that memorable speech in "The Last Day" when Elena mourned the human life she would never have if she became a vampire. Here in flashbacks and echoes, Stefan and Elena experience hyper-real visions meant to draw them together, and it's no surprise that both are teary-eyed when the visions are torn away from them, though they understand that the feelings and experiences were not *real*. In a standout scene in the episode, the two sit fireside and reflect on what they did have, what was real, from a peaceful place of friendship — miles away from where Damon and Elena are now.

Stefan theorizes that you can't be in love with someone *and* be friends (presumably he means this only in the breakup context — let's hope we're all friends with the people we are in love with), and it rings true for Damon, who can't handle being *around* Elena but not *with* Elena. He does make a valiant and totally awkward effort when supernatural hijinks force them to make small talk. But a day spent imagining what she must be seeing in those visions — with snarky, hilarious, needling Enzo making sex-dream joke after sex-dream joke — proves too much for Damon. He can't be her friend, even though she says she needs him in her life. Aside from Enzo making quips about Elena's favorite flavor being vanilla (never change, Enzo), he has some sage insight into the situation when it comes to hope. Just as Enzo held out hope in captivity that he'd one day be free to see Maggie again and thank her, he knows that Damon is holding out hope that his romance with Elena isn't over, that they'll find a way to be together without destroying each other. To agree to be friends, and only friends, is to acknowledge that there's no hope for them in love.

Well, at least the universe isn't against them. As hilarious as it was when Elena implied that the universe doesn't actually exist ("The universe doesn't control anything. It's not real."), she was right about the doppelgänger prophecy being baloney. Were we ever meant to believe it? The characters never really took it seriously; as Caroline says here, they all laughed it off. Unlike the Sun and the Moon Curse of season two, where the twist that it was a ruse smacked you in the face, this story angle felt more like an attempt to get shippers all riled up about their particular pairing. Thankfully, it's all bunk — an ill-conceived ruse by Markos to find the doppelgängers and save his people from an eternity of wandering. The prophecy is all smoke and no fire, but at least it gives us a coda to the Stefan-Elena romance here, a nice counterpart to the exposition-heavy Markos plot.

Mystic Falls finds itself in the midst of an invasion of the bodysnatchers, and all signs point to doppelgänger blood being integral to the Travelers' plan to break the witch curse that's on them. Like Katherine before them, all the Travelers want is a home — maybe one day soon they'll be able to settle down without plagues and disasters befalling them. It's a little apocalyptic, especially when the Other Side is crumbling like Fantasia when we all stopped believing — thunder and rumblings, wind, and beloved characters being whipped off into the nothing. Poor Matt not only gets killed *again* but he experiences losing his sister *again* as Vicki is taken from the Other Side. Where did she end up? The same place as Katherine? Is the whole place going down, as Kol fears? What will happen to Bonnie if there's no place she's anchored to?

COMPELLING MOMENT Stefan and Elena sitting in front of the fireplace. After living the "life that we never could have had," they have a heartfelt and honest conversation. Cheers to a beautiful end to one side of this triangle.

CIRCLE OF KNOWLEDGE

- Resident Evil began as a video game back in 1996, and has spawned numerous gaming sequels across multiple platforms, novels, comic books, and a series of film adaptations starring Milla Jovovich as Alice, who fights to survive increasingly apocalyptic scenarios featuring crazed zombies and the evil Umbrella Corporation. Way scarier than a bunch of chanting Travelers.

- Liv calls Matt, Tyler, and Jeremy the Three Stooges, the famous early 20th-century vaudeville act known for slapstick comedy.
- Thanks to the Travelers passengering themselves into the residents of Mystic Falls, the town has a decidedly *Invasion of the Body Snatchers* thing going on. In the 1956 film and its 1978 remake, citizens of a small town believe that their fellow citizens have been replaced by imposters — and guess what! they are right. Aliens are invading, replicating human forms and gestating them in giant pods! It's creepy as can be, and a classic sci-fi tale of a threat emerging from within the seeming safety of home.

"["Resident Evil"] happened to be an episode that was able to explore the season one roots of the Stefan and Elena love story. We started out just trying to write an episode [Paul Wesley] wasn't in very much, but we needed Stefan to be potent and not feel like he was missing but actually give him less screen time. So we knew we'd need to carve him out and put him in a storyline where he was able to be isolated. And then Brian and Caroline actually came up with the doppelgänger spell that was drawing them together and giving them these flashbacks and these memories, and this kind of alternate universe scenario. And that ended up working like a charm. I *loved* that. When I read their first draft, I was so happy because I'm like, 'This is nostalgic and warm and all the things I love about Stefan and Elena and their love story, and what a great way for Paul to get to play and also direct at the same time.' When all is said and done, the little flourishes and touches that he did and the choices that he made really gave the episode a beautiful and cinematic quality that let those Stefan and Elena pieces really pop and really feel special, which I loved. I just love that relationship and love to be able to visit it again."

— Julie Plec

THE RULES On the Other Side, the dead usually find themselves alone, save for witches who can communicate with each other. But thanks to Markos's escape by overwhelming the Anchor with so many dead Travelers, the Other Side is in flux and chaos. Vicki gets sucked out and up through the trees, in much the same manner that Katherine was removed from the church in "Gone Girl."

Liv, Luke, and Markos each explain some witch/Traveler history: there was a schism among the Travelers after the Silas/Qetsiyah immortality spell, and the witches cursed the Travelers so that they could never settle. When the Travelers did attempt to put down roots, plagues, earthquakes, and fires would destroy them and force them to keep on travelin'. They got around that inability to settle with the passenger spell, which allows a Traveler to stay in one place in someone else's body. Yet the Travelers kept traveling, wanting to destroy the curse for once and for all and have a home in their own bodies.

Markos reveals that he cast a love spell to bring the doppelgängers together and to him, in order to gather the necessary ingredients for breaking said curse. There is no universe-powered prophecy.

PREVIOUSLY ON *THE VAMPIRE DIARIES* The initial fantasy-life visions that Stefan and Elena share are reminiscent of season one: Elena's hair and wardrobe, the emphasis on Elena's diary, their unexpected meeting in the street, and Stefan cooking for Elena in "You're Undead to Me" (1.05), though in their shared visions Stefan is *not* a good cook.

"A dead old guy with a mysterious evil plan," snarks Elena, who knows a thing or two on the subject, having dealt with Klaus Mikaelson (seasons two and three) and Silas (seasons four and five).

Jeremy chuckles that not only has Liz now killed Matt, but Sheriff Forbes shot and killed Jeremy in "As I Lay Dying" (2.22).

Forbes mother-daughter moments tend to happen when the sheriff has been traumatized by supernatural brain-compromising shenanigans: Caroline compelled her distraught mother to forget she was a vampire in "Kill or Be Killed" (2.05) and comforted her after Silas's attack in "She's Come Undone" (4.21).

Bonnie's suspicions about Jeremy and Liv are not without cause: she discovered that Jeremy cheated on her with Anna, a ghost, in "Ghost World" (3.07) after Elena saw Jeremy and Anna kiss and told Caroline, who in turn told Bonnie.

© Glenn Harris/PR Photos

In addition to his two deaths while wearing the Gilbert ring — in "She's Come Undone" and "True Lies" — Matt had a memorable death in "The Reckoning" (3.05), when he purposely drowned himself in order to communicate with Vicki.

It's tricky business dating your brother's ex, especially when romantic visions get in the way, as they have this season. "I am secure enough in our relationship that you having psychic dreams about your ex-boyfriend does not bother me . . . but it still sucks," Damon tells Elena in "True Lies." He doesn't want a play-by-play in "Original Sin," either. Lucky for Damon the era of Stefan-Elena dreams comes to an end here.

Enzo picks up where Katherine left off in "Original Sin": she bugged Elena and Damon about how Elena was having *those* kind of dreams about Stefan all summer.

OFF CAMERA Neil Reynolds says the spirit of the Tom and Elena pairing the writers toyed with in the previous episode, "Rescue Me," became this episode, "when we got to see bizarro-world Stefan and Elena living human lives together."

The mysterious, fresh-from-the-Other-Side, head Traveler Markos is played by stage actor Raffi Barsoumian. "Raffi is delightful," says Melinda Hsu Taylor. "It was so funny: he's from Pasadena, I started chatting with him, and he's just the most normal, pleasant guy that you could imagine, but then he'll come to you on set and say, 'Okay, so this chant' — which is in a sort of made-up version of Czech — 'I've got these two different ways to go — what do you think of these two different readings?' He's thought about the magical chant in a nonsense language, and he wants to give you two options before you roll the camera. He's awesome." Cinematographer Michael Karasick is also a fan. "One of the reasons he's interesting for me is he's got such a cool face," he says. "It's really fun to just point the camera at him."

According to Julie Plec, Paul Wesley threw his hat into the potential directors ring during filming of "The Birthday" (3.01) and was officially the first actor to broach the possibility. "And then [Pascal Verschooris and I] spent a good year basically hoping he would never bring it up again," laughs Plec. "We just knew that the Pandora's box of letting it happen was coming along with a lot of political and logistical complications. So in order for him to earn the spot, he really had to earn it." This included Wesley sitting in on season four prep, concept, and tone meetings; asking directors questions on

Director Paul Wesley on "Resident Evil"

On prepping: I knew going into season five that I would be directing an ep at some point but didn't have specifics. The dates kept shifting, but it got locked down probably a few months prior to the actual filming dates. I had no idea what the ep would center on until probably two weeks prior to shooting.

Reading the script for the first time: I read it as a director and I was absolutely thrilled at the nostalgic quality of the Stefan and Elena fantasy scenes combined with the Matt and Vicki Other Side scenes. I knew I'd be able to take the episode to a new place visually, which I think we achieved quite well.

The shift from actor to director: I needed to be taken seriously as a director and fill those shoes without people thinking I was just limited to acting. Fortunately, due to my personal relationships, I was able to earn people's trust. I also had the advantage of knowing the show very intimately, so people trusted that my instincts were rooted in history rather than some first-time director who has barely seen an episode of the show.

His biggest challenge: I actually thought the most challenging thing, ironically, was the simple acting scenes. There is very limited time on set to actually play around and try different takes. All of the time is spent primarily on technical prep and post, and generally two or three acting takes in television per setup. The time limitations on set can be very constricting when you have to complete a 12-hour day and nine pages of work. This was the most challenging aspect of shooting an extremely technical one-hour show in eight days.

Playing Stefan as a well-adjusted human: It was such a welcome relief. With all due respect, I am a little exhausted with the supernatural element. Playing a human being in the "real world" and not talking about witches and werewolves and daylight rings and endless mythology was like a cool drink of water in a hot desert.

Using the color red in the flashbacks: It was a decision I made. I wanted something to differentiate the flashbacks from the present day. *American Beauty* was one of my favorite films as a young actor, and I was impressed with [director] Sam Mendes' use of the color red. I wasn't exactly stealing it, I just find the color red to be particularly unsettling and I thought it was a good juxtaposition with the tranquil, peaceful, and perfect tonality of the Stefan and Elena flashbacks. It was almost a subtle clue to the audience that this was all too good to be true. It turned out, in the end, that this was entirely the case.

Editing the episode: That was extremely difficult. Because I was shooting the next ep, I essentially had three days to do everything remotely via internet. It was simply me sending off notes to editors. If I had it my way, I would have been in that editing room in L.A. 12 hours a day adjusting every nuance. But we somehow managed to pull through. There is an old saying that a filmmaker is never quite finished with his film, he just abandons it. I did what I could with the limitations and time constrictions, and then I walked away. I felt pretty good about it, though.

His favorite scenes: I particularly like two scenes. One with Malarkey and Candice on the couches eavesdropping on Damon and Elena. These are two good actors, and there were many subtle moments. I enjoy simplicity and truthful human interactions. The scene with Stefan and Elena at the porch when he walks her home from the date is also simple. Just a boy who likes a girl. The less plot-oriented and simple it is, the more potent in my opinion. Aesthetically, the Matt Donovan on the Other Side scenes were interesting.

On whether directing has informed his acting: I feel it has, yes. I think the actor's job is to be subjectively connected, to be truthful and honest in the moment. The director's job is to view it objectively and fit it into the puzzle that is the story. Too many actors on TV use "tricks" and are way too aware of the camera and worry about doing the director's job.

process; "digging in" with the cinematographers; attending director training sessions on the Warner Bros. lot — all on his time off from his work as an actor on the series. With Wesley's commitment came the realization that other actors may express interest in directing. "He's now the first of probably many of our ensemble who will express interest in directing. We have to make sure that we prepare them and that we put them through a trial that makes sure it's not a vanity gig," explains Plec. "Because yes, anybody can come into our show and do a good job, no one's going to let anyone within our team fail — that would be a fate worse than death if we all let any of our own family fail. But nobody wants it to be like that. We wanted it to be a legit directing experience."

Caroline Dries agrees that it was a challenge worth undertaking. "What people don't realize when an actor directs is that the real burden on the show is on the previous episode to the one they're directing." She explains: "Episode 5.17 had to be Paul-light because Paul was in prep — which means there are a series of meetings every day for eight days where the director makes all of his/her decisions regarding location, casting, makeup, etc. It's a crucial time for the director. Of course, being *TVD* writers, we chose 5.17 to be the one where we meet another Stefan doppelgänger. We were like,

'Whoooops, this is terrible timing!' But I think if you look at 5.17, you'll see that Paul's storylines are contained, we could shoot him out in a few days, thus giving him his freedom to prep. Brian and I were also very aware that we needed to have a polished script [for 5.18] in Paul's hands by the start of prep because we had enough working against us. We still tried to limit Paul a bit [in his acting scenes for 5.18] — Caroline says in act one that Stefan was out looking for Travelers at the trainyard. Well, that was convenient, because now Stefan is gone indefinitely until he calls with information. Little things like that helped."

Wesley stepped up to the challenge. "We were tough on him and really made him work for it and he *really* worked for it," says Plec. "He gets the script from the first day we delivered it and he just starts texting Caroline [Dries] and me and Brian [Young] and saying, 'Oh my god, I love this episode. I love it so much. I'm so connected to it, it's beautiful, I'm so excited to do it.' And he really was. He really dialed in to the episode . . . I think ["Resident Evil"] is terrific."

"I absolutely adored Paul Wesley's directorial debut," says fellow director Joshua Butler. "He stepped into the director's chair like he had been there his whole life. I think he has an incredible career ahead of him — both in front of and behind the camera."

FOGGY MOMENTS Granted it's just a fantasy, but there are red table umbrellas behind Stefan when he grabs the loose sheet of Elena's journal, but the Grill's tables wouldn't be across the sidestreet from the restaurant.

When Matt wakes up on the Other Side, in what looks like the old Mystic Falls cemetery, Jenna Sommers' tombstone is right behind him, but she is buried in the *other* cemetery as we saw in the season two finale. Is the Other Side not a precise reflection of the living world or is this a production error?

Liv is very, very careful about who to trust: she makes the boys stab themselves to prove they're not harboring Travelers; she cautions that Jeremy is the only one who is safe from Traveler possession thanks to being a hunter . . . and yet she lets Tyler leave with their only Traveler knife. The Four Stooges might be a more accurate nickname.

The Traveler in Liz knows Tyler by sight and that he daydrinks at the Grill . . . but doesn't know that his mother is dead. How did the Traveler find out about Tyler, and why the limited knowledge?

"I thought the finished product was great. My favorite scene was the Stefan/Elena scene at the fireplace where they decide they're friends who love each other. I think that's a rare relationship dynamic and I truly believe that is what Elena and Stefan were in that moment, so it was great to be able to dramatize it. The process of shooting that episode was interesting. Paul knows the show *so* well, obviously. And he's a filmmaker at heart. He loves movies and directing. I think when you're not connected to the everyday limitations that come with producing a TV show, you don't realize that there are certain parameters we're living with, and the art of it is making amazing drama inside the confines of our budget and time restraints. So we had to crush Paul's cinematic visions here and there, but Paul rolled with things. He had strong opinions and even when we didn't agree on everything, we both agreed that we wanted the show to be awesome. So there's an amount of adjusting and trust that goes into any collaborative process. I hope it made him a better director and me a better producer/writer. That's really all you can ask for when you team up with someone. I'd love to do it again."

— Caroline Dries

Just how did Markos's doppelgänger spell work? He says he cast it 1,500 years ago: has it been drawing all the doppelgängers together since then? This doesn't seem to be the case based on Stefan's comment about how he and Elena fell in love for real, independent of spells. But if Qetsiyah can be counted as a reliable source, doppelgängers have been getting together for centuries. And we saw 1864 Katherine instantly drawn to Stefan. (Which, granted, may just be because he's a handsome devil.) Did the spell only affect doppelgängers while Markos was alive? The visions start for Elena and Stefan once he returns to the living world, which lends credence to that interpretation. But if that's the case, why would Markos draw them to that specific house on Walnut Street when it's no secret who they are or where they are? Sloan has their cell phone numbers and has easily corralled them and got buckets of blood from them. Why the mystical shenanigans?

QUESTIONS

- Where are the Travelers' original bodies?
- In the fantasy-life visions, what was Stefan's backstory and family situation? If he wasn't a vampire then he *probably* wasn't born in the Civil War era. Were the Salvatore parents alive and well too?
- Markos says that Silas and Qetsiyah's immortality spell created a schism within the Travelers, giving rise to the witches. Meaning that the Travelers and witches are in fact the same people divided into two factions following the immortality spell? Do only some witches know about this Traveler-Witch war? Funny we haven't heard about it until recently if it's such a big to-do. (Ahem.)
- Is Kol right? If the Other Side is crumbling, will all the dead supernaturals there be sucked into whatever hellscape Katherine and Vicki are now in? Will none find "peace"?
- How did Matt manage to remember being on the Other Side this time? Sheer force of will? The power of Kol Mikaelson's misty-eyed plea?
- For a leader who's been dead for centuries, Markos seems pretty up on current events — did the Travelers have some way of communicating with the Other Side? Have they had no leader in his absence?
- Was that really the last Traveler knife? How did Gregor come to be in possession of it?

Damon: You want to kill me, you want to hate me, do it. This is between us.
Enzo: That's the problem, Damon. I don't want to hate you.
Because if I hate you, I have nothing left.

5.19 Man on Fire

Original air date April 24, 2014
Written by Melinda Hsu Taylor and Matthew D'Ambrosio
Directed by Michael Allowitz
Edited by Tony Solomons **Cinematography by** Darren Genet
Guest cast Heather Hemmens (Maggie James), Natalie Karp (Young Woman)
Previously on *The Vampire Diaries* Paul Wesley

Enzo wants revenge on Maggie's killer.

As season five nears its end, "Man on Fire" relegates the supernatural-wacky-doodle stuff to the subplot, focusing instead on Damon's only friend, hell-bent on revenge. It's been a season of characters being forgotten, left behind, and abandoned, but Enzo — locked in a cage for 70 years — might get top prize for most hard done by.

Hope dies last, a wise woman once said (actually, it was Joey Potter), and for Enzo the hope that kept him willing to live, willing to keep his humanity (and his sanity) intact, was Maggie James, the kind-hearted Augustine "observer" who felt for him what he felt for her. But in the flashback, we see that instead of taking Maggie up on her half-baked escape plot — she wanted to be turned — Enzo compelled her to leave, and never look back. And 10 years later, when she did look back, when Maggie came for revenge after Enzo's supposed death in the fire, Damon killed her . . . as part of his own revenge scheme against the Augustines.

That "eye for an eye" thing? Really does make the whole world blind. It's no surprise that Enzo reacts to the news of Maggie's 1960 beheading with his "murder voice." When we first met him in "The Cell," Enzo mentioned revenge first (ahead of his affection for Maggie) as the thing that kept him alive and relatively sane in captivity, and he encouraged Damon to plot his own vengeance. While Enzo still retained hope that he would find Maggie — to just see her face again and to thank her, to know that she had a normal life outside the hell he lived in — this dashing, if murderous, vampire was content to play buddy to Damon and banter with Caroline. Michael Malarkey's Enzo has been a *huge* part of the fun of the back half of this season, but his emotional turn in this episode came as a wallop. This character, and this actor, is far more than good looks and British charm. Like Joseph Morgan's Klaus before him, Malarkey proves his acting chops here and gives us an Enzo as compelling (more compelling?) than any other character onscreen. Only to have his heart torn out.

Enzo's breakdown in front of Damon at the Scull bar circles back to one of the core concerns of this series. Enzo doesn't want to hate Damon for killing Maggie: to do so would render him utterly alone, with nothing left. There have been some subtle parallels between Damon and Enzo's relationship and Damon and Elena's this season, and here we get another one. For all the wrong that Damon's done, Enzo loves him — he doesn't want to let go of the friend he knows. Ditto for Elena. And just as we see Stefan rally to protect

> "I know it sounds dumb, but I'm really proud of Damon's 'weird ritual' line while Matt and Jeremy are finding boxers under couches while trying to find the Traveler knife. Anything that mocks Matt Donovan and Jeremy Gilbert, really. But understand that the jabs come from a place of love. I wouldn't make fun of them if I didn't care about them."
>
> — Matthew D'Ambrosio

Bonnie from Enzo, to protect the college-student hostages (by falsely taking the blame for Maggie's murder), Damon comes blazing into the "depressing" scene to set things right — even though it means the destruction of the only friendship he has. And while he told Elena in "Resident Evil" that he didn't want to see her, the two have not lost their connection, as is clear from their silent communication while she's tied up as a hostage, and the more tender Damon-tucks-Elena-in moment.

And in Enzo's final act, he complicates the already complicated brothers Salvatore situation. Should Stefan have just fessed up about what really happened? Yes. Is it a totally understandable and Stefan thing to do to try to protect his big brother with a big lie? Yes. The brothers are *always* trying to manage each other, to fix and protect each other, and while Elena is in on the secret (along with Bonnie), the conflict is, for once, not about her. When this blows up, it will test the brothers' bond once again, and ironically, it will put Enzo's constant reminders to Damon to not give up on his brother to the test.

And until the Other Side actually implodes, Enzo promises to be watching the whole thing go down, with some sure-to-be-dastardly afterlife revenge scheme. If Liv can be trusted, there's nothing that can be done to stop the Other Side from crumbling. Whatever stage of grief Bonnie claims to be in, she is not ready to accept that her life, such as it is, is coming to an end *again*. When the time comes to tell Jeremy, she lies. Will Bonnie and the rest of the Other Siders be lost forever? Is there a way back?

In a very talky subplot, Markos show-and-tells the Travelers' next big move with Tyler as witness, and it's a plan with dire consequences for all the supernatural beings of Mystic Falls. Conflict looms on the horizon: the battle for Mystic Falls is set to begin, just as the supernatural holding ground for the dead crumbles. It's not a good time to die on *The Vampire Diaries*.

COMPELLING MOMENT Enzo's breakdown with Damon. A heartbreaking performance from Michael Malarkey.

CIRCLE OF KNOWLEDGE

- Caroline is conveniently absent in the episode.
- This episode has no cold-open scene, transitioning immediately from the "Previously On" intro to the title card.
- A 1981 novel by A.J. Quinnell that has been thrice adapted onscreen, *Man on Fire* is the story of John Creasy, a former military assassin who takes on a bodyguarding gig. In the Tony Scott adaptation with Denzel Washington (2004), Creasy's alcoholism and guilt for past sins take a backseat to his growing affection for adorable little Dakota Fanning. A religious man, Creasy strives to "not be overcome by evil, but overcome evil with good" — until his precious charge is kidnapped and presumed dead, and Creasy goes on a revenge mission so violent that even Enzo would raise an eyebrow. Protected by St. Jude, the patron saint of lost causes, Creasy ultimately sacrifices himself and ends his "kill 'em all" revenge scheme in order to bring some peace to the innocents caught up amidst terrible circumstance.
- Stefan may have a rep as a tough tutor, but when he's reading Elena the quiz question, the answer on the back is plain to see. Which may be why she gets it verbatim.
- Elena tells Bonnie she's in denial about the Other Side falling apart, but Bonnie insists she's moved on to the fifth stage of grief: acceptance. The "stages of grief" refers to the Kübler-Ross model, the five emotional stages of loss and grief detailed by Swiss-American psychiatrist Elisabeth Kübler-Ross. The five stages are denial, anger, bargaining, depression, and acceptance. Enzo seems stuck in stage two.
- Enzo likes luxury cars: he mentioned a fondness for Jaguars back in "The Cell," and here talks about Lincoln Continentals, first manufactured by the Ford Motor Company in 1939, and Ford Thunderbirds (which weren't in production until 1955, while he was in captivity). Was he allowed to read car magazines or watch TV while locked up by the Augustines? He was able to listen to the radio, after all.

Writers Melinda Hsu Taylor and Matthew D'Ambrosio on "Man on Fire"

D'Ambrosio on the flashback era: It made sense in the timeline of things. Maggie was a human, a real person who ages. So that was the first constraint. Once we realized we'd have to do a flashback we thought about where in the Salvatore brothers' timeline it could take place. It would have to be after the '50s because of Damon's past with Augustine. But we also know from "Because the Night" [4.17] that Damon was in NYC and wearing ripped anarchy tees at CBGBs. I think the '60s was just a natural place for the flashbacks to take place. Plus, Damon Salvatore in a greasers jacket? C'mon. The flashback sequences are hard just in terms of that pesky timeline. We have to go back and comb through everything we've said before, just to make sure we're not contradicting ourselves. But once you know where you have to end up, it's a whole lot easier to fill in the gaps.

Hsu Taylor on working with Malarkey: Michael's a guy who comes so thoroughly prepared and so thoughtful and so ready to try anything on set. He's always on his mark, always on time, always knows his lines — at rehearsal. In "Man on Fire" that scene in the script is probably five, six, seven pages long. And the AD was looking at it and just pulling out his hair and saying, "Oh god we're never going to make this day because we've got to shoot *all* this dialogue" before lunch, because of our schedule. And we did it, and well before lunch, before Malarkey delivered, like, in rehearsal off-book, hit every mark, performed it really well just while they were setting the cameras up, and then we get into actually filming it — he was brilliant.

Michael Malarkey asked me, "Why am I reading to [Stefan] from the journals? Because I understand functionally in the script the audience needs to know Maggie a little bit better to find out why Enzo cares about her. So what is Enzo the character trying to do, to get out of this moment, where he's reading aloud to Stefan?" And I said you're like an interrogator, that's something that you maybe did in the war, and you know that if you break this guy, if you keep going at him, if you pummel him with information, he's going to blink. You're trying to get him to blink first. So if you can break it down into some kind of simple, hopefully act-able, verb then it gives the actor something like, Oh okay now I get it. I'm cross-examining him — it's not a lawyer, it's a cop in an interrogation room.

Hsu Taylor on Markos, mythology, and exposition: Markos had a lot to deliver in that episode because we were at the point in the season where we really needed to get some of the facts out. We had been putting it off a little bit because we like to parse out mythology, so that people don't get overwhelmed or, you know, bored by it. But at the same time you can't hold off forever because it is very mysterious what's going on and it is going to be a special part of the end run of the season. So Raffi, wonderfully, is able to deliver exposition in a way that's entertaining and engaging and very fluid. And that's just a gift from an actor who is saddled with long speeches about his people's intentions and their history and their magic and all of that sort of thing. So it was easy to give those lines to Markos, because he's really good.

There are a lot of different constraints that come about and it made sense for him to say it, because he's the leader and he's very compassionate . . . I liken him to Henry V, because I really like this idea that he was convinced he was doing the right thing. He wasn't doing it for malicious gain or from egomania; he really is trying to do right by his people.

We liked the idea of a little beginning, middle, and end to the Travelers' storyline in that episode; we have our point of view from Tyler/Julian who is able to be the audience's eyes and ears on the ground there, and we have this very dramatic demonstration with Sloan going from zero, being human, to vampire to being dead to alive to dead again. And that all was something that we were able to do in a contained storyline and shoot that in one day in that location, because we only had one day.

Hsu Taylor on shooting the Enzo-Stefan fight: The fight in the rain was Pascal's decision, to shoot on a rainy night, which I think adds this wonderfully cinematic look. It was so hard on the crew that I hope some of them look at this book and know how much we appreciated them all schlepping out in the rain until five in the morning. It's a lot of stunt breaking, a lot of people wiping down the camera lenses and squeegeeing that windshield. When we saw the dailies of the shot that opens . . . I guess it's act five, there's the car windshield and then Enzo's body — actually the stuntman's body — comes whooshing through the air and smashes down on the windshield. That shot took us a long time to set up and almost as long to squeegee the rain off. The dailies are just like *squeegee*; I'd say it goes on for like two minutes of squeegeeing to get it *just so*, and then they finally roll and they launch this guy off of like a chair-canon trampoline thing. Stunt people and our visual effects people — it's just an enormous army of people to create three seconds of screen time. But it's such a great three seconds, you know? And it comes first from this decision by Pascal, rain or shine we'll shoot Thursday night because it's gonna look great if it rains. The forecast was like 100 percent rain, and all of us are like, "Oh well, what's the cover? That we're going to shoot indoors if it rains?" He's like, "Oh no no, we want it to rain — it'll look great!"

But that was really exciting to be a part of because my normal life is sitting in a conference room with people whose company I enjoy tremendously, eating free snacks, watching dailies on DVD, talking about storylines, writing some things on the dry-erase board, checking Twitter when the show is on. It's *so* mild-mannered. Somebody comes in and says lunch is here. We've got a PA who's gone out and picked up things from Tender Greens, or at certain points people will order coffee and somebody comes in and sets down Starbucks. It's all so civilized and sheltered and privileged. Then to be out there in the rain and watching these guys get ready with all this rigging on them and they're, like, bouncing on the trampoline and waiting to get yanked up onto the hood of a car and drenched by rain. The stunt guy's awesome — he goes flying off the car and he's rolling in such a way because they've got these special rigging things that you can roll kind of like a barrel. Another rope is pulling you straight out so you're rolling and flying outward. It's so cool to watch. It's so fun. I love stunts. I'm strangely, like, very mild-mannered in my personal life but on set and in writing I love anything that's like action or crazy torture. The more adrenalin-packed, the better for me. I love that stuff.

D'Ambrosio on watching the final cut for the first time: It was pretty surreal. Just in terms of process, by the time the episode airs I have seen almost 10 various cuts of it. So seeing the final product, with all the sound mixed and VFX shots slipped in and colors corrected . . . it was pretty magical. The worst part was explaining five seasons of mythology to my parents on the phone minutes after it aired. "We really liked the part with the guy chained in the basement! We just didn't realize it would be so bloody." Me too, guys. Me too.

- Damon misremembers Enzo's desire to go to Chile's Cape Horn (which he mentioned in "Total Eclipse of the Heart") as Cape Town, the legislative capital of South Africa.

HISTORY LESSON The circumstances of Maggie's death — and the reveal of her killer's identity — unfold against the backdrop of the "unseasonably cold" election night of Tuesday, November 8, 1960, in Mystic Falls, Virginia. The U.S. presidential election race between Senator John F. Kennedy and Vice President Richard Nixon was one of several historical firsts: it was the first presidential election after Alaska and Hawaii were granted statehood (on January 3, 1959, and August 21, 1959, respectively); the first election where both candidates were born in the 20th century; John F. Kennedy was the first Catholic and the youngest candidate elected to the office of U.S. president; and it was the first election in which both the presidential and vice presidential victors were current sitting U.S. senators, with Kennedy representing Massachusetts and Lyndon B. Johnson representing Texas. The election was also one of the closest presidential races in history, with Kennedy winning by 0.1 percent of the popular vote. Even though the *New York Times* declared Kennedy the victor before midnight, the results in several states were still uncertain on the morning of Wednesday, November 9th, and Nixon actually won the popular and electoral votes for Virginia.

THE RULES A prophecy of unknown origin states that the Travelers can undo witch magic with the blood of the last two doppelgängers (Stefan and Elena, as it turns out). After turning Sloan into a vampire, Markos has her drink the last vials of Stefan and Elena's blood in Traveler possession, the Travelers chant, and — presto, chango — she's a human again. The injury she suffered in her final moments as a human (Markos having slit her throat) kills her.

PREVIOUSLY ON *THE VAMPIRE DIARIES* The Lockwood floor safe is handy for hiding things, like the moonstone in season two. Unfortunately, the Traveler knife is not there. Maybe try the soap dish in Damon's bathroom?

Amnesiac Stefan burned his diaries in "For Whom the Bell Tolls," so alas that fact-checking resource is no longer available to revenge-seeking vampires.

This is the second time "Tweedle-dee and Tweedle-dum" is used as an insult this season: Tessa called Amara and Elena Tweedle-dee and Tweedle-dum in "Death and the Maiden."

This isn't the first time a vengeance-seeking lover has come after Damon: Lexi's boyfriend, Lee, tried to avenge her death in "Bloodlines" (1.11), and Alaric's motives for moving to Mystic Falls — to find and kill the vampire who he believed killed his wife, Isobel — was revealed later in the same episode.

"Well, this is depressing," Damon says of the bar full of compelled college students, recalling Rebekah's same pronouncement to Damon and Sage in "Break on Through" (3.17).

Elena tells Enzo she knows what he's feeling, because she turned off her emotions after losing a loved one in "Stand By Me" (4.15) and experienced all her feelings come rushing back in "She's Come Undone" (4.21).

Damon has memorably carried Elena a few times, as he does here: after the car crash in "Bloodlines" and out of the hospital, where Klaus was draining her blood, in "The Reckoning" (3.05).

> "I loved the Damon/Stefan scene at the end of 5.19 where Damon told Stefan he never gave up on him. Originally, that wasn't in the ep, but we needed to fill time because it came in short for airing, and watching that scene, I was like, 'Oh whoops, the episode wasn't complete until that scene was in there.' Melinda wrote that."
>
> — Caroline Dries

Elena wakes up after Damon has dropped her off in her dorm room, in a callback to his first moment of tenderness toward her, stroking her cheek while she slept in "Friday Night Bites" (1.03).

In "Total Eclipse of the Heart," Stefan pressed a shovel into Enzo, and Enzo pulled it deeper inside him. "What I do to you, Enzo, will be final," the younger Salvatore warned the vampire. And here Enzo makes good on Stefan's promise by forcing Stefan to yank out his heart.

Damon killed Stefan's only friend one time too: Lexi in "162 Candles" (1.08).

OFF CAMERA Heather Hemmens, who plays Enzo's lost love Maggie, is no stranger to The CW, having been a series regular on the network's short-lived *Hellcats*. Born and raised in Maine, Hemmens has also directed and produced a few short films and made guest appearances on *CSI: New York*, *CSI: Miami*, *Grey's Anatomy*, and *Without a Trace*. In a fun bit of *TVD* trivia, *TV Guide*'s Robyn Ross tweeted during the episode's initial airing that Hemmens had auditioned for Tessa, a role that ultimately went to Janina Gavankar, but producers had wanted to find a spot for her on the show ever since.

Michael Malarkey told *Just Jared, Jr.* that the episode's script was "a peach," and he was genuinely grateful for the opportunity to explore Enzo in a new way. "I think Enzo is basically at wit's end with the whole situation that happened in the bar," he said of his character's dramatic suicide-by-heart-rip. "He could not deal with it, so he was like, 'Screw it all. What can I do to screw these people's lives up because mine is screwed up?' It's a very selfish act in a sense. He's hurt and he doesn't know what else to do, so he does that as his last act of retribution."

This episode marked long-time writer's assistant (and season six script coordinator) Matthew D'Ambrosio's first writing credit on the show. "Every season the show will do an episode to be written by a freelancer," he says. "On our show, that person is usually one of the assistants in the office. The process is that one of the head writers (in my case it was Melinda Hsu Taylor) will send out a list of scene prompts to the assistants. We write a few of the scenes and then anonymously send them back to whoever is judging the scenes. Then that person will choose whichever assistant wrote the best scenes. I'd lost this 'contest' two times before I finally won in season five."

Originally, Melinda Hsu Taylor wanted the episode to introduce its '60s flashbacks via dialogue and the Kennedy election newscast (which is still present during the scene), but editor Tony Solomons suggested a much simpler option for the transition: a song. "He said, if you just play a song people are going to understand right away that they're back in the '60s," says Hsu Taylor. "I'm like, 'Okay.' [laughs]" Solomons calls music an integral part of *The Vampire Diaries*, "especially when transporting the viewer to a different era. Our stories take place over many generations and nothing orients an audience faster than corresponding music for a particular setting because music speaks to our intellect and our emotions."

Two of director Michael Allowitz's favorite scenes he directed in season five are from this episode. "I really like when Enzo learns that Damon killed Maggie and he turns his humanity switch off," he says. "I also thought the beheading of Maggie worked quite well with the Kennedy election playing in the background." Allowitz also designed the episode's distinctive flashback transitions — the silhouette of characters in present day over the flashback scene — but the blending of those scenes fell to Solomons. "I wanted a new way to connect the present day with the past and link the two," Solomons explains. "I am a fan of the TV show *Sherlock* and I was inspired by how they visually link storylines. We experimented with the transitions in After Effects and settled on a look that is unique to this episode." Allowitz was happy with how they turned out, adding, "I thought it worked great and gave that episode's flashbacks a unique style." Shooting in the rain, however, was tricky. "Real rain is very difficult to shoot in for many reasons — mostly for matching the entire night's work," explains Allowitz of filming the Stefan-Enzo battle royale. "Well, it kept raining all night; while the crew was miserable, the scene has a very cool look — unlike if we shot it without rain."

"Damon wants to rally Stefan to his side to save Enzo, and Stefan wants Damon to forget Enzo forever and walk away," says Hsu Taylor of the episode's final scene, one of Caroline Dries' favorites. "So those two actions, even though it's not in their dialogue, it's pretty clear — and I think they played it well in the scene — that they're driving at each other at 180 degrees, opposite viewpoints."

Welcome to Scull

Garreth Stover: The Scull bar [where Liv works, featured in "Man on Fire"] was the main [new] set for the year. We had awhile to design that set and its surroundings, the street outside. The best thing about that set, besides all the details and size, was how we worked out almost every issue a shooting company might have while shooting in it. Now granted, I designed it after I had directed an episode ["Because the Night" (4.17)], so I did it with real knowledge of how hard it is to shoot at breakneck speeds for the shooting crew and its director, so I think that really helped. Also Pascal [Verschooris], our producer, insisted that every possible shooting angle be achievable in the set, so it became an engineering feat, which I think we pulled off pretty well. It's really a great set.
Melinda Hsu Taylor: It's beautiful. I want to rent it out for parties — I mean, of course you couldn't for liability reasons. It's all the brainchild of our production designer Garreth — he's a genius at this — and also our set decorators. There are all these layers of stuff going on in that bar. It's everywhere you look: there's a button, like a push-button to turn on the lights, that looks like it's from 1920. There's a light fixture that can go up and down on a pulley if you want to change the lighting, or you want to have it in frame or out of frame. All the walls move, and the bar itself splits up into three pieces. That big painting behind the bar also moves back. Like when Enzo is toasting Maggie James, they moved out the back wall of the bar and put the camera there instead, so they can get that nice shot of him over the liquor bottles with the bar behind him. But what you don't see is that we've removed that painting, we've removed that whole back wall of the bar so that we can stick the camera exactly where it needs to be. All that was planned for by Garreth and Pascal. He just loves his Scull-de-sac — that's the location outside of Scull bar, there's a little fake Main Street [of] just shops and stuff that has a little curve and so we call it the Scull-de-sac.
Michael Karasick: My favorite place [to shoot] is the Scull bar. I haven't really shot a lot in there; Darren [Genet]'s done a lot in there but I've only done a couple of scenes so I'm looking forward to spending more time in there. Pretty much anything built by Garreth is pretty spectacular. I mean between him and Pascal — because they work hand in hand in building these sets, and they're just beautiful. It's like candy to a lot of us, getting in there on these stages and working in these sets because they're wonderful.

FOGGY MOMENTS How did Enzo know that Elena and Stefan had a study date at the Scull bar at 9 a.m.?

Enzo takes Bonnie's phone when she's trying to secretly contact Damon, Enzo calls Damon from Bonnie's phone, and Damon answers knowing it's Enzo, despite the fact that his caller ID would've said Bonnie.

Enzo threatens the "neck membrane," but humans don't have neck membranes. (Some insects do.) Back to Augustine with you, Enzo, for more anatomy lessons!

Where did Caroline disappear to? Damon leaves her a voicemail giving her grief for not picking up, but seriously where is she? Why establish the friendship/flirtation between Enzo and Caroline and then *not* have her around in the moment of crisis?

What was Maggie's job exactly? She was observing Enzo doing what? Heal? Make moony eyes at her? Since the Augustines didn't even refer to their subjects by name, it's hard to believe they'd be interested in a detailed personal history. And what did Maggie think was going on at Augustine: a man is kept in a cell, is not fed properly, is always covered in blood, and his wounds heal rapidly? In what universe would that seem like a normal, okay non-violation of basic human rights? Why was becoming a vampire her only way to get Enzo free? What about the old steal-the-keys-while-the-guard-is-sleeping routine?

Why was Maggie seeking revenge for Enzo's (supposed) death by trying to kill *Damon*? Why did she think that Damon was (a) responsible for the fire, and (b) had some obligation to save Enzo? No one knew about their pact to escape other than Enzo and Damon. Wouldn't a more likely revenge target have been the Augustines themselves — the people who captured and tortured Enzo for decades, who had him trapped in the cell he couldn't escape from during the fire?

This episode's flashback complicates what we know about Stefan and blood control and his journey in seasons one and two. Here he says he's barely feeding on human blood by 1960, and certainly not killing. Except what has been established about Stefan — before he painstakingly built up blood control by having a pinprick of Elena's blood every day, as we saw in "Kill or Be Killed" (2.05) — was that it was an all-or-nothing feeding situation for him. Human blood drinking equalled ripper Stefan. He had to stick to bunny blood, or risk murdering. That was the lesson from the "1912" (3.16) Sage flashback: Stefan couldn't just have a little blood, he went full-on ripper

> "I have a real fondness for some of the flashback characters that we played with, like Dr. Whitmore and Maggie, all of the Augustines. I joke in the writers' room that I'm going to write a spin-off called *Augustine* [laughs]. That will never come to pass, but they are my favorite."
>
> — Melinda Hsu Taylor

and only came back under control after Lexi spent decades working him through it.

What is the source of this prophecy that Markos keeps talking about? Where did Markos get his info, and why have the Travelers waited so long to kill off the extra doppelgängers and get them down to two? Were the deaths of Silas and Amara necessary to this master plan, and if so, why not knock them off earlier — since, in addition to knowing where Silas was, they knew Amara was the Anchor to the Other Side, had her in their possession, and could easily overwhelm her, as they did Bonnie? Have they been searching for doppelgängers for 2,000 years with no luck?

Why not try the doppelgänger-blood magic on an existing vampire, instead of killing off Sloan? The Travelers sure seem cool with dwindling their numbers.

QUESTIONS

- What would've happened if Enzo had killed Bonnie, since — as he says — she is already technically dead? Would the Other Side collapse? Can she be killed on this side of the living/dead boundary, if she's already a ghost?
- Liv says that, like a math equation or a recipe, taking away one ingredient from the Other Side disrupts the whole. But Esther left the Other Side without it crumbling. As did Qetsiyah. Is Markos important to the fabric of the Other Side in a way that those two powerful witches weren't? Why is the stability of that dimension dependent on him? Or is it a cumulative thing?
- How much of the Travelers' guinea pig experiment did Tyler witness versus Julian, his passenger? We see his eyes flip black and then back to

normal — can we safely assume it's Tyler, not Julian, who sees the magic undone by doppelgänger blood?

- What makes Markos vital to the Travelers' plan? Why did they have to resurrect him? Is there something special about him that we haven't yet seen?
- Will Stefan tell Damon the truth about Enzo?

Damon: Did you think I was going to go on a rampage,
slaughter a bunch of innocent people, go bowling with human heads?
What'd you think I was gonna do?
Stefan: Hate me. I thought you would hate me.

5.20 *What Lies Beneath*

Original air date May 1, 2014
Written by Elisabeth R. Finch and Holly Brix **Directed by** Joshua Butler
Edited by Marc Pollon **Cinematography by** Michael Karasick
Guest cast Tamara Austin (Maria), Sonny Charles (Traveler #5), Chauncey A. Jenkins (Traveler #6), Brian Kinnett (Traveler #4), Alex Lukens (Traveler #3), Shelby McDaniel (Traveler #1), Anna Murphy (Traveler #2)
Previously on *The Vampire Diaries* Paul Wesley

As the Travelers hunt the doppelgängers, the doppelgängers hide out in a cabin in the woods . . . with a vengeful ghost.

When you're on the run from an evil magic nomadic people and you could hide anywhere in the world, where do you go? Isolated cabin in the woods. It's picturesque, perfect for boozing it up, and chock-full of opportunity for a ghost to get its vengeance.

While there was a lot of fun and snark and awkward in "What Lies Beneath," it wasn't too heavy on that thing called "plot," making it one of the filler episodes of the season. Thankfully, in *TVD* tradition, the secret of Enzo's death is revealed before too long, but his master plan is well-trod territory on this show: revenge. Damon killed Maggie, Stefan's lying about Enzo's death, so Enzo shall punish the ones Damon loves for the ultimate revenge. Got it. The problem is that there's no palpable threat: will Stefan or Elena or Caroline or Damon get knocked off by a ghost in the third-to-last episode of the season? On the Travelers' front, Jeremy and Matt and Tyler (while he's Tyler) decide the best way to get the info they need is to torture Julian with wolfsbane and assorted pain, while Bonnie continues to keep the secret of just how dire her situation is since the Other Side is crumbling. There's a halfhearted attempt to play this episode as a romantic weekend gone wrong between Jeremy and Bonnie, but given that all these two have are romantic weekends, the stakes there, as in the cabin plot line, are more fizzle than sizzle. The ramp-up to the final two episodes, though, is clearly on — Tyler's in danger of losing his body to Julian permanently, Bonnie's about to be whooshed away by the destruction of the Other Side, Stefan and Elena are under all kinds of threats thanks to their doppelgänger status, and Enzo's still a live wire (though pacified by episode's end). Though you'd miss out on some good old-fashioned *TVD* entertainment, you could skip this episode without losing the plot.

The same is true emotionally speaking, especially on the Damon-Elena on-again, off-again, rinse-and-repeat front. Damon was confused. Elena was confused. He had a bad day. He kissed her. She was full of wonder that a guy could be both good and bad . . . Though she's had *years* of experience dating Salvatores, she is still baffled by romantic complications; it's a little too naïve even for Elena. On the Stefan-and-Caroline "are they more than just friends?" front, Caroline jumps to conclusions about the closeness demonstrated by Stefan and Elena, completely misreading the clues in a manner that reveals more about her true feelings than it does about their secret. The scene between Caroline and Stefan by the blazing woodshed is nicely understated: Stefan's rationale for keeping the secret that he "murdered" Enzo from Caroline is that he didn't want her to think less of him — and it certainly further endears him to her. Although the jealous turn from Caroline in this episode sours their building connection just a smidge, it's a poignant change of pace to see the relationship potential between these two so slowly and carefully built over the course of three seasons, especially on a show known for its propensity to race through plots. When it comes to character and matters of the heart, *The Vampire Diaries* takes its time.

COMPELLING MOMENT The drinking game scene. Full-on entertainment with A+ reactions around that table.

CIRCLE OF KNOWLEDGE

- For a bathtub experience more harrowing than Elena's in this episode, see Robert Zemeckis's 2000 supernatural thriller *What Lies Beneath*. Michelle Pfeiffer stars as Claire Spencer, a woman who's given up her dazzling career as a cellist to be wife to Dr. Norman Spencer (Harrison Ford) and mum to a daughter who's just left for college. In a big old house by the water, Claire starts experiencing spooky, spooky things but wrongly pins her suspicions on the passionate next door neighbors, accusing the husband (played by Papa Salvatore, James Remar) of murdering his wife. Just like Caroline in this episode, Claire's suspicions are off the mark but she ain't crazy — something *is* terribly wrong. There is a vengeful ghost plaguing the house. Aside from some overlap in scares — be careful when you wipe fog from a bathroom mirror, there will likely be a ghost in the reflection! — the movie, just like the episode named after it, is about the lies told and the horrors forgotten in order to maintain the status quo.
- Tyler's brazen escape from Traveler headquarters is the only time we see a wolf transformation this season.
- Damon must really love classic cartoons. He refers to Liv and Luke as "the Wonder Twins," which is actually his second reference to the show within the series ("1912," 3.16). Zan and Jayna, the Wonder Twins, are part of the DC Universe's *Super Friends* and have the power to physically transform after bumping fists to activate their powers.
- Damon calls Caroline "Meryl Streep," referring to the multiple award-winning American film and stage star widely regarded as one of the greatest actors of all time, in a reminder of Ms. Forbes's chosen path at college: drama major.
- In the Salvatore basement, Jer opens up an awesome-looking cabinet of poisons to get some vervain and wolfsbane in order to torture Julian. Also in the drawers is a label that looks like it reads "cyanide" and, next to the wolfsbane, "Amorita muscaria" — a possible misspelling of amanita muscaria, or fly agaric. It is a fungus with psychoactive (hallucinogenic) properties and, with its iconic red-and-white speckled cap, it has become the typical visual touchpoint for toadstools. While it's considered a poisonous fungi, human death by ingestion is very rare. Let's assume these drawers of poison are Damon's.

> "I have to say that the final scene between Elena and Damon in 'What Lies Beneath' is the one I'm most proud of. I had always wanted to use Kerli's 'Chemical' in a *TVD* episode when I first heard it, and planning the moment so that the song would climax when Damon kissed Elena . . . that was truly satisfying to me as a director."
>
> — Joshua Butler

HISTORY LESSON Not only is Caroline Forbes the type of person to think up charades clues, she will give all of those clues a theme; in this case, the theme is the super-subtle "secrets that people think they're getting away with." Clues include: Area 51, the secret military installation in Nevada connected to Edwards Air Force Base and ground zero for everyone's favorite alien-related conspiracy theories (as if that place could be any weirder than Mystic Falls); the JFK assassination, the ultimate American conspiracy theory surrounding Lee Harvey Oswald's shooting of President John F. Kennedy; and Watergate, which, as Damon points out, is nearly impossible to portray as a charade without talking, considering the scandal surrounding Republican President Richard Nixon's eventual resignation dealt with hours of taped conversations in which he plotted to cover up a 1972 break-in at the Democratic National Committee headquarters housed at the Watergate Hotel. (But if anyone could reenact this as a charade, Caroline could.) Later, during the actual game, Elena acts out Skull and Bones for her teammate Stefan, which is the infamous secret society founded in 1832 at Yale University in New Haven, Connecticut, which conspiracy theorists have posited to be a global conspiracy, a branch of the world-controlling Illuminati, and in control of the Central Intelligence Agency. The mysteries surrounding Skull and Bones were the basis of the 2000 film *The Skulls*, though there is no historical evidence that real society members were as handsome as the film's stars, Paul Walker and Joshua Jackson.

THE RULES A passenger cannot be called forth when the host body is transitioning into a wolf, as we see with Maria and Julian-Tyler in the cold open.

Luke does a cloaking spell to hide the location of the doppelgängers from the Travelers, while the Travelers do a locator spell to find said doppelgängers.

As the Other Side crumbles, ghosts are able to physically interact with the Land of the Living. We've seen a determined ghost do this in the past: Vicki could mess around with stuff thanks to the added assistance of a witch on the Other Side in "Smells Like Teen Spirit" (3.06).

The Travelers give Julian "permanent" control of Tyler's body with some more chanting and by burning Julian's body; Mia did a similar spell for Katherine to take control of Elena's body, but as we learned when Elena came back, the word "permanent" is loosely defined here. When Travelers do the passenger spell and hang out in someone else's body, their own bodies go into a coma-like state (and they apparently need no food or water).

PREVIOUSLY ON *THE VAMPIRE DIARIES* Damon's line about him and Stefan and their ex-girlfriend is reminiscent of Damon asking Stefan "Where'd our girlfriend go?" in "A Few Good Men" (1.15). Here Elena has evolved into their common "ex-girlfriend."

Caroline's dad, the late Bill Forbes, left behind a cabin much like the Gilbert lake house, first seen in "Crying Wolf" (2.14).

In "The Devil Inside," Caroline muses that there's a possible nickname in "Elena and Damon, Damon and Elena," and here she uses the shipper name "Stelena" to express her displeasure at Elena and Stefan's secretive behavior.

Elena prepares to clink glasses with Caroline on the "kiss a Salvatore" round of Never Have I Ever because Caroline and Damon shared kisses (and decidedly more) in "Friday Night Bites" (1.03) and "Family Ties" (1.04).

Damon's line "Enter the complication" evokes Elijah's "complication speaking" phone greeting to Klaus in "American Gothic" (4.18).

A ghost staking his brother in a burning shed is a "dick move" to Damon, on par with getting stabbed while wearing a John Varvatos shirt in "Family Ties."

OFF CAMERA "It was such fun character work," Holly Brix says of the episode's drinking game sequence, which was mainly driven by "ping-ponging looks and building tension." Joshua Butler concurs, calling the scene one of his favorite moments throughout the series. "I think it works so well because it allows viewers to play along with Elena, Stefan, Caroline, and Damon," he says. "In a way, it's like the ultimate *TVD* trivia night. If you know the series well, each

The Murder Buddy Fan Club

Melinda Hsu Taylor: It's no secret in the writers' room that I'm Enzo's champion, not that he really needs one because he's so popular. He's *really* popular.

Michael Allowitz: Enzo turned out to be a crowd favorite and what a great actor Malarkey is. Really enjoyed his arc and being able to be part of it.

Rebecca Sonnenshine: Of course Enzo has been the *most* fun to write for (and hang out with). Michael is a great actor and is always up for anything.

Neil Reynolds: Enzo is a delight to write for, in part because we're still figuring out his voice, energy, and origins. He captures some of the loose-cannon energy of Klaus in his heyday but has a perspective all his own.

Julie Plec: The first episode that [Malarkey] shot, I wasn't there, but Melinda was there, and she kept emailing like, "Oh my god, *Enzo Enzo Enzo*," and you just could tell. And then I went to Atlanta in the midst of all that, and the actors were like, "Oh my god, Michael Malarkey's so good, he's such a good actor, he's so nice." And then I got to meet him and hang out with him a little bit and I thought, "Oh, this guy is *so* charming and delightful," and his little English accent or whatever it is.

Hsu Taylor: I love his British accent. I'm a sucker for a British accent, I don't know about anybody else. So that helps for me.
Matthew D'Ambrosio: He's just such a fun antihero. He's charming, cute, speaks with an accent (oh man, that accent). Plus, Michael Malarkey stops hearts with his acting abilities. I mean, really. The man has range and presence. Even scenes where Enzo is simply walking down the street and talking on his phone, you can't help but stop and just be absorbed by his performance.
Holly Brix: He's an amazing actor and, like a lot of our cast, he can perform anything — he adds these little touches that really make everything pop.
Plec: We had a close call where we were literally on holiday — and he got offered a series regular job on *True Blood*. And that would have completely taken him out of not just the episode — right when we got back from Christmas, which was already written and prepped — but the rest of the season. So it was either let go of him right then and re-shoot a piece of the previous episode and have that storyline end until next season when he's available to us — because it was the last season of *True Blood* so we could have him back once we got into season six — or really dive in and embrace the character and know that he would ultimately be a series regular for us. So it sort of forced our hand in a way that wasn't *fun* in the moment. But when we were victorious, it was thrilling, because we knew we wanted him around for the long haul; we just couldn't decide if we could live without him for half the season or not. Thankfully, we got to keep him, and we got to continue on.
Hsu Taylor: This guy is really great as the character, and really *useful* as a character because he's this weird kind of foil between Damon and Stefan in a way that there's kind of like a bro-triangle in a sense. And he's always vying for Damon's affections and loyalty. And he can deliver exposition effortlessly — very helpful. He had chemistry with Caroline — that's fun. He had a bad streak, he had a vendetta against the Augustines, and all of those things were really good in generating story.
Plec: I just knew the audience was probably hungry for that kind of snarky, Klausian element in the show, having lost Joseph Morgan and just needing that kind of Spike presence, especially while Damon was in the midst of whatever he was going through with Elena. I was figuring people would take to him and I'm glad that they did.
Hsu Taylor: This is something that you can't plan for — how much an audience will like a character or not. Some characters are set up to be really likable and the audience just doesn't go for them. Enzo's a character where we could have gone a number of different ways with him based on how story was evolving in the later part of the season, and we quickly got into the mindset of "Well, we love him, the audience loves him, he's doing a great performance, and let's keep mining his character."
Heather and Crissy: Enzoooooo.

'Never have I ever . . .' question references character moments and underlying relationships and plot details that we're all familiar with. As a director, I was very cognizant of finding every unspoken moment and every meaningful look that would trigger memories for the characters and the audience."

Brix and Butler share a passion for horror films, which contributed to the episode's homage feel. Brix loved this episode, revealing that originally "we were thinking of doing a riff on the old Alfred Hitchcock film *Rope*," the 1948 movie based on the 1929 play by Patrick Hamilton inspired by notorious child-murderers Nathan Leopold and Richard Loeb, two University of Chicago students obsessed with committing the perfect crime. Due to changes in "Man on Fire," they "ended up riffing a little on the Michelle Pfeiffer film *What Lies Beneath*, which is where we got the title." Butler says filming the episode was a blast, giving him "the chance to create the bathtub scene in the vein of Hitchcock's *Psycho*," as well as including "the deliberate throwbacks to '80s vampire movies like *Near Dark* and *The Lost Boys*."

Meanwhile in New Orleans . . .

Genevieve: I asked around. It's not just your father. The purgatory where supernatural souls are trapped is disintegrating.
Elijah: What do you mean "disintegrating"?
Klaus: She's right, more or less. It's actually imploding. I made a call to a rather reluctant Bennett witch in Mystic Falls who said the same thing. The dead are being torn away into nothingness. And they're not interested in going quietly.

As the Other Side collapses, the side effects begin to reverberate throughout New Orleans in *The Originals* episode "A Closer Walk with Thee" (1.20). The episode opens with sadistic Original patriarch Mikael invading Klaus's dreams, which Klaus interprets as "impeccable Freudian timing" as the birth of his child draws near, but he soon learns that Elijah is also dreaming about Mikael. Davina performs a seance to contact her dead friend Tim but Mikael appears instead, blasting out the windows in the witches' greenhouse. Just like Enzo in "What Lies Beneath," Mikael is able to physically affect matter in the Land of the Living.

The witch Monique casts a spell on Hayley that stops her heart, causing her to cross over to the Other Side, where Mikael awaits her, intent on killing Klaus's child. While Genevieve is able to break Monique's spell in time, saving Hayley and the baby, Mikael appears to Davina and tells her he is the only person who can make Klaus pay for killing Tim and that she can bring him back to life.

In order to get the shot of the Travelers coming over the hill at the end of the episode, the extras had to start on their knees behind the sightline. "It was kind of funny to have that many adults kneeling in the dirt offscreen," says Brix.

The writers wanted the Travelers and Markos to be distinct from previous seasons' villains. "We didn't want to make any villain super-strong and then make our plot [all about] wanting to kill them," explains Caroline Dries. "We did that with Klaus and the Originals. We also liked the idea that the Travelers' goal was a little mysterious and then emerged as a fundamental thing everyone wants: having a home."

The set of the Traveler camp in "Man on Fire" and this episode's opening scene is actually in the basement of a Macy's department store. "It's a beautiful space. Darren, our DP, lit it wonderfully and made it look like day and night and made it look like a camp," says Melinda Hsu Taylor. "Like [the Travelers] had found and repurposed a bunch of department-store basement stuff; they pirated electricity. Every single thing that goes on in one of these locations, somebody has to think of the real-world reason behind them, why the Christmas lights are lit up. Well, this is a department store, they broke in, they have to go to places that are abandoned, but they probably are not paying the electric bill so how do they get power? So we have to have those conversations beforehand, which are pretty fun."

FOGGY MOMENTS This episode features some bizarre-for-vampires behavior: Stefan and Elena have top secret conversations in places where they could *easily* be overheard by prying vampire super-hearing. Stefan and Elena are unpacking bags of groceries from the car: they are hiding from Travelers who want to destroy them and they stop for groceries? Luke's the only one who needs food. Call for delivery! Damon and Stefan don't immediately sniff out that everything's covered in gasoline in the shed. Nor do they use their vampire speed and strength to escape the burning shed. An overall complaint: if characters decide to have big old emotional heart-to-hearts when they are supposedly in dire situations (Caroline and Elena in the woods searching for Luke, Damon and Elena by the car), the situations read as Less Than Dire to the audience. If they're not in fear for their lives, we're not in fear for their lives.

It's an understandable shortcut, but as Julian takes over Tyler's mind, Tyler sees flashes of Julian's life . . . but only the last few days when Tyler's

> "I will always and forever (heh) fight for Caroline Forbes. She's had such a journey from mean girl to team player. She became a vampire out of Katherine's revenge. Her dad tried to kill her. The Green Arrow (Stephen Amell) shot her in the head. Tyler put her through the emotional ringer and she came out from the other side in one piece. Plus her dialogue is always so snappy. I just love her. She's someone I could see myself being really good friends with. Like if you needed someone to pick you up from jail, who would you call? I'd call Caroline. She'd give you just enough guff to put you in your place, but all in the name of friendship and loyalty because she cares about you and doesn't want you to do that again."
>
> — Matthew D'Ambrosio

been his man-suit. When Katherine took over Elena, we saw the major moments of her life, not recent events.

Why does Markos want Julian to be in permanent control of Tyler, knowing that Tyler fled back to his friends? Isn't Julian more likely to give away Traveler secrets if he's in permanent control? And isn't he guaranteed to die when Tyler's body is killed by reversal of spirit magic? Why not leave Julian in semi-control of Tyler so he can return to his original body when the spell is done, and in the meantime protect his body from Tyler's friends?

QUESTIONS

- Caroline says that the vampires do not need an invitation into her dad's cabin because he's dead. But someone must own the cabin — did Caroline inherit it or is it stuck in estate hell?
- What would happen if the gang just killed all the Traveler bodies in that cave?
- Will Damon figure out a way to resurrect Enzo before the Other Side crumbles?
- *Will* the Other Side crumble? Will Bonnie survive?
- Is Tyler a goner?

Damon: Yeah, I know: find Markos, kill Markos, save Mystic Falls from becoming Traveler homeland. It'll be a busy day for me, Stefan. Time to strap on the hero hair.

5.21 Promised Land

Original air date May 8, 2014
Written by Rebecca Sonnenshine **Directed by** Michael Allowitz
Edited by Glenn Garland **Cinematography by** Darren Genet
Guest cast Cadarious Tyrez Armstead (Businessman Traveler), Tamara Austin (Maria), Wayne Austin (Truck Driver), Cynthia Barrett (Soccer Mom), John Eddins (Mr. Douglas), Cigie George (Businesswoman Traveler), Paul Hamm (Mailman), Chad Marvin (Bike Messenger Traveler), Randall Newsome (Mr. Sikes), Vince Pisani (Fruit Stand Worker), Kathleen Walsh (Young Mother Traveler)
Previously on *The Vampire Diaries* Paul Wesley

The Travelers take over Mystic Falls.

You know you've just witnessed a *TVD* classic when you're left thinking, *Did that really happen?* "Promised Land" delivers a *Vampire Diaries* master class: the dialogue crackles, it looks insanely beautiful, it's gory and gruesome and full of wonderful character moments. And on top of all that we spend some time with "the beautiful citizens of Mystic Falls," as Damon would call them. The town is not just home to our gang, but to Mr. Sikes who gave Caroline a lollipop after she signed up for her first savings account. To the guidance counselor Pam Douglas, who we've seen give a hoot about Jeremy . . . and now she's a Traveler named Karl who sticks her husband in the neck with a pair of scissors. That scene in particular is wonderfully quirky and well played, an unusual detour away from the main cast. These little moments make it more powerful, and tragic, when all those possessed citizens die in the town square as the Travelers' spell takes hold. As Caroline asks Julian, does Markos have to be so violent about things?

That conversation between Julian (in the body of the former love of her life) and Caroline yields interesting philosophical debate in an episode with a particularly loaded title. He argues that Markos is doing the *right* thing by undoing all the spirit magic in the world. He's hitting the reset button, taking things back to the way they *should* have been if Silas and Qetsiyah hadn't mucked things up. No witches using spirit magic to create and control and destroy. But Markos's plan renders his people the dominant species, the only ones left with access to extra-human gifts. Markos has not even a speck of concern for collateral damage — be it human or Traveler. To prove that point to Damon, he stabs one of his own Traveler husk people in the neck. Hostage taking? Not an effective plan against Markos. And, like every other wrongdoer in the history of this show, he's partially fueled by a need for revenge, in his case against the witches and all the entitled folks who've taken for granted everything they have, while the Travelers have suffered (along with homeless people, aging hipsters, and Matt Donovan — thank you, Damon). The origin story of the witches and Travelers, how they split, and just how different their magic is remains vague and muddled (and will likely never be explained on the show), but suffice it to say there are two very determined groups at play here. The Travelers have had their screen time this season. How about passing equal time over to Luke and Liv's reportedly crazy-ass coven in season six?

Thanks to the helpful (though ill-fated) Traveler named Maria, Stefan and Elena are freed from the longest continuous blood donation in recorded history, which means Damon can focus his efforts on being the Savior of the Universe. Despite his cracks about donning the hero hair, his endless and enjoyable snark, and what Caroline calls his "too cool to care" attitude, Damon is determined and doesn't seem to mind taking on the role of leader. He's delegating all over the place, and though he's ultimately unsuccessful in saving the town or killing Markos, it's more than a little bit awesome to see him rally in Stefan and Elena's absence. Damon is determined to protect his home — the "Salvatore boring house" and the town he claims is "kind of a dump."

During the first few acts of "Promised Land," Bonnie is in the opposite headspace from Damon. To protect Jeremy and her friends from further heartache, she has them believing a big whopper of a lie: that Liv has a spell she's willing to do that will save Bonnie from the Other Side. And everybody wants to tag along. When Caroline suggests that they kill Tyler, and then Tyler can hitchhike back to life along with Bonnie and Enzo, Bonnie's exasperation hits a breaking point. And it's Enzo who makes her rally with his hope-dies-last speech. However false or unfounded, however irrational his hope is that there's a way back to life, he refuses to give up. He'll fight (or pester) for a way back until the moment he's taken into the Great Beyond. It's just the rallying call Bonnie needs. While Caroline panics as she packs (what do you need for an apocalypse?), Bonnie plots. Bonnie has long been relied upon by her friends to be the one who will come up with the Hail Mary pass that somehow saves the day and their lives. But she's not a witch anymore, and she's facing a problem the likes of which literally no one has seen before. *Definitely* skip finals, Bonnie.

One of the highlights of these last few episodes has been the relationship that Elena and Stefan now share — they love each other, they know each other so well, and they have pushed past the awkwardness and the hurt to become true friends. The scenes of these two punchy, blood-starved vampires on a hot deserted highway are some of the best in a brilliant episode: their shared love for Caroline Forbes; Elena rearranging her boobs to flag down a truck; their conversation about toxic relationships, love, and the nature of vampirism. Imagine if that were their last day together — it's the kind of peace and connection that would make for a beautiful end to a love story.

Though Markos advises Damon to say his goodbyes, there's a decided lack of "hey we might all die" hugs and farewells when the gang gathers in the Whitmore College parking lot, outrunning the spell that's removing magic from Mystic Falls. There's no Salvatore-brother bonding moment or a proper goodbye between Elena and Stefan. With no foreshadowing or swelling-music signaling the end, the fatal fight between Julian and Stefan is simply shocking — Stefan, heart snatched out of his chest, turning gray and veiny and vampire-dead with Caroline's reaction mirroring that of the viewers at home. Stefan is on the Other Side. The Other Side is collapsing. Bonnie has no plan. In a moment like this, Enzo's words seem wise to take to heart: "I will accept it when it's done."

COMPELLING MOMENT For sheer shock factor alone, Stefan having his heart torn out.

CIRCLE OF KNOWLEDGE

- The idea of a "promised land" has its roots in Judeo-Christian lore. In the Torah and Old Testament book of Genesis, God tells Abraham to leave his native land of Mesopotamia for Canaan, an area roughly defined as

> "I think we all love writing Damon, because he's the master of snark. So 'Promised Land' was fun, because when Damon is pure of heart, he's basically a heroic, super-clever snark machine who's getting shit done and saving the day. For one scene, due to a change in blocking in the previous scene, I had to rewrite his opening line — which was a snarky joke. That's the worst — trying to be funny in five minutes. So I was really sweating it out in the Salvatore library (where we often set up video village), trying to come up with something that wouldn't suck. I ended up with something about Traveler cuisine consisting of gruel and trail mix, and I had to write it out by hand and give it to Ian. 'Sorry, I had to change your line,' I said. He read it and smiled, so I figured it didn't suck."
>
> — Rebecca Sonnenshine

stretching from the Nile to the Euphrates river, which was promised to the descendants of Abraham. This divinely endowed "promised land" is at the root of the modern-day conflict between Israel and Palestine.

- Continuing his tradition of on-point pop culture references, Damon drops a classic from the 1983 comedy film (and TBS marathon staple) *A Christmas Story*, telling Stefan "she'll shoot your eye out" when Stefan explains he and Elena have been drained of blood by Markos and need to hunt for food. During this scene, Elena is (rather hilariously) trying to perfect her aim with a slingshot and not, thankfully, the Red Ryder BB gun that the film's Ralphie Parker so desperately wants for Christmas and with which he does in fact ping himself in the eye.
- Enzo says Markos managed to "Houdini" himself from the Other Side and back to the Land of the Living, turning famous Hungarian-American illusionist and escape artist Harry Houdini (1874–1926) into a verb meaning "to escape."

HISTORY LESSON Damon finds a vintage treasure in the Salvatore wine cellar — a bottle of 1945 Bordeaux. In addition to being an exemplary specimen of wine from the Bordeaux region of France, French wines of the World War II era have a fascinating and turbulent history. While Stefan was serving as an ambulance driver on the Egyptian front, the winemaking families of

Nazi-occupied France were struggling to save their livelihood and an important part of their country's cultural identity. Not only were their vineyards in danger of being destroyed by invading troops, but Hitler himself appointed men called *weinführers* to find stores of bottled wine so it could be sold by the Germans. Many French vintners went to great lengths to protect their wine, including burying it, hiding it behind false walls, and storing it in caves. When Hitler's home was seized by Allied forces in May 1945, many bottles of French wine were found in its cellar. A 1945 Bordeaux is also highly prized because of the region's adverse weather conditions that year; winemakers struggled against frost, drought, and heat, yet the wine ultimately prevailed.

THE RULES Luke and Liv's coven is powerful enough to not only shake a diner table but to enable the brain-pain spell on Luke (it's unclear whether it's from the Other Side or remotely from the realm of the living).

Markos has transfused himself with doppelgänger blood: this enables him to channel the power of all of his people, rendering him strong enough to battle Damon and hybrid Julian and live.

The Travelers' big spell requires chanting (obvs) and each Traveler to crush a vial of mixed doppelgänger blood. As the spell takes effect, the bodies the Travelers are passengered in bleed from the nose and ears, and then drop dead. When their human hosts die, the Travelers return to their own bodies. This explains why the Travelers bothered with all the passengering in the first place: the bodies that performed the spell would be destroyed by it.

The purpose of this big bad spell? It destroys spirit magic (also referred to as "witch magic") layer by layer, spreading outwards from Mystic Falls until — eventually — the whole world would be free of spirit magic *and* all that it has ever created. That includes the curse the witches put on the Travelers that prevented them from ever settling down and having a home. It also includes vampires, the product of a witch's spell. We see Luke's and Liv's magic "sputter out" and daylight rings stop working. Though the vampires' original human death wounds appear, they don't die instantly . . . the spell moves slowly enough that they can outrun it. Phew.

Spirit or witch magic is distinct from Traveler magic, which Markos refers to as being "pure." How "Nature," the force behind both spirit and Traveler magic, is involved in all this remains unclear. (And just forget that Expression magic ever existed, okay? It's off the table.)

Killing a doppelgänger halts the Traveler spell, presumably stopping the

© PRN/PRPhotos.com

spread of the spell rather than undoing the spell entirely. Doppelgänger blood is finicky stuff when it comes to spells: in the past, the blood had to be from a living human doppelgänger (e.g., in Klaus's break-the-hybrid-curse spell), and here the doppelgängers need to at least be the living undead in order for the magical properties of their blood to work.

PREVIOUSLY ON *THE VAMPIRE DIARIES* The Salvatores love their references to hero hair: Stefan mused that he should groom his hero hair in "Graduation" (4.23), and Damon told him to "put your hero hair on" in "Fifty Shades of Grayson."

Need help with a move? Don't ask Matt for help. Here he knocks over a vase while moving Traveler husks, and in "Plan B" (2.06), Carol Lockwood admonishes Matt and Tyler ("Boys!") for sloppily moving antique furniture from the 1800s while prepping for the masquerade ball.

We first learned that the tunnels beneath Mystic Falls were accessible from the Mystic Grill's stock room in "The Killer" (4.05).

As the Traveler spell undoes the magic that keeps our vampires alive, flashes of Elena's death from "The Departed" (3.22) and the Salvatore brothers' deaths from "Blood Brothers" (1.20) are shown.

OFF CAMERA The plot of this episode was undetermined for a long time. "At the end of the season, we have a list of things we *must* accomplish," explains Rebecca Sonnenshine. "But we don't necessarily know if they go into episode 21 or 22. So there were probably four completely different versions of this episode."

She calls Stefan's death the fun "no one will see this coming!" card, and it turns out even Paul Wesley was surprised by the twist. "Truth be told, it was a shock," he says. "But I then quickly came to realize it was impermanent, so my shock was replaced by curiosity as to how they would get my character out of the situation and bring him back to life."

Adds Sonnenshine, "The funny thing is, we get so wrapped up in moving the story forward, we don't necessarily think about what the audience reaction will be. We're just sweating away, trying to land on the best version of events. And after we decided Stefan's death would be the thing that stops the spell from spreading, it became fact. It wasn't until deep into postproduction — during a spotting session, where we go over music and sound plans — that I thought, 'Oh my god. Stefan dies.' I walked back into the writers'

Julie Plec on the Love Triangle

I loved being able to bring the love triangle to a close. It doesn't mean it's closed forever, but it's closed for now. For so many years it's been the back and forth of who would [Elena] choose and every year it's that decision. Things change and things shift and all that, and to be able to make the audience believe for half the year that that love story had been fated by some ancient prophecy — which, of course, was complete bullshit. For one, because I would never do that to Stefan and Elena. Like, never. Never, ever, ever. And writers have pitched that to me for years — writers that come in and no longer work for us were like, "There needs to be some reason why their relationship is so special," and I said, "Yes, it's called love." It doesn't need to be mystically fated. But to make the audience *believe* that perhaps it was mystically fated, only to then learn that no, it was truly a spell created when there were only two doppelgängers left on this earth, that they would find their way to each other. But that didn't apply to their entire relationship. So being able to get Stefan and Elena to a place where they can acknowledge "our love was real, what we had was beautiful," to be able to see both in episode 5.04 ["For Whom the Bell Tolls"], when he had no memories, and then again in ["Resident Evil"], their alt-universe, to be able to be respectful and pay homage to the beauty of that relationship. But also put it to bed for now because, like it or not, this is the part of the series where Elena's with Damon, true and true. To not have to worry about sustaining a love triangle as we move into next year — I'm so excited. And again, you never know, people find their way back to each other. The longer the show goes, you don't know how Damon and Elena will end and if Stefan and Elena can ever begin again and anything's possible. But I just love the freedom of it.

For me, personally, I love that they can be friends in spite of everything that they've gone through because they do love each other. Again, they'll be able to fight and they'll be able to walk away from each other and they'll be able to make up and they'll be able to have all those things if you take the romantic stuff out of it. It's still powerful and it's still potent. And I've been rooting for [Stefan] and Caroline to get together since he helped her in the bathroom in episode 2.02 ["Brave New World"]. Not wanting to force that, and wanting to let it play as long as possible — because we might never earn our way there. The worst thing you can do is to force that and have people reject it. I want it to be earned and if it takes three more frickin' years to earn it properly, then we'll take the three years. And if it isn't going to work, then we'll go another direction. But I still love that idea.

Meanwhile in New Orleans . . .

Elijah: So not even death can stop my mother from seeking the annihilation of her own flesh and blood.

As the witches prepare to sacrifice Klaus and Hayley's newborn daughter in *The Originals*' season one finale, "From a Cradle to a Grave" (1.22), the rapid deterioration of the Other Side results in two surprising turns of events. The witch Davina pulls Mikael from supernatural purgatory into the real world, and she seemingly has full control of him and is intent on using him as a weapon against Klaus.

Elijah, Klaus, and Hayley learn from Genevieve that Original mother and witch Esther has been influencing the Quarter witches since being consecrated in New Orleans' soil, planning to sacrifice her newborn granddaughter. When Hayley kills Genevieve, the witch's power returns to the earth, allowing the fourth and final Harvest girl to resurrect. Esther not only manages to hijack that power to return to life in the girl's body, but she is able to save one of her children from the Other Side before it collapses, and this child too is in a different body. Finn, Kol, Henrik, and a sibling who died a witch before the family arrived in Mystic Falls could all have been on the Other Side, and the season ends without identifying which Original sibling was saved, only the revelation that it is one of Esther's children in its final line: "Yes, Mother."

room and said, 'I think people might be really upset by the end of this episode.' And Caroline probably said, 'You're just realizing that now?'"

"Setting up the finale is always delicate," says director Michael Allowitz of helming this episode, which involved extensive prep and storyboarding of the truck crash and Maria's pull into Oblivion; the production built an elaborate blue screen in order to film both sequences. "I wanted to make sure the audience was, most importantly, involved in the story and ready for the season's climax. The episode had a bit of everything, from torture to rekindled love to a very big stunt sequence. [Shipper] fans got another Delena kiss and action fans got a truck being slammed into an invisible wall. I especially enjoyed the Travelers unraveling and the building of the possible end with Markos."

Attentive viewers may notice a vehicle switcheroo in this episode. "Jeremy's car driving down the street to pick up Damon as he's escaping the anti-magic bubble is actually a different SUV than the one that pulls over and Damon gets into," reveals Caroline Dries. "It's stock footage. We had

"[With *The Originals*] we're not saying there will be future crossovers, but I also don't want the shows to get so far away from each other that we can't do it — that it would be a big rule break. But the end of this season basically was a crossover — it was a mythology crossover. It was funny as people started figuring that out: they realized, 'Wait a second, if the Other Side's going away, then that means everybody else over there is gone forever.' And so we're sitting over in the *Originals*' writing room and I said to them all year long, 'The Other Side's going away, keep that in mind . . .' Then it started impacting — you know, really with losing Claire [Holt] and losing Rebekah, the question of 'Okay, there's more Original family but they're dead, so what do you wanna do about that?' So that's really where the big, true mythology crossover came into play."

— Julie Plec

to rearrange that moment a little bit and it wasn't working with the existing footage. No one noticed. The editor had to point it out to me."

Of all the characters' various sufferings this season, Caroline Dries says that, though they are "equal opportunity misery-givers" in the writers' room, she'd "have to say Stefan's had it the toughest this season. Drowning all summer, then losing his memory, then witnessing Elena and Damon's love. His biggest breakthrough was realizing that he was finally over his love for Elena, which is not very optimistic, is it? Poor guy!"

FOGGY MOMENTS Forget the Traveler apocalypse: zucchini is spelled incorrectly on two signs at the fruit and vegetable stand!

Elena says to Maria the Traveler that Julian ran from Markos, and later Markos calls him a traitor. But it was *Tyler* who escaped from the Traveler camp. He faked being Julian, then turned into a wolf and ditched the camp in the opening scene of "What Lies Beneath," and ever since the Travelers made Julian the permanent "owner" of Tyler's body, he has been imprisoned by the Mystic Falls gang. How does that make Julian a traitor to the Travelers?

Bonnie tells Enzo that when the Travelers used doppelgänger blood to bring back Markos from the Other Side, they "basically" destroyed the magic that was holding the Other Side together. How so? Qetsiyah was a Traveler and created the Other Side (presumably) using Traveler, or "pure," magic, not spirit magic, to make Amara the Anchor for the spell. Was Amara's blood essential to that spell, and we just never heard about it? If the Other Side could withstand an "Anchor swap," why can't it withstand a doppelgänger-fueled spell?

When asked on Twitter about why Matt and Jeremy, who have both died multiple times and been resurrected by magic, were unaffected by the Travelers' No-More-Magic spell, Julie Plec replied that it isn't magic that is *keeping* them alive. The magic line has to be drawn *somewhere*, but it seems a little arbitrary that when the spell of the Gilbert ring broke, it didn't throw Matt back to his last moments of his most recent death and Jeremy back to the Other Side, with Bonnie's spirit-magic spell that resurrected him erased.

How did Julian get to Whitmore College? How did he "hear" that Maria brought Stefan back to Mystic Falls? How did he know that Stefan would be at Whitmore College?

QUESTIONS

- When not spritzing torture victims like Mr. Sikes, what does Damon use that atomizer for?
- What is the deal with Luke and Liv's coven and the family that Luke has repeatedly referred to as bad news? Are there any living members of the coven (besides the Parker twins)? If the coven is all or mostly (or even partly) on the Other Side, are they brainstorming a way to save it too?
- Just after Maria agrees to help Enzo and Bonnie, *whoosh* off she goes. Is there some rhyme or reason to who is being whooshed off to the Great Beyond? Who are the Powers That Be on the Other Side? Or is it just random chaos over there? (i.e., are characters whooshed off at the writers' mercy and as the plot demands?)
- Is the Travelers' spell permanent? Is Mystic Falls a spirit-magic-free zone forever?
- Can Bonnie save the day and herself?
- Is there a way to bring Stefan back to the Land of the Living? Can Enzo tag along too please?

Bonnie: Do you think it'll hurt?
Damon: I don't kn—.

5.22 *Home*

Original air date May 15, 2014
Written by Caroline Dries and Brian Young **Directed by** Chris Grismer
Edited by Tony Solomons **Cinematography by** Michael Karasick
Guest cast Matt Davis (Alaric Saltzman), Lennon Harrison (Sign Traveler #2), Arielle Kebbel (Lexi), Trevor Scot Schliefer (Passing Traveler), Jarred Sonnier (Sign Traveler #1), Cornell Austin Willis (Van Traveler)
Previously on *The Vampire Diaries* Ian Somerhalder

The gang saves Mystic Falls from the Travelers. The Other Side collapses.

And so it ends. Season five closes with a heartbreaking implosion (and an impressive explosion) that leaves our characters unmoored — some loved ones lost, others returned. Home is where the heart is, as the saying goes, and in this finale, the Mystic Falls gang proves willing to go to the ends of the earth to be together and to protect each other, even when that means risking not only their lives but their eternal existence.

While Markos and the Travelers may not rank on the list of most compelling antagonists this series has seen, their single-minded mission to take away the place the characters call home provokes a similar single-mindedness in the ensemble of characters. As the episode opens, Markos and the Travelers (with all their half-sensical, mystical mumbo-jumbo) have managed to destabilize the entire universe as these characters know it: Mystic Falls is a no-spirit-magic zone, meaning vampires will die, witches are powerless, and its inhabitants have been either evacuated or killed (after being used as meatsuits for the Travelers). The Other Side is on the brink of collapse because of Markos's return, and that means all the dead supernaturals who've made that purgatory their home are either headed for Oblivion or in a race to find that ever elusive "peace." The ship, to use Sheriff Forbes's metaphor, is going down.

In an act one scene that nicely pairs with the final one, Damon and

Bonnie — the gang's de facto leaders — have a charged conversation about the stakes of their situation. Not only is this one of the least annoying recap-the-previous-episode scenes we've had in a while but it demonstrates how neither one of them needs *any* help being "motivated" (though Damon smashes some stuff for good measure). All that matters to these two is saving the ones they love — Stefan and that ever-growing list of Other Siders, saving their home. From start to finish, the characters make choices in "Home" that serve that one clear purpose: to save, to protect, to die for one another.

While it may be in her job description to serve and protect the people of Mystic Falls, Sheriff Forbes steps up, playing a key role in orchestrating Project Kaboom. When Markos's suspicions keep her at the Grill despite the ticking clock, Liz doesn't waver in her resolve to oust these interlopers from her home, even if she won't live to see it happen. The captain goes down with the ship, and she chooses to stay, knowing that she's moments away from an explosive death with no safety net of an Other Side to be rescued from. The last Mystic Falls parent sees it through alive, thanks to Damon and Alaric stopping to save her — and risking their own passage back to the Land of Living in doing so.

Another matriarch willing to risk herself for her loved ones, Sheila "Grams" Bennett may not have succeeded in teaching her grandchild not to rush her elders, but she has instilled in Bonnie the most important Bennett family value: she protects her own. Grams doesn't try to stop Bonnie from making the sacrifice she's committed to making — she respects her granddaughter's choice — but Grams has made a selfless choice of her own. Somehow Bonnie has been taken care of, and combined with Grams's comment that she's not the only one in her *family* who knows how to make a sacrifice and that slow pan over the graves of other Bennett witch ancestors, Grams may not have been the only Bennett working to protect Bonnie from the pain of Oblivion.

An episode with no time for mincing words or for hesitation — after all, the end is nigh — "Home" sees those in the gang who are more morally sound make strong choices that they may not make on a regular Thursday night. Bonnie may not like it but she readily works with the man who murdered her father, despite the risk that bringing Silas back would pose to humanity, in order to save the people she loves. She also awesomely spits his "bygones" line back at him and lets him be whisked off out of the Other Side. Her father's murder (not to mention countless others) gets some measure of justice in a

> "What surprised me [about "Home"] is how emotional the final product turned out to be. We were blessed by great performances from our actors who truly gave it their all. After building the episode, my challenge was to find music that did not detract from those great performances, but enhanced them. We often rely on the music of singer-songwriter type artists, and for the final sequence I returned to one artist I was very familiar with, Birdy. We had featured her music in 5.04 ["For Whom the Bell Tolls"] during a very emotional farewell-to-Bonnie sequence. Fortunately, I found a little-known Birdy track called 'Wings' that was familiar to her U.K. fans but was at the time unreleased in the States."
>
> — Tony Solomons

moment that ties back to the beginning of the season. While no one (except Damon) is willing to blow up the whole town, the idea of committing a mass Traveler massacre is one that no one flinches at. And when Liv refuses to take the risk of bringing back Stefan and company from the Other Side (and potentially allowing the Travelers to restart their no-magic spell, should they live to chant again), Caroline does what she couldn't do earlier in the season: she kills to save Stefan. By sending Luke to the Other Side, she ensures that Liv feels as motivated as the rest of them do. With Stefan dead and the Other Side collapsing, Caroline is as ready to take desperate measures as Damon is. Stefan has to come back.

It's been a slow burn and build on the Caroline-Stefan romance front, but Caroline seems more and more self-aware about her feelings for Stefan, especially after seeing him die. But more important than whether or not they ever go on that first date, which Lexi so brilliantly chides Stefan about, Caroline is there for him in what is arguably the worst moment of his life — having, by the end of the episode, lost the two people he knew and loved longest and best. Though she did once have an epic love of her own in Lee, Lexi has had one singular role these past five seasons whether we saw her alive, as a ghost, or in flashback, and that was to be the best best friend a guilt-ridden closet ripper could have. Lexi is willing to sacrifice another shot

© Emiley Schweich/PR Photos

in the Land of the Living, and she risks Oblivion in order to do right by Stefan. She won't overwhelm Bonnie by passing through her; instead, she gives up her spot for Stefan's brother, the man who killed her. She is there to chuck Markos into Oblivion — with that trademark Lexi grin, to boot — and Stefan knows without having to be told that Lexi fought for him 'til the end. Selfless and determined, Lexi almost wills herself to find peace, and having "earned her stripes," she does find peace in a beautiful send-off to a great character.

But though the audience gets a final moment with Lexi, Stefan doesn't get a goodbye. Not with Lexi, not with Damon. Jeremy is also denied a proper goodbye: try not to cry at the thought of Little Gilbert, who's lost so much, tearing through the forest screaming Bonnie's name, ultimately in vain. Like Damon and Elena and their decisions to be the spark that blows up the Grill, Bonnie makes a choice and demands it be respected. She not only decides *how* to spend her last days — happy, with Jeremy, with hope — but she willfully decides how she will view her time since she died, just shy of a year ago in *TVD* time. Instead of bemoaning her death, she tells Jeremy that she considers her extra time a gift, time she did not waste. Bonnie does what her Grams tells her to do in their perfect final moments together: she stays strong, Grams proud of Bonnie and her choices.

Despite the fact that there is no earthly way that "Home" will be the last we see of Damon and Bonnie, somehow *The Vampire Diaries* — with its own special brand of magic — manages to make their final moments utterly devastating. After a season of turmoil, Damon and Elena are together, at peace and in love, and just as Elena is forced to respect Damon's suicide-mission choice, he respects hers. In a perfect line, considering what they've been through this season, Elena looks at Damon and says she knows what she signed up for — she's all in. "Home" was an episode full of heroic moments, ones that required trust and teamwork, sacrifice and suffering, but one that definitely stands out after so much angst is Elena and Damon sharing an ever-so-slight smile at each other, as the car races toward the Grill. There's no place they'd rather be than at each other's sides, live or die; that's their home.

"Damon finally had everything he wanted. He was happy. He should be here," says Stefan, in a line that synthesizes what both Damon and Elena are feeling on opposite sides of the living/dead divide in the Salvatore tomb. Damon says he has "peaked," that there's no better way to die than in knowing he's loved by Elena. It's a beautiful goodbye, made ever so much

© Andrew Evans/PR Photos

"Our biggest issue writing the finale — I know Brian will attest to this — are those GD rules we had to live up to in terms of passing through the Other Side. Like, first you pass through Bonnie when you die, then you wake up, then you have to pass through her again — I'm so glad we got rid of that place! Anyway, it wouldn't have been that big of a deal if every character didn't have to do it. So just the mere logistics drove us nuts. The fun parts though, the parts you love writing, were all [about] the buildup. It wasn't until the end of the season that we realized how and why Damon was going over to the Other Side. We realized, of course, it has to be Stefan. This came from hours and hours of discussion of how we actually destroy the Other Side, who should be over there. I mean, days of discussion and changing our minds. Luckily, we knew we wanted to blow up the Grill, so it helped to have one stationary moment to build to. There were so many possibilities I'm having anxiety remembering the damn process. I will say, in all the hijinks of getting our people in place for the ending to work, there was a scene in the finale where Damon is sitting on his car being pensive. I love that scene because we rarely see Damon alone, and he's about to do something he may not come back from. I just loved that. He was finally, after 170-whatever years, content with himself and he was finally ready to be a true hero. I loved it. To me, that's what the show is about."

— Caroline Dries

more heartbreaking because Elena can't hear a word he says. She only knows he's there, at least for a few minutes more. From the moment Elena gets thrown back into the Land of the Living by Bonnie (Bonnie flat-out refuses to accept Elena's insistence that she wait for Damon, and Stefan gives a subtle "do it" nod to Bon) to the end of the episode, Nina Dobrev gives us a performance that is achingly real. It gets hard to describe the level of performance she brings to her characters without resorting to hyperbolic and overused terms, but watch her breakdown-goodbye to Damon and try not to use the phrase "tour de force." After seasons of grief and loss and pain and suffering, Elena reaches a new depth of despair in losing Damon. With the promise he'd made to her — "I will make it back to you" — broken (for now, at least), Elena is gutted. She loses the man she loves and her best friend. But at least she and Jeremy have the comfort of Alaric alive again. Thank you, *TVD* Powers That Be, for that.

Like any good finale (and this show *knows* from finales), "Home" ends with a million questions and a million possibilities for season six: Tyler human, Enzo alive, Alaric resurrected, Elena without Damon, Stefan the only living Salvatore brother. Without the Other Side, death is now a permanent sentence. The town may be safe from vampire attacks, witch magic, and creepy blood rituals, as Matt says, but it's no longer home to those who've lived there their whole lives. And Damon and Bonnie? They have to make it back.

COMPELLING MOMENT Bonnie and Damon — their final exchange is so perfectly in keeping with their characters and their fraught relationship, and to see them hold hands and face Oblivion together, terrified and unflinching, is a special kind of emotional torture. The fade to white and Damon's last line cut off? Brutal, in the best *Lost*-ish way. Bravo.

CIRCLE OF KNOWLEDGE

- "Home" is not only the shortest *Vampire Diaries* episode title ever, but a simple statement of the season's predominant theme.
- It's a good thing the Travelers were blown out of Mystic Falls; they had a lot to learn about town governance, like how moving a sign doesn't constitute "resetting the official border" of a municipality. The current population of Mystic Falls is 6,923, minus those residents who died in the town square last episode. How often do you think they have to update that population?
- "You need to go be a younger, hotter Bruce Willis," Bonnie tells Jeremy, referring to the American actor's penchant for playing action heroes, like the Die Hard series' yippee-ki-yay cop John McClane or *Armageddon*'s hero astronaut Harry Stamper.
- Julie Plec revealed on Twitter that the "Bygones?" moment, where Silas flippantly asks Bonnie to get over him murdering her dad, was a homage to the legal dramedy *Ally McBeal* (1997–2002). One of the show's main characters, Richard Fish (Greg Germann), constantly said "bygones" as a way of deflecting uncomfortable conversations, and the series finale was titled "Bygones."

Endearing Insults and Insulting Endearments

Bon. Jer. Stef. Ty. Care. The gang is called many a name in each episode, and most of them? Not that nice. Here be a list of nicknames and insults slung in season five.

Elena: America's Most Boring Self-Righteous Vampire, Condescending Bitch, Show Off (Katherine); Queen of Nature Versus Nurture, Miss Avoiding Me for Days, Sunshine (Damon); Whatever You're Supposed to Be (Aaron); Sleepyhead (Caroline); Darling, College Girl (Enzo).

Damon: Douche (Random College Guy); Safe Brother (Amnesia Stefan); Brother, George (Stefan); Mr. So Far So Good, Mr. I Can Handle My Brother, Mr. I Know What I'm Doing (Elena); Soldier, Mate, Big Brother, Grumpy Pants (Enzo); Professor Salvatore (Caroline).

Stefan: Brother, New You, Amnesia Stef, Buddy (Damon); Insatiable and Bloodlusting Vampire Ripper of Monterey, Fun Brother (Amnesia Stefan); Me (Silas); Gorgeous, Sleepyhead, Sweet Pea (Tessa); Stranger (Katherine); Professor Salvatore, Tutor From Hell (Elena); Tutor Guy (Bonnie).

Caroline: Roomie, Dr. Forbes (Elena); Blow-Off Girl, Hot Shot (Jesse); Roomie, Honey (Katherine); Dr. Forbes, Prude-y Trudy, Blondie, Munchie, Meryl Streep, My Sexy Blonde Frenemy (Damon); Suzie Sunshine (Katherine-as-Elena); Goldilocks, Blondie, Gorgeous (Enzo).

Jeremy: Freak Who Faked His Own Death (Jeremy); Genius, Little Punk, Pocahontas, Little Gilbert, Buddy, Idiot, Gilbert, Man of the Hour (Damon); Hunter (Silas); Little Rugrat, Little Gilbert (Katherine).

Matt: Matty Blue Eyes, Matty Blue, Matty Blue Blue, Matty Pants, Elena Gilbert Cheat Sheet (Katherine); Dumbass, Quarterback, Donovan, [Jer's] Xbox Buddy (Damon); Quarterback (Klaus); Matty (Katherine-as-Elena); Captain Responsible (Tyler); Darling, Mate (Kol).

Tyler: Poor Lad (Klaus), Dude (Matt), Wolf Boy (Damon).

Bonnie: Bon-Bon (Damon, Katherine), Mr. Miyagi (Liv), Precious Anchor to the Other Side (Luke).

Katherine: Brown-Eyed Bitch of a Cure for Immortality (Nadia); The Cute One, Absentee Mother (Katherine); Corpse to Be (Caroline); Kitty Kat (Damon).

Silas: Dick (Jeremy); Control Freak (Damon); Bastard, Genius (Qetsiyah).

Qetsiyah: Qetsi-whatever, Ray of Sunshine, Miss Crazy, Vindictive Prehistoric Witch (Damon); The Other Crazy (Elena).

Amara: Crazy Pants, [Silas's] Nutter Butter Soulmate (Damon); Ancient Boyfriend Stealing Bitch, Love (Qetsiyah); Idiot (Katherine).

Dr. Maxfield: Dr. Dickfield, Doc (Jesse); Creepster Professor, Professor Blondie, Doogie, Dr. Frankenstein, Dr. Creepy Ken Doll, Doc (Damon); Dr.

Whoever, Dr. Wes (Katherine); Slippery Little Devil, Dr. Frankenstein, Our Good Dr. Wes (Enzo); Dr. Creepenstein (Caroline).
Aaron: Whatever Your Name Is (Elena); Moody Mystery Guy, Mini Wes, Cowboy (Damon).
Jesse: Flyer Guy (Elena); Killer, Sweetie (Damon).
Enzo: Mate, Bastard, Mr. Butterfingers (Damon); Other Enzo (Caroline); Casper the English Ghost (Luke).
Nadia: Street Rat (Rebekah); Eurobitch, The Devil's Spawn (Damon); Scary Vampire Daughter, Mildly Abusive Daughter (Katherine).
Gregor: Creepshow Boyfriend, Czech Freak (Matt).
Markos: Your Highness (Julian).
Travelers: Eurotribe, Salvation Army (Damon); Singing Witches (Enzo); Tribe of Ancient Wannabe Witches (Stefan).
Augustine Society: Freaks (Damon).
Liv: Little Witch Friend, Crazylocks (Damon); Hot Shot, Little Pocket Witch (Bonnie); Newbie Emo Witch Type with a Bad Attitude (Caroline); Show Off, My Ray of Sunshine Sister (Luke); Good Soldier, Little Witchy Friend (Enzo).
Luke: Wonder Twin, Stupid Witch (Damon); Witch Twin (Enzo).
Tom Avery: Other You, Stefan's Doppelhim (Caroline).
Bill Forbes: Dickwad (Damon).
Mr. Sikes: Sweetie Pie (Damon).
Rebekah: Blonde Original Chick (Vicki).
Alaric: Buddy (Damon).
Caroline and Elena: Chatty Girls in the Back (Dr. Wes), Jerks (Liv).
Caroline and Tyler: Goldilocks and the Big Bad Wolf (Katherine).
Caroline and Enzo: Atlanta Assassination Squad (Enzo).
Damon and Elena: Frenemies (Silas).
Damon and Enzo: Murder Buddies (Stefan).
Stefan and Elena: Doppeltargets, Team Stelena (Caroline).
Elena and Amara: Tweedle-dee and Tweedle-dum (Qetsiyah).
Jeremy and Matt: The Gilbert Donovan Brain Trust, Clowns, Braindead Teenagers, Tweedle-dee and Tweedle-dumber, The Hardy Boys, Geniuses (Damon).
Matt, Jeremy, and Tyler: Three Stooges (Liv).
Tyler and Matt: Townies (Luke).

- We see a cluster of Bennett ancestors' gravestones in the cemetery: Marie Bennett ("beloved mother and daughter"), Amelia Bennett ("she was well esteemed and loyal to all she knew"), and Ernestine Bennett ("sacred," "R.I.P."). Bonnie's relationship with her ancestors has been fraught: they punished her for using dark magic at the end of season three and again at the beginning of season four, cutting her off from it and paving the way for her to turn to Expression, under the influence of Shane. But now she's "earned her stripes," and it seems plausible that her ancestors may have been willing to do her a *big* favor with Grams leading the charge . . .

- After five seasons, we finally learn how old Damon was when he was shot and killed by his father: 25.
- Every time someone dies while wearing the Gilbert ring, they awaken further and further away from their body. Here we see that the regular supernatural folks who die — Elena, Damon — awaken on the Other Side right next to where their corpses are on the mortal side of the divide. Damon ends up far from his car because, unlike "Safety First" Elena, he didn't buckle up his seat belt before driving into the Mystic Grill.
- The Other Side clearly does not follow Klaus's rule about no death on birthdays. Judging by comments made in "Gone Girl" about Bonnie's birthday being "next week," Bonnie dies either on or just after her birthday.
- Now that Tyler is only a *potential* werewolf again, he may want to drop a line to his old pal Hayley in New Orleans. They're making magic free-werewolves-from-monthly-change rings over there; maybe he can get his paws on one . . . just in case he kills someone and triggers his curse again.
- Season five is the most suicide ridden of any in *TVD* history. Here Damon and Elena sacrifice themselves willingly (as does Sheriff Forbes), adding their deaths to the list of countless Travelers who self-sacrificed and those who committed or attempted suicide, like Amara, Silas, Qetsiyah, Katherine, Elena in "While You Were Sleeping" (who, thanks to werewolf-venom, was on the brink of hurting herself), and Enzo, who kills himself by forcing Stefan to remove his heart. The season also had a case of the crazies, with characters and situations being described as crazy with great frequency, as well as genuine mental health issues — PTSD, Amara's insanity — cropping up as plot points.

THE RULES Bonnie explains that the Anchor is a gateway to the Other Side, usually one-way only, but the combination of Liv's magic (using a spell learned from Silas) and the weakening of Bonnie with so many Travelers passing through her allows for the gateway to become two-way. The spell that Liv does is different from the one the Travelers did to let Markos come back:

they all chanted together, and when Markos returned, he didn't blink back into existence but emerged from collapsed Bonnie's shadow.

In order to make it to the Other Side, a supernatural person needs to die before the Travelers' spell removes all their supernaturalness. (Elena is concerned that she and Damon explode while they are still vampires.) A human with a werewolf gene not yet triggered is supernatural enough to go to the Other Side (since Tyler went there and came back).

Luke does a quick spell to interrupt Liv's sustained spell — a handy one to know! — concerned that her spell will kill her, as we've seen spirit magic spells do to witches before.

With the Other Side now gone, when a supernatural person dies, they pass into one of the remaining afterlife options: they find peace, or they go to that unpleasant-seeming Oblivion place, or, perhaps, they are just dead. In season six, Jeremy won't have any ghosts to talk to, and, save for transitioning vampires, death will be permanent.

PREVIOUSLY ON *THE VAMPIRE DIARIES* During their last hang in Stefan's car, Lexi encouraged him to go to Portland ("Graduation," 4.23), which she asks him about here.

Damon reminds Elena of a recurring theme in many of their fights when he insists on being the spark that sets the Grill aflame: him not respecting her choices, such as when he forced her to drink his blood in "The Last Day" (2.20) or his repeated refusals through seasons two, three, and four to agree with Elena being a martyr or sacrificial lamb.

In "Graduation," it was the hunters who were determined to blow up the Grill; now it's our heroes.

Jeremy quips that the Salvatore brothers will make a generous donation to rebuild the Mystic Grill after exploding it, just as Damon offered the Mystic Falls hospital after he and Klaus blew up part of it in "The Rager" (4.03).

Perhaps Elena Gilbert should just avoid automobiles altogether. Before this episode's smash-up, she was in the car crash that killed her parents, she flipped her car in "The Turning Point" (1.10), she died and turned into a vampire after Rebekah forced her and Matt off Wickery Bridge in "The Departed" (3.22), and she got witch-whammied by Liv while in Maria's truck in "Promised Land."

Alaric's friendly advice to Damon in the Grill — "when you finally get the girl, don't blow her up" — echoes his words to Damon in "Graduation," after Elena chose Damon: "You got the girl."

Like Silas with his bygones line, Klaus is also a big believer in letting bygones be bygones, at least when it comes to *him* doing horrible things, as he expressed to Stefan in "Homecoming" (3.09) and to Rebekah in "The Five" (4.04).

Bonnie wondered if the Other Side's collapse would hurt when she thought it was a goner in "Death and the Maiden," and here her last words to Damon repeat that fear. Poor Bon-Bon.

OFF CAMERA "The season finale was awesome," says editor Marc Pollon. "It was big, tense, very emotional — fitting of a season finale. Tony Solomons is a terrific editor who nails all his shows, but especially that one." Solomons credits Caroline Dries and Brian Young's script and he trusted director Chris Grismer to provide a solid foundation. "The finale is always one of the more ambitious episodes," he explains. "The expectation is that not only will this episode neatly wrap up the season, we hope it also promises that something special is in store."

Of the unexpected team-up of Bonnie and Damon in the finale, Julie says, "[Ian] and Kat, in the last two years, three years now, started coaching with the same person — Ivana Chubbuck, Ian's fabulous acting coach and mentor — and they really connect on a level of chemistry when they're in scenes with each other. Ian really respects Kat's process and respects her as an actress and loves working with her. They made it a perfect pairing moving into the next season. They really enjoy their acting connection with each other, so it stimulates them in ways that, when you're five years deep in a show, can be really exciting."

"Bonnie wasn't initially involved in that very last moment," says Caroline Dries. "I don't even think she was meant to die. The idea was that Damon died and was supposed to come back but instead Bonnie says, 'You guys, he's not over here. The Other Side is gone.' Something like that. Then one day Julie was like, 'You know, I was talking to Ian and he really enjoys working with Kat,' and we all started thinking, we too love seeing them together onscreen. So what if we ended them together? And it was kind of perfect — their dialogue about 'couple thousand at most' that Brian wrote pretty much sums up their relationship and fate."

The Death Toll

Now that the Other Side is gone, death promises to become permanent on *The Vampire Diaries*. Here's a look back at our core characters' death counts in the era when it wasn't so sticky . . .

Caroline (1): smothered by Katherine ("The Return")

Stefan (2): shot by his father ("Blood Brothers"); heart-snatched by Julian ("Promised Land")

Damon (2): shot by his father ("Blood Brothers"); killed in a suicide-mission car crash ("Home")

Tyler (2): neck snapped by Klaus ("The Reckoning"); killed by the Travelers' no-magic-zone ("Home")

Elena (3): killed by Klaus ("The Sun Also Rises"); drowned after car crash caused by Rebekah ("The Departed"); killed in a suicide-mission car crash ("Home")

Bonnie (4): self-inflicted death by magic ("The Last Dance"); self-inflicted death by magic ("Growing Pains"); accidental death by magic while resurrecting Jeremy ("The Walking Dead"); blipped out of ghost-Anchor existence with the Other Side's destruction ("Home")

Katherine (4): hanged herself in order to become a vampire ("Katerina"); drained of blood by Silas ("Monster's Ball"); died of old age ("500 Years of Solitude"); expelled from Elena's body by Stefan ("Gone Girl")

Jeremy (4): neck snapped by Damon ("The Return"); shot by Sheriff Forbes ("As I Lay Dying"); heart stopped by Bonnie to desiccate Klaus ("Before Sunset"); drained of blood by Silas ("Down the Rabbit Hole")

Matt (4): drowned himself to see his sister on the Other Side ("The Reckoning"); neck snapped by Damon ("She's Come Undone"); neck snapped by Silas ("True Lies"); stabbed in the neck by possessed Sheriff Forbes ("Resident Evil")

Alaric (7): staked by Damon ("A Few Good Men"); killed by Stevie ("Crying Wolf"); neck snapped by Damon ("Disturbing Behavior"); run over by hybrid-driven SUV ("The New Deal"); stabbed by Elena ("Bringing Out the Dead"); staked by Esther ("Do Not Go Gentle"); killed when Elena dies because of a magical link ("The Departed")

FOGGY MOMENTS The Julian-is-a-traitor plot point gets further confused here: Markos calls him a traitor for killing the doppelgänger, an act Julian committed *after* Markos had already labeled him a traitor for no good reason. Rest in Oblivion, the both of ya!

Markos says that Julian/Tyler will be stripped of his hybrid side first, then his vampirism. But there is no "hybrid" side — there's the vampire side, there's the werewolf side; Tyler was a hybrid of vampire and werewolf.

It's a dramatic moment and a great callback to the previous episode when Caroline and Elena stopped Liv and Luke's car, but . . . why didn't Liv and Luke whammy them with magic and keep on driving? (Or use defensive driving tactics and swerve around Elena?) They are clearly in the magic-still-works zone since Caroline and Elena are still alive and vampires.

Unless Whitmore College's finals are in early March, and not in May, the sun would not have set by 7 p.m. when Damon and Elena drive into the no-magic zone. The Mystic Falls clock tower strikes 7. The bell rings ominously! A nice moment, but that clock tower has no bell.

How large is Mystic Falls and how far away from the town square is that "Welcome to Mystic Falls" sign? We see a stretch of highway by the sign (which at night is dark save for the streetlights lining it; i.e., we're not in the center of town), but the map with the no-magic perimeter shows five, maybe six, city blocks — no big stretches of field and road. The distance needs to be short enough that Damon and Elena don't have their vampirism removed

"I think that there are more favorite episodes in this season — even if the season itself had its highs and its lows, I can count so many episodes that I would consider of my favorites of the entire series. One of them is Bonnie's funeral in episode 4. One is the 100th. I love the one that follows the 100th when Katherine becomes permanent in Elena. I love 'Gone Girl' so much, I think it's a beautiful episode of television. I love Paul's episode. I loved the finale. Oh! And the triple-gängers! I loved episode 7 so much! The death of Silas, the triple-gängers, the whole thing; that episode, with the bus stop scene. Off the top of my head, I can list five or six episodes that I love, and that makes me really proud of the season. And of the job Caroline [Dries] did. She really had to carry a lot of the luggage and do a lot of the heavy-lifting and it was not easy on her, and she just handled it like a pro, and she's brilliant and beautiful."

— Julie Plec

before they die, but judging by how quickly it happens to Tyler/Julian, this spell operates with plot outcomes in mind rather than any sort of internal story logic.

The scenes where Bonnie is only talking to ghosts (e.g., Enzo, Silas) do not consistently take place on the Other Side (with the blue haze), rather than in the Land of the Living. Can the recently dead see ghosts (and can ghosts see them) before they've passed through to the Other Side? Just before Tyler passes through Bonnie, he reacts to what Enzo says, as if he can see and hear him. But in "Promised Land," Enzo doesn't see Stefan when he arrives to pass through Bonnie.

Why doesn't Luke help Liv with the spell after he returns to the Land of the Living? We've seen the Travelers chant en masse all season long, and we've seen witches share power through touch — why not hold Liv's hand to share his power?

QUESTIONS

- Alaric is back — but he's still a super-vampire. How will he adjust to his new normal?
- Will the Parker twins be back?
- Matt says to Jer that killing the Travelers doesn't necessarily get rid of the no-magic zone: is Mystic Falls still a no-magic zone? Is the Salvatore house within the no-magic zone? Where will our supernatural pals live — Whitmore?
- Will Tyler manage to remain a human with a werewolf gene, or will his temper lead him to kill again and re-trigger the curse?
- Without the Other Side, does Matt's resurrection ring still work?
- Grams doesn't say she *won't* pass through Bonnie to the Land of the Living, she says she *can't*. What did Grams do to ensure Bonnie's peace — and is there a plus-one for Damon? How and when will Bonnie and Damon find their way back to the Land of the Living from wherever they ended up?
- In the meantime, how the heck are Elena and Stefan and Caroline and Jeremy and the rest of the gang going to survive without Bonnie and Damon?

Julie Plec on Death in *TVD*

It wasn't hard [to destroy the Other Side] because it was time. When Kevin came up with the great gag at the end of season two — Vicki and Anna standing there and appearing before Jeremy — that was our big cliffhanger and so then in season three, we were saddled with creating the rules of why that could be possible. [laughs] And within that came the whole idea of this supernatural purgatory that Jeremy had access to, and then that kind of took on a life of its own. But that was really special for us because as we lost characters that we loved, we could have either Jeremy connect with them or have the audience privileged to see that particular ghost. I think one of the best uses of it was that great moment at the end of episode 4.02 ["Memorial"] when Damon's sitting there giving the toast to Alaric after all the funeral stuff and Alaric's sitting there, and we're able to see him and we're able to acknowledge that he's in that space.

So there were so many beautiful benefits of having something like the Other Side in our pocket; then in a weird way, it almost became like the Hellmouth. We were trying to decide if there were too many redundancies between the end of last season and this season when we were breaking early on. And I was like, "You know what, on *Buffy*, every year they try to blow up that damn Hellmouth and every year they fail, you know, until the bitter end." And so we were able to get so much great stuff out of it, and along with that, of course, came the critical issue of death not meaning anything. We knew at some point that we'd have to give death severe stakes again, and the only way to do that was to make sure the Other Side was destroyed completely, which cuts us off from a lot of loved ones. Which is why this last episode was sort of a free-for-all, 'cause, you know, when you're saying goodbye to people forever, it really makes you take stock of what it would feel like to never see them again. And then there were some that we just couldn't live without, like Alaric, hence the return.

Every time, every time I see [Jeremy running, screaming Bonnie's name], the tears just — I mean, I cry at seven different spots in that episode, but it's pretty much Elena crying her head off, Jeremy running to Bonnie, and then the final moment where I'm just like ... Each time it just gets me, I don't know why. I've seen it 50 times and it's just so powerful. And I think, for me, that goes to the whole "death has no stakes" criticism. Because I watch that stuff — like Bonnie's funeral in episode 5.04 ["For Whom the Bell Tolls"], Alaric's goodbye in "Do Not Go Gentle," and then "Home" — I know where we're going, I know what we're doing, right? And I knew Alaric would resurrect at the end of ["Do Not Go Gentle"] and be around until the end of the season, I knew that Bonnie would come back. But when you watch those moments, they're so potent and so emotional that I feel it still does give you that gut punch that you want.

And, in a way, you get to feel the cathartic release of death and then you get the cathartic joy of resurrection for a lot of these characters. So for me personally, screw the criticism because when all's said and done, I like that we had the opportunity to see these characters again. But, that being said, you can only dip into the well so often. And so, we had to blow up the well.

A lot of reporters asked me [about the finale] because I tweeted once last year that we just came up with the end of season five and it's a total mindfuck, and that was what it was. We all thought of that: we're going to destroy the Other Side and Damon's going to get caught over there . . . and nobody knows what happened to Damon and it seems like he was potentially gone for good. So it was fun to get there, you know?

In that finale, that was a true goodbye; that was a Damon and Elena true goodbye, that was the Other Side going away, that was the characters' fundamental belief that there's no way out of this. It's ultimately Elena's realization there's no way out of this.

And I think the whole next season is about trying to figure out the story, trying to figure out — where is he? How do we get him back? What form will he come back in? What happened? Will Bonnie come back with him? What is going to happen? And the beauty of it is that six months will have passed by the time we start the season again, both in our lives and the show. Our characters will have profoundly moved on. And it's not a take-back; it's a mystery, and something our characters will have to experience after they've put at least a temporary lid on their grief.

Music in Season Five
Songs by Scene

5.01 "I Know What You Did Last Summer"

1. "Unbelievers," Vampire Weekend: *Opening montage of Elena's email to Bonnie, including scenes of Damon and Elena in bed, Caroline talking to Tyler on the phone as she packs for college, Matt and Rebekah in a threesome, and Bonnie coaching Jeremy on how to reply to Elena's email.*
2. "Royals," Lorde: *Damon bids Elena goodbye as she leaves; the girls move in at Whitmore College.*
3. "Falling," Amy Stroup: *Damon and Elena talk on the phone about Megan.*
4. "Pumpin Blood," NONONO: *Rebekah finds Matt at the town square BBQ party.*
5. "Dreaming," Smallpools: *Elena and Caroline arrive at Whitmore House for the party.*
6. "Destroy," In-Flight Safety: *Damon tells Jeremy that he is no longer expelled from school.*
7. "Here We Go Again," Johnny Stinson: *Caroline and Elena leave the party, unable to enter the house. Elena leaves Megan a voicemail.*
8. "Time," The Fast Romantics: *Silas-as-Stefan and Damon discuss Katherine over a drink at the Grill.*
9. "Run Away," Cary Brothers: *Damon finds Jeremy in the middle of the road; Caroline listens to Tyler's voicemail.*

5.02 "True Lies"

1. "Don't Give Up," Ferras: *At Whitmore, Elena tells Caroline about Megan's memorial.*
2. "Better Life," Paper Route: *Caroline and Elena show up for Dr. Maxfield's applied microbiology class.*
3. "Say Now," The Rival: *Matt buys cold medicine for Katherine at the gas station.*
4. "Burn," Ellie Goulding: *Caroline and Damon arrive at the bonfire.*
5. "This Moment Now," Tyrone Wells: *Caroline and Jesse talk.*
6. "Don't Deserve You," Plumb: *Damon gives Elena Stefan's daylight ring.*

5.03 "Original Sin"

1. "Way Out," Bass Drum of Death: *Stefan enters the bar and attacks the bartender, then tells her to run.*
2. "Hello Lover," Empires: *At the Salvatore house, Damon, Elena, and Katherine prepare to follow the clues in the doppelgängers' dream.*
3. "Dear Mr. President," Fitz & The Tantrums: *On the phone with Nadia who's at the Grill, Silas reveals he doesn't trust her.*
4. "Breathing Underwater," Metric: *Elena, Damon, and Katherine drive along Route 29, looking for Jo's Bar.*
5. "Hard Times," J. Roddy Walston & The Business: *Elena and Damon encounter Nadia in the bar.*
6. "Satellite Call," Sara Bareilles: *Fireside at the Salvatore manse, Elena and Damon discuss what Qetisyah said about the fate of doppelgängers.*

5.04 "For Whom the Bell Tolls"

1. "I've Got Friends," Manchester Orchestra: *Stefan reads his journal in the car with Damon . . . before Damon crashes it.*
2. "Cards with the Devil," Von Bonneville: *At the Grill, Damon explains the bell-ringing ceremony to Stefan.*
3. "Back Against the Wall," Cage the Elephant: *Jeremy does push-ups at the Salvatore mansion.*
4. "Happy Faces," Babe Youth: *At the Grill, Elena and Damon discuss Stefan's progress.*
5. "Longest Night," Howie Day: *Elena and Stefan jump onto the Mystic Falls High School roof.*

6. "Hearts Like Ours," The Naked & Famous: *In the cemetery, Jesse quizzes Caroline on microbiology.*
7. "Gravity," Sara Bareilles: *At Wickery Bridge, Stefan and Elena come close to kissing.*
8. "Without a Word," Birdy: *The gang gathers for Bonnie's memorial.*

5.05 "Monster's Ball"

1. "You Don't Know," Brooke Annibale: *On Whitmore campus, Elena writes in her diary.*
2. "Send Him to Me," Barbara Brown: *Katherine scarfs down some diner food while Nadia tells her a tall tale about her mother.*
3. "Bad Things," Meiko: *Caroline and Tyler arrive at the Whitmore Historical Ball.*
4. "Most Wanted," Cults: *Qetsiyah arrives at the ball and heads straight for Stefan.*
5. "Never Tear Us Apart," Cary Brothers (INXS cover): *Qetisyah and Silas-as-Stefan knock back tequila shots and then dance.*
6. "Waves That Rolled You Under," Young Summer: *Elena asks Dr. Maxfield to dance.*
7. "Au Revoir," OneRepublic: *In her dorm room, Caroline gives Tyler an ultimatum, and he leaves for good.*

5.06 "Handle with Care"

1. "Bitter Rivals," Sleigh Bells: *Katherine orders all the food at the diner, celebrating the fact that she's not dead.*
2. "Elephant," Tame Impala: *Silas greets the day (and Damon and Elena), and Tessa wakes up sleepyhead Stefan who's passed out on her couch in the creepy cabin.*
3. "Shine," Wild Belle: *After dyeing out her gray, Katherine halfheartedly pretends to be Elena when Caroline comes in.*
4. "Stars," The Delta Riggs: *Elena calls Damon with the news that Stefan's with Tessa.*
5. "Keep Your Eyes Peeled," Queens of the Stone Age: *Silas, Damon, and Jeremy arrive at the warehouse in New Jersey.*
6. "The Walker," Fitz & The Tantrums: *With Dr. Maxfield tied up, Caroline calculates how much of his blood they must drain before she can compel him.*

7. "Spark," Fitz & The Tantrums: *Katherine-as-Elena crosses the threshold into Whitmore House and makes a beeline for the food table.*
8. "Coming Down," Dum Dum Girls: *Elena and Stefan arrive back at the Salvatore mansion; Damon recaps their total failure of a day to Elena.*

5.07 "Death and the Maiden"

1. "You," The Aquatones: *Silas chitchats about love with two strangers at the bus stop, then liquefies the guy's internal organs and steals his bag.*
2. "Don't Swallow the Cap," The National: *On the bus to Mystic Falls, Silas takes a call from Damon, who pleads with him to follow through on his pinky promise.*
3. "Afraid of the Dark," Ejecta: *In his bedroom, Elena tries to convince Stefan not to do anything crazy.*
4. "With Love," Christina Grimmie: *Amara dies, and Bonnie returns.*
5. "Afraid," The Neighbourhood: *Stefan buries Silas and is overcome.*

5.08 "Dead Man on Campus"

1. "Harlem," New Politics: *Bonnie records a video update for her mom, also known as "proof of life."*
2. "Bad Intentions," Digital Daggers: *At the Grill, Katherine offers to translate Matt's Czech video in exchange for booze.*
3. "Slipping Away," Barcelona: *Jesse is amazed at the healing powers of vampire blood; Katherine approaches Stefan at the Grill.*
4. "The Night Out," Martin Solveig: *The party for Bonnie kicks off.*
5. "Come a Little Closer," Cage the Elephant: *Bonnie talks to the dead witch; Jesse and Caroline dance and smooch.*
6. "All Night," Icona Pop: *Elena hands out Jell-O shots and talks to Aaron.*
7. "The Other Side," David Gray: *Stefan finds Katherine's suicide note, and Katherine jumps from the clock tower.*
8. "My My Love," Joshua Radin: *Bonnie and Jeremy "register for classes"; Jesse passes on to the Other Side.*

5.09 "The Cell"

1. "A New Pair of Shoes," Buddy Stewart: *Damon returns to Mystic Falls in 1953.*
2. "Creeplife," Deap Valley: *Katherine takes a crack at journaling.*

3. "Yes Yes," The Colourist: *Aaron and Elena talk about Jesse's "suicide" on the way to find Damon and Wes.*
4. "Walkin' After Midnight," Patsy Cline: *Damon is led back to his cell, and Enzo welcomes him. Reprises when Enzo is returned to his cell after a bout of torture; Damon asks Whitmore why he's torturing them.*
5. "Oo Wee," The Hearts: *Enzo and Damon talk about pretty ladies.*
6. "No Other One," Buddy Stewart: *Dr. Whitmore demonstrates the healing power of vampire blood at the 1957 New Year's Eve party.*
7. "A Girl Like You," Eddie Robbins: *Enzo and Damon choose who will drink the rations and gain his strength.*
8. "I Need You," Buddy Stewart: *The Whitmore Society celebrates New Year's Eve, 1958.*
9. "My Superman," Santigold: *Katherine and Stefan make out.*

5.10 "Fifty Shades of Grayson"

1. "Slave," Yeah Yeah Yeahs: *Damon breaks his way out of his cell in the basement of Whitmore House.*
2. "Fitzpleasure," Alt-J: *Katherine not-so-gracefully exits Stefan's room.*
3. "Where It Ends, Where It Begins," Sacco: *Damon and Stefan question Aaron about where Wes could be hiding Elena but get sidetracked into a doppelgänger hookup conversation.*
4. "The Love Club," Lorde: *In the forest, Matt plays trainer to Ms. Katherine Pierce.*
5. "All I Want," Kodaline: *In his bedroom, Katherine asks Stefan for a little redemption.*

5.11 "500 Years of Solitude"

1. "Love Don't Die," The Fray: *Damon and Elena deal with the morning after their breakup separately but similarly: with booze.*
2. "Come Save Me," Jagwar Ma: *In the Salvatore library, Damon outlines the rules of the Katherine Pierce Impending Death drinking game.*
3. "Illusory Light," Sarah Blasko: *As she lies dying in his bed, Stefan says goodbye to Katherine by giving her peace from the memory of the worst day of her life.*
4. "Let Her Go," Passenger: *The brothers Salvatore enjoy a bourbon on the steps outside; the gang gathers, waiting for Katherine to die.*

5.12 "The Devil Inside"

1. "Tongue Tied," Grouplove: *"Elena" approaches Matt in the town square.*
2. "21 Flights," Heavy English: *Matt looks for his phone while Tyler does morning shots.*
3. "Fa Fa Fa," Datarock: *Matt tells Tyler he's going to throw him a welcome-back party; Caroline goes on a stress-cleaning spree.*
4. "Flirting with Thieves," Heavy English: *Stefan makes his "you're a dick" face to his brother while playing pool at the Grill.*
5. "Your Body Is a Weapon," The Wombats: *"Elena" arrives at the party, and Matt invites her in; "Elena" and Stefan talk.*
6. "Thunder Clatter," Wild Cub: *Caroline confesses to "Elena" that she had sex with Klaus.*
7. "Live in This City," Dragonette: *Damon arrives at Tyler's welcome-home party and can't get in.*
8. "Bravado," Lorde: *Post-party, Tyler has an existential crisis and Matt comforts him.*
9. "Soften and Shake," Olivia Broadfield: *Stefan and Caroline have an epic friendship moment by the fire.*
10. "I'm a Man," Black Strobe: *With Enzo watching on, Damon kills Aaron in the road.*

5.13 "Total Eclipse of the Heart"

1. "Best Day of My Life," American Authors: *On campus at Whitmore, Katherine writes in her diary about how awesome she is.*
2. "Who I Belong To," Pink Frost: *At the Grill, Nadia compels Matt to forget Katherine's questions.*
3. "Lady in Waiting," U.S. Royalty: *In the Salvatore basement, Enzo and Damon question and kill Whitmore's head of campus security.*
4. "I Want It All," Jules Larson: *In their dorm room, "Elena" asks for Caroline's help choosing accessories.*
5. "It Ain't Over," The Rival: *Nadia gets a text from Katherine while drinking at the Grill.*
6. "Female Robbery," The Neighbourhood: *Tyler, Matt, and Nadia do shots.*
7. "Best Part of Me," St Leonards: *"Elena" and Stefan meet up at the Bitter Ball.*
8. "Beer Pressure," Wildcat Strike: *Tyler tells Matt that Nadia has been compelling him.*

9. "Ever Love," Beginners: *Caroline takes "Elena" to the Shredding Station.*
10. "Love Me Again," John Newman: *Bonnie and Damon arrive at the Bitter Ball.*
11. "Restart," Little Daylight: *On the phone with Nadia, Katherine makes a pros and cons list about letting Jeremy die. Well, only pros.*
12. "Background," Barcelona: *Stefan checks on "Elena" to see if she's okay.*
13. "Say Something," A Great Big World ft. Christina Aguilera: *"Elena" gets Stefan to take a sexy splinter out of her back and they bond.*

5.14 "No Exit"

1. "Radioactive," Imagine Dragons: *Enzo and Damon chitchat in a farmer's house, waiting for Farmer John to revive as a newbie vampire so Damon can feed on him.*
2. "You Belong Here," Leagues: *Stefan and "Elena" stop for gas and talk about saving Damon.*
3. "Fleur Blanche," Örsten: *Katherine showers and seduces Stefan in the motel room.*
4. "Poisonous Spider," Company: *At the diner, Nadia harshes Katherine's chipper mood by revealing that she's been bitten by Tyler Lockwood.*

5.15 "Gone Girl"

1. "Good Mistake," Mr. Little Jeans: *Bonnie and Jeremy approach Liv on campus to ask for another locator spell.*
2. "White Collar Whiskey," Emily Wolfe: *Katherine says her goodbyes. The song reprises as dead Katherine explains her very last diabolical plan to Other Side Anchor Bonnie.*

5.16 "While You Were Sleeping"

1. "Alive," Empire of the Sun: *Elena dreams of Katherine-as-Elena dancing on top of a bar.*
2. "Avant Gardener," Courtney Barnett: *At Scull, her place of employment, Liv fills up salt shakers and brags about her spell prowess to Bonnie.*
3. "Fire Breather," Laurel: *Damon and Elena break up (again) and then have shirt-ripping sex.*

5.17 "Rescue Me"

1. "Shake," The Head & the Heart: *In Damon's bedroom the morning after their sex-a-thon, Elena tries to make a quick escape while Damon suggests another round.*
2. "Weekend Warrior," Eytan and the Embassy: *Damon daydrinks at the Grill and insults Tyler and Matt, "Mystic Falls' amateur therapists."*
3. "Walking Backwards," Leagues: *Liv and Jer talk at the Grill, while Tyler tries unsuccessfully to listen in. Thanks, silencing spell!*
4. "Do I Wanna Know?" Arctic Monkeys: *In an empty hallway at Mystic Falls High, Damon tells Elena how he'd make minivan-driving eavesdroppers jealous.*
5. "Girls Chase Boys," Ingrid Michaelson: *At the diner, Tom eats waffles like he's been trapped in a basement subsisting on an IV drip for four months, while Caroline explains what's been going on.*
6. "Far From Yesterday," Amy Stroup: *Caroline and Stefan have the perfect end-of-a-bad-day conversation in the junkyard minivan; Elena asks Damon to let her go, and he does.*

5.18 "Resident Evil"

1. "Mad World," Sara Hickman (Tears for Fears cover): *In the opening fantasy sequence, Elena meets Stefan after he catches a page that flutters away after she tears it out of her journal.*
2. "Woman," Wolfmother: *Damon and Enzo play pool at the Salvatore mansion as Enzo recaps the previous episode.*
3. "Warm / Happy," The Lonely Forest: *At the Grill, Elena and Caroline talk about Elena's super-intense Stefan dreams.*
4. "It Was Blue," Angus Stone: *Liv makes Tyler and Matt stab themselves with the Traveler knife.*
5. "Kids," The New Division: *Elena tries to get ahold of Damon, but he screens her call. Caroline gets through to Enzo. Temptation: one!*
6. "Outro," M83: *In Damon's bedroom, Elena tells him that unlike the visions of the perfect life, what they have is real, if messy and complicated, and he rejects her offer to be friends.*

5.19 "Man on Fire"

1. "Be What You Be," Angus Stone: *Stefan helps Elena study over coffee and ignored bagels.*
2. "Breathless," U.S. Royalty: *Bonnie asks Liv how to fix the imploding supernatural purgatory.*
3. "Locked in a Cage," Brick & Mortar: *Enzo drinks, as he has mini flashbacks of his halcyon moments with Maggie while he was . . . locked in a cage.*
4. "Ninety Nine Pounds of Dynamite," Buddy Stewart: *Election night in Mystic Falls, 1960.*
5. "Poor Little Girl," Buddy Stewart: *After compelling Maggie, Enzo gives her back her vervain bracelet.*
6. "Starlight," Johnny Angel: *Damon meets up with Maggie James on election night.*

5.20 "What Lies Beneath"

1. "River," together PANGEA: *Damon makes cocktails while Caroline brainstorms secrets people think they're getting away with.*
2. "Turn It Around," Lucius: *Team Stelena dominates charades.*
3. "Chemical," Kerli: *Damon and Elena talk about how feelings can be confusing, then they kiss.*

5.21 "Promised Land"

1. "Torture," Rival Sons: *Stefan collect-calls Damon from a derelict gas station.*
2. "The Truth in You," The Garden District: *Walking down the country road, Elena and Stefan talk about the nature of vampirism.*
3. "Cherry Licorice," The Felice Brothers: *Luke and Liv discuss their angry coven at the diner.*
4. "Bad Blood," Bastille: *Elena asks herself What Would Caroline Do? and then rearranges her bosom before flagging down a car.*
5. "Future Bolt," Hotpipes: *Damon and Markos sass each other; Julian suggests Damon use him for a surprise attack on Markos.*
6. "I'll Be Honest," The Privates: *Elena and Stefan rush into the Grill after their daylight rings stop working.*
7. "Don't Let Me Go," RAIGN: *Stefan passes through Bonnie to the Other Side.*

5.22 "Home"

1. "No Rest for the Wicked," Lykke Li: *Lexi and Stefan pop by the Grill (Other Side edition) looking for fellow ghost Alaric.*
2. "Walking," Ash Grunwald: *As the Travelers party at the Grill, Markos blocks Liz from leaving.*
3. "Love Is Just a Way to Die," I Am Strikes: *Damon tells Elena that Project Kaboom requires him to go kaboom.*
4. "Buried Alive," Yeah Yeah Yeahs ft. Dr. Octagon: *At the Grill, Markos and Liz have an awkward hang.*
5. "Finished Sympathy," Glasvegas: *The only time it's okay to drink then drive: Damon knocks back a few, then gets in his car ready to drive into Mystic Falls and certain death. Elena joins him.*
6. "Be Alright," Lucy Rose: *Damon says goodbye to Elena.*
7. "Wings," Birdy: *Jeremy runs to Bonnie. Bonnie and Damon stand together as the Other Side goes down.*

The Vampire Diaries Timeline

Though the writers make no attempt to keep a strict timeline, especially with the present-day events, here is the *TVD* timeline is all its messy glory. ● indicates a full moon.

In the Beginning . . .

c. 10 CE — In Ancient Greece, Silas becomes immortal along with his lady-love Amara, having stolen the immortality elixir meant to be consumed at Silas's wedding to Qetsiyah. Qetsiyah creates the Other Side and the Cure and entombs Silas. ("Down the Rabbit Hole," "After School Special," "Original Sin," "Handle with Care") Nature creates doppelgängers of Silas and Amara to restore balance ("Original Sin"). Witches put a curse on the Travelers so that if they try to settle down as a people they will be plagued and forced to move on ("Resident Evil," "Man on Fire"). Liv says her coven of witches has been tracking the Travelers for "thousands" of years ("Resident Evil").

c. 510 CE — Markos casts a spell on doppelgängers, drawing them together with the promise of "true love." It's unclear when Markos dies and goes to the Other Side but he has been dead for "centuries." ("Resident Evil")

The Origin of the Species

c. 975?–1000 — Esther and Mikael lose their first child to a plague, travel to the New World, and live in peace as they raise their six children ("Ordinary People").

c. 1000 ● — Henrik is killed by a werewolf ("Ordinary People").

c. 1000, shortly thereafter — Esther turns her remaining children and Mikael into vampires and places the hybrid-binding curse on Klaus. The white oak tree is burned. Klaus kills Esther; Ayana preserves Esther's body with magic. Klaus and Elijah begin faking documents that tell about the curse of the Sun and Moon. At some point in this era, the "witches," perhaps Ayana, create the daggers that can put an Original into a death-like state when coated in the oak's ash. ("Klaus," "Ordinary People")

Between c. 1000–1114 — At some point while still in what would become Mystic Falls, Finn and Sage fall in love and he turns her ("The Murder of One"); the Original siblings go back to the Old World ("Ordinary People," "All My Children").

1110 — A "dying witch" creates the Brotherhood of the Five, at the behest of Qetsiyah; the hunters spend four years translating their own tattoos and killing vampires ("The Five").

1114 — Klaus slaughters the Five after they dagger all of his Original siblings; Rebekah buries Alexander along with his sword ("The Five").

Shortly thereafter — Klaus daggers Finn ("Bringing Out the Dead"), who spends 900 years in a coffin. Interestingly, Klaus daggers his first sibling while suffering from the torment of five simultaneous Hunters' Curses.

1166–7 — Klaus's Hunters' Curses break, after 52 years, 4 months, and 9 days, suggesting there were no active hunters from 1114 until this point ("We All Go a Little Mad Sometimes").

Dark Ages — Vampires punish those who threaten to expose their kind with 50 years in solitary confinement, according to Stefan ("You're Undead to Me").

1300s — Kol "runs with witches" in Africa ("A View to a Kill").

The 1400s–1700s

c. 1400 — Calendar markings on the cave wall under Mystic Falls indicate a white oak tree grew in the town and was a spot for worship for the native people ("All My Children").

1400s — According to Vanessa, the Sun and the Moon Curse dates back 600 years to when the Aztecs were being plagued by vampires and werewolves ("Bad Moon Rising"); later Elijah reveals to Elena that the historical documents were fakes ("Klaus").

1450 — Rose is born ("The Descent").

1464? — Pearl becomes a vampire; she has "400 years on" Damon who is not turned until 1864 ("There Goes the Neighborhood"). Presumably, Anna also becomes a vampire around this time.

June 5, 1473 — Katerina Petrova's birthdate ("Because the Night").

1473–1490 — Katerina's father, a Traveler, forbids his family from practising the "devil's work" a.k.a. magic ("Fifty Shades of Grayson").

1490 — Katerina Petrova gives birth to a baby girl, Nadia, who is taken from her ("Katerina," "Monster's Ball").

1492 — In England, Katerina meets Klaus at his birthday celebration; she and Elijah spend time together ("Klaus").

April 6, 1492, Night before the sacrifice — Katerina escapes and becomes a vampire; Trevor and Rose begin running from the Originals ("Katerina," "Rose," "Monster's Ball").

1498 — Katerina discovers that her entire family has been killed by Klaus ("Katerina," "Monster's Ball").

1515? — Nadia becomes a vampire so she can hunt down her mother ("Monster's Ball").

1520 — Nadia is in Northern Europe knocking on doors trying to find Katerina Petrova ("Gone Girl").

1600s — Kol "runs with witches" in Haiti ("A View to a Kill").

1659? — Lexi is born; she lives to be 350 years old ("162 Candles").

1692 — The Bennett family moves from Salem to Mystic Falls ("Haunted"). They are among a larger group of settlers who moved to the area to flee persecution ("The Dinner Party").

1700s? — A few hundred years prior to present-day events, Kol runs into a group of Silas worshippers and kills them ("Catch Me If You Can").

1700s — Klaus helps build up New Orleans from a "backwater penal colony" ("The Originals").

Winter 1720 — Nadia Petrova is in France, following up on a rumor that Katherine killed a man outside Versailles ("Gone Girl").

1755 — The Saltzman family comes to America from Germany ("History Repeating").

1790? — A hundred witches are rounded up and burned at the stake in Mystic Falls ("The Dinner Party").

1792 — Mystic Falls cemetery is established ("Pilot").

The Rise of the Salvatores

October 9, 1810 — Giuseppe Salvatore is born ("Children of the Damned").

1820s/1830s — A cholera outbreak in Mystic Falls gives rise to the bell-ringing holiday of Remembrance Day ("For Whom the Bell Tolls").

1821 — Honoria Fell is born ("For Whom the Bell Tolls").

1839 — Damon is born ("Home").

Early November 1847 — Stefan Salvatore is born ("Lost Girls," "162 Candles").

October 1852 — Damon breaks Stefan's nose trying to teach him how to throw a right hook ("Death and the Maiden").

1860 — The town of Mystic Falls is founded ("Under Control"); the town jail is built, with a special cell for vampires ("Disturbing Behavior").

1861–1865 — The American Civil War. At some point in this era, Giuseppe Salvatore impregnates a maid, who bears him a child; the child carries on the Salvatore name after Stefan's and Damon's human deaths, despite being illegitimate ("1912"). Whitmore College is established initially as a Civil War hospital ("True Lies").

January 23, 1864 — According to his tombstone, Giuseppe Salvatore dies ("Children of the Damned"). This date conflicts with many other details in the timeline and is likely a production error.

April 1864 — According to Vanessa (and Isobel's research), Katherine arrives in Mystic Falls ("Bad Moon Rising") but see September for conflicting detail.

June 1864 — Johnathan Gilbert begins writing the journal that Jeremy finds ("History Repeating").

September 1, 1864 — The beginning of the Atlanta Campaign fires, which Katherine uses as a cover story ("Children of the Damned"). Presumably, Katherine arrives at the Salvatore estate shortly thereafter. This date conflicts with Isobel's research ("Bad Moon Rising").

September 24, 1864 — The first Founders' Ball is held ("Family Ties"). Katherine confronts George Lockwood at the ball ("Memory Lane"). Damon is rebuffed when he visits Katherine in her bedroom after the ball; Stefan has just professed his love for Katherine ("Memory Lane"). Some time soon after the ball, Katherine reveals to Stefan that she is a vampire ("Lost Girls").

1864 — A comet passes over Mystic Falls ("The Night of the Comet").

The Battle of Willow Creek / The Vampire Purge — Mr. Tanner says that the Battle of Willow Creek took place in 1865 ("Pilot"), but the flashbacks suggest it was actually in late 1864. On the day of the battle, Katherine meets with George Lockwood to go over their plan to fake her death ("Memory Lane"). Damon is also with Katherine at some point on that day and sees her in possession of Emily's crystal ("History Repeating"). Stefan speaks to his father about the vampire situation and unwittingly drinks vervain, which leads to Katherine's capture ("Children of the Damned"). Damon makes a bargain with Emily for Katherine's safety ("History Repeating"). Stefan and Damon are shot trying to rescue Katherine ("Family Ties," "Blood Brothers"). Either one or both of the brothers watch the church burn ("History Repeating" conflicts with "Blood Brothers" on this detail). Before Katherine leaves Mystic Falls, having been released from the church before it was set afire, she gives George Lockwood the moonstone and she sweetly promises (the then-dead) Stefan that they'll be together again ("Memory Lane").

The day after the Battle of Willow Creek — Emily gives the Salvatore brothers their rings; Stefan confronts his father and inadvertently kills him; Damon promises Stefan an eternity of misery ("Blood Brothers").

Shortly thereafter, 1864 — Stefan kills Thomas and Honoria Fell, and Johnathan Gilbert (temporarily); Stefan meets Alexia Branson (a.k.a. Lexi); Damon leaves Stefan in Lexi's care ("The Dinner Party").

1865 — Damon "made sure" vervain won't grow in Mystic Falls ("Family Ties").

Sometime thereafter — Katherine surreptitiously lets the founders know that Emily Bennett is a witch, and she is killed ("The House Guest"). Somehow, Emily's grimoire ends up buried with Giuseppe Salvatore despite the timeline problem ("Children of the Damned").

Sometime thereafter — The Salvatore crypt is built sometime after Giuseppe's burial but before Zachariah Salvatore's murder ("Children of the Damned," "1912").

April 15, 1884 — According to her tombstone, Bonnie's ancestor Marie Bennett is born ("Home").

The 20th Century

1900s — Kol "runs with witches" in New Orleans ("A View to a Kill").

1900? — The Salvatore boarding house is built ("Lost Girls").

July 2, 1910 — Construction begins on Wickery Bridge ("Break on Through").

c. 1910 — Klaus daggers Kol ("Bringing Out the Dead").

1911? — Lexi tries to set up Rose on a date with Stefan ("Rose").

1912 — The brothers see each other for the first time since 1864 for their nephew Zachariah Salvatore's funeral. Samantha Gilbert murdered him as well as another councilman. Sage teaches Damon to seek pleasure in killing. Stefan lets the ripper out. ("1912") The white oak tree is used to build Wickery Bridge ("Break on Through").

February 11, 1912 — Construction of Wickery Bridge is completed ("Break on Through").

1917 — Stefan slaughters a migrant village in Monterey ("As I Lay Dying").

December 4, 1919 — Mikael runs Klaus out of New Orleans ("The Originals," *The Originals*' "Le Grand Guignol").

1922 — Samantha Gilbert confesses to her murders and is put in an asylum, where she kills a nurse, a guard, and eventually herself ("1912," "Break on Through").

March 12, 1922 — Stefan is in Chicago and writes in his diary about meeting a woman, presumably Rebekah ("The End of the Affair").

April 1922 — Stefan records in his diary that Lexi found him and is trying to help him again ("The End of the Affair").

June 1924 — According to his diary, Stefan is back feeding on animal blood after his ripper stint ("The End of the Affair").

1935 — Stefan is managing his cravings, and Lexi's project is to get him to laugh ("The End of the Affair").

1942 — The start date for Anna's research into vampire attacks in the Mystic Falls area ("Bloodlines"). Damon, in New Orleans with Charlotte, gets a visit from his brother and Lexi; Damon kills 12 people in the hopes of breaking Charlotte's sire bond; Stefan leaves to serve in World War II, while Damon stays behind at Lexi's behest ("We'll Always Have Bourbon Street").

The Augustine Years

1943 — World War II field hospital doctor Whitmore discovers that soldier Enzo is a vampire, captures him, and brings him back from Europe to conduct experiments on him ("The Cell"). According to her tombstone, Bonnie's ancestor Marie Bennett dies ("Home").

1950s — Marcel studies law ("The Originals").

1950 — Compelled by Enzo, Maggie James quits her job as an observer at the Augustine Society ("Man on Fire").

June 10, 1951 — Maggie writes in her journal about having a job at a preschool ("Man on Fire").

1952 — After 30 years of Lexi's help, Stefan finally begins to feel like himself ("The End of the Affair").

March 1953 — Maggie writes in her journal about not finding love ("Man on Fire").

Early June 1953 — Joseph Salvatore telegrams his vampire relations — Stefan and Damon — to summon them to Mystic Falls with the intent of passing them over to the Augustine Society ("The Cell").

June 11, 1953 — Damon kills Joseph Salvatore; Damon is captured by the Augustine Society's Dr. Whitmore, beginning five years of imprisonment and torture ("The Cell").

June 12, 1953 — "Uncle" Joseph Salvatore is found dead at the Salvatore boarding house; Stefan is caught on camera outside the house by the local news station ("Family Ties," "You're Undead to Me").

1953 — Four people are killed in "animal attacks" in Mystic Falls ("Bloodlines"); since Damon is imprisoned at this time, he's not the vampire responsible ("The Cell").

April 2, 1954 — The first restoration of Wickery Bridge begins, according to the preservation society's sign ("Break on Through").

December 31, 1956 — Dr. Whitmore shows his gathered guests the healing properties of vampire blood with a demonstration on Mrs. Fell; Enzo hatches his escape plan with Damon ("The Cell").

December 31, 1957 — Damon escapes the Augustines, leaving Enzo to die in a fire (which he survives); Damon turns his emotions off ("The Cell").

1958 — Maggie James finds a box with medical journals from 1950, detailing patient 121444, Enzo ("Man on Fire").

Sometime shortly thereafter — Maggie returns to Whitmore and believes Enzo died in the fire; she spends the next two years searching for Damon ("Man on Fire").

November 8, 1960 — Damon kills Maggie ("Man on Fire").

November 9, 1960 — Maggie's death is reported as a mugging turned fatal ("Man on Fire").

1962 — Five people are killed in "animal attacks" in Mystic Falls ("Bloodlines").

October 1969 — Stefan meets Sheila Bennett at an antiwar demonstration ("Bloodlines").

August 16, 1972 — Abby Bennett is born, according to the document from the DMV ("The Ties That Bind").

1974 — Three people are killed in "animal attacks" in Mystic Falls ("Bloodlines"). Slater is made a vampire and begins accumulating college degrees ("Katerina").

October 17, 1975 / January 18, 1978 — Isobel Flemming is born: the earlier date is on her driver's license ("A Few Good Men"), the later one on her tombstone ("Know Thy Enemy").

February 4, 1976 — Alaric Saltzman is born ("Break on Through").

1977 — Damon is enjoying himself in New York, Lexi spends six months with him trying to get him to flip his emotions back on; Stefan is in Mystic Falls at the time ("Because the Night").

1980s — Elizabeth Forbes and Kelly Donovan go to high school together ("Lost Girls"); Kelly Donovan and Miranda Sommers are best friends ("There Goes the Neighborhood"). Miranda is also best friends with Abby Bennett ("The Ties That Bind") and Liz Forbes ("Bring It On").

1983 — Anna sees Katherine in Chicago ("Fool Me Once").

Late 1980s? — Liz Forbes and Logan Fell have known each other since he was six ("The Turning Point"). Kelly Donovan babysits Jenna Sommers ("There Goes the Neighborhood").

Spring 1987 — Lexi and Stefan attend a Bon Jovi concert; Katherine stalks Stefan ("Masquerade").

1989? — Damon meets Bree and asks for her help getting into the tomb ("Bloodlines").

August 20, 1991? — Vicki Donovan is born ("Lost Girls").

Early to mid 1990s — Jenna Sommers and Mason Lockwood attend high school together, along with Logan Fell ("Memory Lane").

1992? — Megan King is born ("Fifty Shades of Grayson").

1993? — Isobel leaves her hometown of Grove Hill; Elena is born in late August/early September ("A Few Good Men," "The Birthday"), but Elena's birthday is later specifically stated to be June 22 ("The Devil Inside"). Caroline is born in the fall ("Our Town"), and Bonnie in the spring ("Gone Girl").

1994 — Stefan and Damon see each other for the last time before fall 2009 ("Pilot").

March 14, 1994 — Aimee Bradley is born ("Rose").

October 13, 1994 — Jeremy Gilbert is born ("The Night of the Comet," "The Devil Inside").

1996 — Abby lures Mikael away from Mystic Falls, entombs him in a Charlotte cemetery, and stays in North Carolina ("The Reckoning," "The Ties That Bind"). The Augustines (perhaps Dr. Gilbert) experiment on

Enzo's ability to stay conscious after having blood drawn; he passes out after 2.9 pints ("Fifty Shades of Grayson").

Late 1990s — Logan babysits Caroline ("The Turning Point"); Pastor Young teaches first-grader Tyler Lockwood the importance of teamwork and community ("Memorial"). Six-year-old Aaron Whitmore loses his parents, thanks to Damon's vengeance scheme; Wes Maxfield finds the bodies and joins the Augustine Society ("Dead Man on Campus," "Fifty Shades of Grayson").

January 1999 — Dr. Grayson Gilbert gives seven-year-old Megan King vampire blood to cure her terminal heart condition ("Fifty Shades of Grayson").

June 25, 1999 — Dr. Gilbert notes in his journal that he subjected a vampire to 3,000 volts of electricity ("Fifty Shades of Grayson").

June 26, 1999 — Dr. Gilbert's notes indicate he bumped that voltage up to 4,000 volts ("Fifty Shades of Grayson").

The 2000s

2000? — Caroline demonstrates her control freakiness while building a Barbie castle with Elena in the second grade ("Promised Land").

Pre-2003 — Caroline and Elena visit the family's cabin with Bill and Liz Forbes; Bill tells excellent ghost stories ("What Lies Beneath").

2003? — Ten-year-old Tyler sees his uncle Mason; he doesn't see him again until after Mayor Lockwood's death ("The Return"); Caroline's parents split up ("Bringing Out the Dead").

May 4, 2007 — The date of "death" on Isobel's tombstone ("Know Thy Enemy"); presumably her parents chose the date she disappeared, which conflicts with the timeline established in "Blood Brothers" that suggested Damon turned Isobel in 2008.

2007? — To prevent the humiliation of her son flunking out of eighth grade, Carol Lockwood writes Tyler's English essay for him ("Total Eclipse of the Heart").

2007/2009? — Elena babysits April Young ("Growing Pains").

May 23, 2009 — Elena meets Damon, but he compels her to forget their encounter ("The Departed"). Grayson and Miranda Gilbert die in a car accident ("Pilot"); Stefan rescues Elena ("Bloodlines").

A few days later, 2009 — At the Gilberts' funeral, Elena sees April for the last time before the events of "Memorial."

Summer 2009 — In Mystic Falls, Stefan observes Elena and investigates her family history ("Bloodlines"). Matt and Bonnie work as lifeguards together ("The Reckoning").

August 2009 — Katherine compels a guy to attack Mason; Mason kills him, which triggers his curse ("Kill or Be Killed").

August 31, 2009 — Mason writes in his journal about how different he's felt since killing the guy who attacked him ("The Sacrifice").

Season One Begins

September 6, 2009 —Damon kills a couple who are driving home from a concert ("Pilot").

September 7, 2009 — First day of school at Mystic Falls High ("Pilot").

September 8, 2009 — Damon attacks Vicki during the party by the falls ("Pilot").

September 9, 2009 — The comet passes over Mystic Falls ("The Night of the Comet").

September 10, 2009 — Caroline wakes up with Damon; Stefan tries out for the school football team; Caroline and Damon crash Elena's dinner party with Bonnie and Stefan ("Friday Night Bites").

September 11, 2009 — Stefan gives Elena the vervain-filled necklace; Damon kills Coach Tanner ("Friday Night Bites"). (This date actually *was* a Friday.)

September 15, 2009 ● — Mason turns into a wolf for the first time ("The Sacrifice").

September 24?, 2009 — The Founders' Ball is held; the date here is based on the original Founders' Ball, which was held on the 24th. Stefan captures Damon and locks him in the cellar ("Family Ties").

September 27?, 2009 — Three days after leaving Elena a cryptic voicemail message, Stefan tries to fix their relationship by making dinner for her ("You're Undead to Me").

September 28?, 2009 — The Sexy Suds Car Wash is held at the high school; Damon attacks Vicki and kills her friends; Elena figures out that Stefan is a vampire; Stefan asks her to keep his secret ("You're Undead to Me," "Lost Girls").

September 29?, 2009 — Damon turns Vicki into a vampire; Logan is killed ("Lost Girls").

October 31, 2009 — In terms of plot, only a few days pass between "Lost Girls" and "Haunted," but "Haunted" takesplace on (or near) Halloween. Vicki is staked by Stefan and dies ("Haunted").

Early November 2009 — Bonnie reveals her powers to Elena; Stefan turns 162; Damon kills Lexi ("162 Candles").

Mid-November? 2009 — Emily possesses Bonnie and destroys the crystal; Logan returns, now a vampire. Stefan has been asking Damon for "months" why he returned to Mystic Falls; Alaric mentions to Jeremy that they are halfway through the school semester ("History Repeating").

The following day ● — With a full moon overhead, it's Career Night at Mystic Falls High School; Elena and Stefan have sex for the first time; she discovers the portrait of Katherine; Noah causes Elena to crash her car ("The Turning Point"). Damon rescues her from the car wreck ("Bloodlines").

The following day — Damon takes Elena to Atlanta to visit Bree; Bonnie falls into the tomb and Stefan rescues her ("Bloodlines").

The following day — Elena arrives back in Mystic Falls, and Stefan reveals that he rescued her from the car crash that killed her parents in May and that she is adopted ("Bloodlines").

December? 2009 — The 1950s Decade Dance is held at the high school; Caroline passes a Christmas display in a store window ("Unpleasantville").

Shortly thereafter — Stefan unearths the grimoire that was buried with his father; both Elena and Bonnie are kidnapped by Ben the Bartender, working for Anna ("Children of the Damned").

The following day — The tomb opens; "Duke from Duke" throws a party at the old cemetery where people are wearing winter coats and hats; Sheila Bennett dies ("Fool Me Once").

Christmastime, 2009 — Jenna takes Jeremy and Elena to celebrate the holidays at the lakehouse ("O Come, All Ye Faithful"); this detail conflicts with Elena's assertion in "Crying Wolf " that it is her "first time" back to the lakehouse since her parents died.

Winter 2010 — An ill-fated hiker tells a tomb vampire named Harper the year; the Bachelor Auction is held at the Grill ("A Few Good Men").

Sometime thereafter — Vicki's body is found ("Let the Right One In").

One month before Founders' Day ● — Johnathan Gilbert returns to Mystic Falls; the Kickoff to Founders' Day party is held on the night of a full moon; Stefan gives in and drinks human blood ("Under Control").

Three weeks or so before Founders' Day — Bonnie returns to Mystic Falls; the Miss Mystic Falls competition is held; Elena and Damon lock up a blood-drunk Stefan ("Miss Mystic Falls").

A few days later — Stefan refuses to eat; Elena convinces him not to commit suicide; Isobel shows up at the Grill ("Blood Brothers").

The following day — The Mystic Falls High students prepare floats for Founders' Day; Elena meets her birth mother, Isobel ("Isobel").

The following day — Isobel gets the Gilbert invention from Elena and gives it to Uncle John ("Isobel").

Founders' Day — The tomb vampires, Anna, and Mayor Lockwood are killed; Tyler, Matt, and Caroline are in a car accident; Katherine impersonates Elena, kisses Damon, and attacks Uncle John ("Founder's Day").

Season Two Events

The following day — Mason returns to Mystic Falls for his brother's wake; that night, Damon "kills" Jeremy and Katherine "kills" Caroline ("The Return").

The following day — Caroline completes her transition to vampirism; the school hosts a carnival ("Brave New World").

Full Moon ● — Alaric, Damon, and Elena go to Duke University. Caroline gets a daylight ring from Bonnie. Mason turns into a werewolf. Tyler discovers the Lockwood secret. ("Bad Moon Rising")

The following day — Caroline wakes up to find Katherine in her bedroom ("Bad Moon Rising").

The following day — (Assuming this is not the same day that Katherine wakes up Caroline in her bedroom, because Katherine's wearing a different outfit when she shows up at the Salvatore boarding house.) Jenna hosts a barbecue; Katherine reveals to Stefan the real story behind the Vampire Purge of 1864 ("Memory Lane").

August 2010 / The following day — The day of the Historical Society Volunteer Picnic; that night, Sheriff Forbes is put in the Salvatore holding cell until the vervain is out of her system ("Kill or Be Killed"). The flashback to "one year ago" in "Kill or Be Killed" is later revealed to have taken place in August 2009 ("The Sacrifice"), meaning the present-day events take place in August 2010. (The timeline is later muddled, because "The Birthday" also takes place in August or early September 2010, a year after the events of the pilot episode.)

Three days later — It takes three days for the vervain to leave Liz's system ("Kill or Be Killed"). The gang sets up for the masquerade ball. Mason is tortured and killed by Damon. ("Plan B")

Masquerade Ball — Katherine kills Aimee; Tyler triggers the werewolf curse by accidentally killing Sarah; Katherine is captured and put in the tomb; Elena is kidnapped by a man compelled by Rose and Trevor ("Masquerade").

The following day — Elijah arrives and kills Trevor; Damon and Stefan rescue Elena ("Rose").

The following day — The Martins arrive in Mystic Falls; Elena visits Katherine at the tomb; Rose and Damon visit Slater; Elijah compels Slater to kill himself ("Katerina"). It's not clear how many days, if any, pass between "Katerina" and "The Sacrifice," but since Slater's body is still undiscovered in "The Sacrifice" it's safe to assume the timeline is contiguous.

That night — Late at night, Jonas steals various artifacts from Elena's room ("The Sacrifice").

The following day — Jeremy manages to get the moonstone out of the tomb; Stefan is stuck in the tomb with Katherine; Elijah kills three vampires ("The Sacrifice").

The following day — Tyler calls Mason as he gets ready for the full moon ("By the Light of the Moon"). (Assuming this is a separate day since he's wearing a different shirt than in "The Sacrifice.")

Full Moon ● — Tyler makes his first transformation. Rose is bitten by Jules. ("By the Light of the Moon")

The following day — Jules wakes up in a campground bloodbath; Rose dies ("The Descent").

The following day — The werewolves kidnap and torture Caroline ("Daddy Issues").

The following day — Stefan and Elena go to the lakehouse. Tyler leaves town with Jules. ("Crying Wolf")

The following day — (Assuming it's the next day, since news of Tyler's departure is just spreading.) Elijah is killed (twice). Katherine is freed from the tomb. ("The Dinner Party")

The following day — The Grill burns down; Luka and Jonas Martin are killed ("The House Guest"). Jenna meets Isobel ("Know Thy Enemy").

The following day — Under Klaus's compulsion, Isobel kills herself; Katherine is kidnapped; Alaric is possessed by Klaus ("Know Thy Enemy").

The 1960s Decade Dance — Bonnie fakes her death to fool Klaus; later that night, Elena takes the dagger out of Elijah ("The Last Dance").

The following day — Elena spends the day with the newly resurrected Elijah, learning the true curse ("Klaus").

The Sacrifice ● — Damon force-feeds Elena his blood; Stefan and Elena go for a climb by the falls; Damon gets bitten by Tyler ("The Last Day"). Klaus breaks the curse, killing Jenna, Jules, and Elena, and transforming into a true werewolf-vampire hybrid ("The Sun Also Rises").

Next morning — Elena and Jeremy bury Jenna and John ("The Sun Also Rises").

The following day — Klaus daggers Elijah. Jeremy dies but Bonnie resurrects him. Stefan gives himself over to Klaus. ("As I Lay Dying")

By moon cycles, it is two months from Founders' Day to the events of the finale. By time markers within episodes, it is only 26 days.

Season Three Events

Summer — Klaus and Stefan chase werewolves (and kill tons of people), while Elena and Damon track them ("The Birthday").

Day 1 of season three timeline | late August/early September 2010 — Two months after the events of "As I Lay Dying," Elena turns 18; Stefan kills Andie Star ("The Birthday").

Day 2 ● — Elena, Alaric, and Damon track down Stefan in the Smoky Mountains; Klaus's hybrid experiment fails ("The Hybrid").

Day 3 — Caroline is tortured by her father; Elena and Damon go to Chicago; Rebekah is awakened ("The End of the Affair").

Day 4 — In Chicago, Katherine kills Gloria to save Stefan; Damon attacks both Alaric and Bill Forbes at the barbecue at the Lockwoods' house ("Disturbing Behavior").

Day 5 — Bill Forbes leaves town; Damon and Katherine go on a road trip; Klaus drags Stefan back to Mystic Falls ("Disturbing Behavior"). That night, Tyler is turned into a hybrid, Stefan is forced to flip the switch, and Katherine and Jeremy locate Mikael ("The Reckoning").

Day 6 and 7 — Katherine tries to revive Mikael but he is unresponsive ("Smells Like Teen Spirit").

Day 8 — The first day of school, established as one year after the events of the pilot (which took place on September 7, 2009). Vicki tries to kill Elena at the Spirit Squad bonfire; Bonnie's magic is used to open the door to this side for the ghosts. ("Smells Like Teen Spirit")

Day 9 — The Night of Illumination ("Ghost World").

Day 10 — Elena learns the Original family history from Rebekah; Mikael confronts Stefan and Damon ("Ordinary People").

Day 11 — As part of their plot to fool Klaus, Elena stakes Mikael; Klaus leaves Portland to return to Mystic Falls ("Homecoming").

Homecoming — Rebekah is daggered; Mikael is killed ("Homecoming").

Day 13 — Klaus discovers that his coffins are missing ("Homecoming").

Day 16? — Sunday, likely the one directly following Homecoming Friday. Alaric is run over by a hybrid-driven car while saving Jeremy; Stefan enlists Bonnie to help him hide the coffins ("The New Deal").

Day 17 — Caroline turns 18; a fundraiser for the Wickery Bridge revitalization is held at the Lockwoods' ("Our Town").

Day 18 — Jeremy leaves Mystic Falls for Denver; Brian Walters is found dead ("Our Town").

Day 19 — Bonnie tracks down her mom; Damon undaggers Elijah ("The Ties That Bind").

Day 20 — Bill Forbes refuses to transition and dies; Kol, Finn, Rebekah, and Esther are resurrected ("Bringing Out the Dead").

Day 21 — The Mikaelson family holds a ball ("Dangerous Liaisons").

Day 22 — Esther tries to kill her family; Abby is turned into a vampire ("All My Children").

Day 23 — Alaric spends the day in jail; they realize he is the Mystic Falls Murderer ("1912").

Several days later — Damon, Sage, and Rebekah manipulate each other; Alaric attacks Meredith ("Break on Through").

Next day — Abby leaves Jamie and Bonnie ("Break on Through").

Next day — Bonnie breaks the "united as one" spell; Matt kills Finn; Rebekah tortures Damon ("The Murder of One"). Damon and Elena leave for Denver ("Heart of Darkness").

Next day — Tyler returns; Esther possesses Rebekah ("Heart of Darkness").

Next day — The 1920s Decade Dance; Alaric is turned into a super-vamp ("Do Not Go Gentle").

Next day — Alaric terrorizes the gang; Klaus is desiccated ("Before Sunset"). Late that same night, Elena dies and Alaric along with her ("The Departed").

By time markers within episodes, it is approximately 31 days between "The Birthday" and "The Departed."

Season Four Events

One year prior to season four — Pastor Young teaches a theology course at Whitmore College and meets Professor Shane ("We All Go a Little Mad Sometimes"). Shane visits the island where Silas is entombed ("Into the Wild").

Three weeks prior to Day 1 — Shane says that Silas's tombstone is donated to Whitmore College ("We All Go a Little Mad Sometimes").

Day 1 | Morning after Elena dies — Pastor Young and the council take over the town (basically), and Elena becomes a vampire ("Growing Pains").

Day 2 — Shane and Young call each other frequently ("We All Go a Little Mad Sometimes"). The Young farm explodes ("Growing Pains"); Stefan and Elena leave for a learn-to-feed-on-Bambi camping trip ("Memorial").

Day 3 — News of the Young farm explosion hits the newspapers; Stefan and Elena return, and Connor Jordan arrives in town ("Memorial").

Day 4 — The memorial for the 12 dead is held ("Memorial").

Day 5 — Elena returns to school; Rebekah throws a party ("The Rager").

Day 6 — Connor is held prisoner by Klaus; Damon, Elena, and Bonnie go to Whitmore College for the day; Stefan learns about Elena's sire bond to Damon ("The Five").

Day 7, Sunday? — Connor takes hostages at the Mystic Grill in an attempt to lure and kill vampires; Klaus excavates Alexander's sword; Elena kills Connor ("The Killer").

Day 8 — Elena suffers from the Hunter's Curse and nearly kills herself; Jeremy activates his hunter status by killing the hybrid Chris ("We All Go a Little Mad Sometimes").

Day 9 — Elena wakes up free from the Hunter's Curse; Stefan and Elena break up ("We All Go a Little Mad Sometimes").

Day 10 — Caroline organizes the gang (and a guest-star Olympic athlete) to help set up on the day before the Miss Mystic Falls competition ("My Brother's Keeper").

Day 11 — At Miss Mystic Falls, Jeremy tries to kill his sister; Elena and Damon sleep together ("My Brother's Keeper").

Day 12 — Damon and Stefan go to New Orleans; Elena finds out she is sired to Damon ("We'll Always Have Bourbon Street").

Day 13 — Damon and Stefan return; Damon and Elena discuss the sire bond ("We'll Always Have Bourbon Street").

Day 14 | December 2010 — At the Winter Wonderland event, Klaus slaughters 12 hybrids and then kills Carol Lockwood ("O Come All Ye Faithful").

Days 15–17 — Damon trains Jeremy in the ways of vampire slayage at the lakehouse, with Matt along for team spirit; Klaus quells his urge to kill Stefan ("After School Special").

Day 18 — Rebekah holds the gang hostage at the school; Klaus turns a bar full of people into vampires so Jeremy can kill them ("After School Special").

Day 19 — Kol compels Damon to kill Jeremy; Stefan and Rebekah consummate their partnership ("Catch Me If You Can").

Day 20 — Day of the 1980s Decade Dance: Jeremy kills Kol, Bonnie traps Klaus in the Gilbert living room. Bonnie uses the new moon to power the spell, which will last three days, four at most. ("A View to a Kill")

Day 21 — The gang travels to Silas island and begins their hike ("Into the Wild").

Day 22 — Jeremy is missing, and the gang spends the day trying to find him ("Into the Wild").

Day 23 — The gang reaches Silas's tomb; Silas kills Jeremy ("Down the Rabbit Hole").

Day 24 — Elena and Stefan return with Jeremy's body; Damon finds Bonnie and brings her back to Mystic Falls; Elena turns off her emotions and burns down the Gilbert house with Jeremy's corpse in it ("Stand By Me").

Day 27? — It has been a "couple of days" since Elena turned off her emotions: the cheerleading invitational is held at Mystic Falls High, Elena throws an impromptu party at the Salvatores, and leaves that night for New York City with Damon ("Bring It On").

Day 28? — Elena, Damon, and Rebekah spend the day in Manhattan; Caroline kills 12 witches ("Because the Night").

Day 29? — Elena and Rebekah steal Damon's car and head out to find Katherine ("Because the Night").

Day 30? — Elena and Rebekah arrive in Willoughby; Katherine gives Elijah the Cure ("American Gothic").

Day 39? — Elena hasn't killed anyone for "eight or nine days"; Mystic Falls High holds its prom ("Pictures of You").

Day 41? — Klaus and Elijah learn that Hayley is pregnant, and they decide to stay in New Orleans ("The Originals").

Day 42? — Elena, who's been at the Salvatores for days, is tortured back into having feelings ("She's Come Undone").

Day 43? — Liz Forbes says that the blood banks were raided "last month," but it is more like two weeks ago; the veil drops within the Expression triangle ("The Walking Dead"). Qetsiyah sneaks through from the Other Side to the Land of the Living and manages to stick around after the veil goes back up ("Original Sin").

Day 44? ● / June 2011 — It's graduation day at Mystic Falls High. Since Elena and company started their junior year in 2010, they graduate as the class of 2011. Katherine becomes human again. ("Graduation")

Gotta love Mystic Falls where it's only 30 days from Christmas to graduation!

Season Five Events

Summer 2011 — Matt and Rebekah travel around Europe and have a threesome with Nadia; Damon and Elena hang out in Mystic Falls making sweet vampire love; Caroline preps for college; Tyler hangs out with werewolves; and Stefan drowns over and over again. ("I Know What You Did Last Summer") Damon takes a weekend break to Charleston to kill Aunt Sara Whitmore; Dr. Wes Maxfield becomes Aaron Whitmore's guardian, since Damon murdered the rest of the boy's family ("Dead Man on Campus," "The Cell"). Traveler Sloan spies on Dr. Maxfield's Augustine experiments for "months" before she introduces herself ("Total Eclipse of the Heart"). Doppelgänger Tom Avery is witch-napped and held in a basement for four months before Caroline and Enzo find him ("Rescue Me").

September 2011 | Day 1 of Season Five — Damon and Elena enjoy a last day sex-a-thon and bubble bath. Caroline packs. ("I Know What You Did Last Summer")

Day 2 | First day of school — Jer's back at school, presumably it's a Monday; Elena and Caroline leave for college; their roommate, Megan, is killed. Silas mind-controls the entire town square and kills Bonnie's dad. ("I Know What You Did Last Summer")

Day 3 — Silas mind-controls Elena to kill Damon; Matt and Jeremy are on the lam with Katherine ("True Lies").

Day 4 — The Sheriff, Damon, and Elena open the safe but Stefan's not in it ("True Lies").

Day 5 — Qetsiyah tells Stefan the story of her and Silas, then wipes his mind in a spell that takes away Silas's powers. Nadia captures Katherine. ("Original Sin")

Remembrance Day, Friday — Damon and Elena try to jar Stefan's memories; Jeremy reveals that Bonnie is dead ("For Whom the Bell Tolls").

Day 7 — The gang holds a memorial for Bonnie; Dr. Maxfield turns Jesse into a vampire ("For Whom the Bell Tolls").

Day 10 — The Whitmore Historical Ball is held; Jesse has been held by Dr. Maxfield for three days. Silas drinks the Cure from Katherine's blood and becomes mortal ("Monster's Ball").

Day 11 — Silas discovers that Amara is the Anchor; she drinks the Cure from him. Qetsiyah returns Stefan's memories to him. ("Handle with Care")

Day 12 — Qetsiyah makes Bonnie the Anchor to the Other Side; Qetsiyah, Silas, and Amara die ("Death and the Maiden").

Day 21 — Dr. Maxfield says it's been "approximately" 14 days since Jesse turned (genius scientists, so imprecise!). Despite the nine day jump in the timeline, the girls are only now throwing Bonnie a welcome party, Matt is only now dealing with the passenger video he recorded, and Stefan is still in the height of his PTSD. Katherine kills Gregor, who's passengering in Matt, and later Stefan saves her from her suicide attempt. ("Dead Man on Campus")

Day 22 — Elena is captured by Wes, and Aaron Whitmore learns about the Augustine Society; Stefan and Katherine rekindle their flame ("The Cell").

Day 23 — Elena is nearly turned into a vampire-eating vampire by Wes; Enzo is freed after 68 years in captivity. That night, Katherine has a heart attack. ("Fifty Shades of Grayson")

Day 24 — Katherine, on her deathbed, passengers herself into Elena; Caroline and Klaus have scandalous sex ("500 Years of Solitude"). Rebekah makes a comment about not being gone even three months, but she was actually last in Mystic Falls just over three weeks ago.

Day 25? — Though there is no explicit timeline reference in "The Devil Inside," Damon buries Katherine's body (and the corpse is still fresh when she's found) and "Elena" has only been AWOL for a short period of time, so it's safe to assume it's the day after Katherine died. Mia does a spell to put Katherine in control of Elena's body. Damon kills Aaron Whitmore. ("The Devil Inside")

Day 26 — Damon and Enzo kidnap Jeremy in order to motivate Bonnie to find a witch who can find Wes; the gang attends the Bitter Ball at Whitmore College; Damon is injected with the ripper virus ("Total Eclipse of the Heart").

Day 29 — After two days, Nadia returns a compelled Matt to his friends. Vampire-eating Damon is trapped in a farmhouse with Enzo by Wes and the Travelers, nearly killing Enzo and "Elena." Stefan locks him up in the Salvatore holding cell; Stefan and Caroline figure out that Katherine is in Elena's body ("No Exit").

Day 30 / "Weeks" after Katherine's death on day 24 — Stefan tells Damon that Katherine has been in Elena's body for "weeks" but it's actually just been six days by timeline references within the show. Damon kills Dr. Wes. Nadia dies from Tyler's bite. Katherine is sucked into Oblivion. ("Gone Girl")

Day 31 / Spring Break, 2012 — Stefan tells Elena that the time from Day 26 to Day 31 is about "three weeks"; it's also spring break, despite the school year starting one month earlier. Enzo and the Travelers cure Damon and Elena of their viruses. ("While You Were Sleeping")

Day 32 / Next day — Enzo kills witch Hazel and doppelgänger Tom in Atlanta; Liv attempts to kill Elena and then makes an alliance with Jeremy; Markos returns to the Land of the Living ("Rescue Me").

Day 33 / Next day — The Travelers passenger themselves in the residents of Mystic Falls; Matt temporarily dies and Vicki is taken from the Other

Side; Stefan and Elena experience elaborate shared fantasies ("Resident Evil").

Day 34 / Next day — While college students study for finals, Enzo holds them hostage believing Stefan is guilty of Maggie's murder; he forces Stefan to kill him ("Man on Fire").

Day 35 / Next day — After a day at the Forbes cabin, Stefan and Elena are doppel-napped by the Travelers. Damon refers to Markos as being resurrected a "good week or two" ago, but it's just been three days. Damon says if he were Stefan he would've killed Enzo *months* ago. ("What Lies Beneath")

Day 39 / 4 days later — Stefan and Elena escape the clutches of the Travelers; Julian kills Stefan ("Promised Land").

Day 40 / Next day — The gang blows up the Grill with the Travelers inside. Stefan, Enzo, and Alaric are resurrected. Lexi, Grams, Damon, and Bonnie — along with countless others on the Other Side — disappear when the supernatural purgatory collapses. ("Home")

Going by time-passage cues within each episode, the season ends only 40 days after it began, but it's finals week, a.k.a. May 2012, in the season finale — eight months since the start of the school year in the season premiere. It's magic!

Selected Sources

Bargh, Renee. "*Vampire Diaries* Has a New Star!" *Extra TV*. October 3, 2013.
Bondeson, Jan. *Buried Alive: The Terrifying History of Our Most Primal Fear*. New York: W.W. Norton & Company, 2001.
Bricker, Tierney. "Olga Fonda Dishes on Nadia's 'Surprising' Agenda and Receiving Warnings from Matt Fans," *E! Online*. October 31, 2013.
——. "Olga Fonda Sounds Off on Tonight's Mother of a Reveal and What Lies Ahead," *E! Online*. October 31, 2013.
Bucksbaum, Sydney. "*The Vampire Diaries*: Kat Graham Dishes on Bonnie's Death, the Other Side, Why She's Happy with her Season 5 Story Line, and More," Zap2It.com. October 10, 2013.
The Cell. Directed by Tarsem Singh, 2000.
CivilWar.org.
Decanter.com. "100 Wines to Try Before You Die."
Duncan, Lois. *I Know What You Did Last Summer*. New York: Little, Brown and Company, 2010.
Guliadis, Theo. "Candice Accola Dishes on Caroline's Romances, College Life, and *The Vampire Diaries* Season 5," AlloyEntertainment.com. October 2, 2013.
Hemingway, Ernest. *For Whom the Bell Tolls*. New York: Scribner, 1940.
HomeoftheNutty.com/vampirediaries/screencaps.
I Know What You Did Last Summer. Directed by Jim Gillespie, 1997.
JaninaGavankar.com.
KendrickSampson.com.
Man on Fire. Directed by Tony Scott, 2004.
Márquez, Gabríel Garcia. *One Hundred Years of Solitude*. New York: Alfred A. Knopf, 1995.
Monster's Ball. Directed by Marc Forster, 2001.
Ng, Philiana. "*Vampire Diaries*: Kendrick Sampson on Jesse's 'Ulterior Motives,' Romancing Caroline," *The Hollywood Reporter*. October 24, 2013.
"Nov. 8, 1960: Kennedy Is Elected President," *The Learning Network*. Learning.Blogs.NYTimes.com. November 8, 2011.
Platini, Estelle. "Saving French Wine During WWII," Cellarer.com. July 29, 2008.
RaffiB.com.
Richenthal, Matt. "Candice Accola Teases *The Vampire Diaries* Season 5, Caroline's Unhappy College Adventure," *TV Fanatic*. October 2, 2013.
RickCosnett.com.
Ross, Robyn. "*The Vampire Diaries*' Paul Wesley: Stefan Is Screwed Up in the Head This Season," *TV Guide*. October 2, 2013.

Sartre, Jean-Paul. *No Exit and Three Other Plays*. New York: Vintage International, 1989.
Snopes.com.
True Lies. Directed by James Cameron, 1994.
Twitter.com/CarolineDries.
Twitter.com/CMollere.
Twitter.com/JuliePlec.
USElectionAtlas.org.
The Vampire Diaries. TV series. Executive Producers Leslie Morgenstein, Bob Levy, Kevin Williamson, Julie Plec. The CW. 2009–.
Vampire-Diaries.net.
VampireDiaries.Wikia.com.
Villarreal, Yvonne. "Ian Somerhalder teases *Vampire Diaries*' Future — Love Troubles?" *L.A. Times Showtracker*. October 2, 2013.
Weaver, Michael. "What Happens to the Human Body After We Die?" MadSci.org. April 25, 2005.
What Lies Beneath. Directed by Robert Zemeckis, 2000.
While You Were Sleeping. Directed by Jon Turteltaub, 1995.
Wieselman, Jarett. "Claire Holt's Journey from *TVD* to *Originals*," *ET Online*. October 2, 2013.
——. "Is *TVD*'s New Educator Evil?" *ET Online*. October 24, 2013.
Wikipedia.com.

Acknowledgments

Thanks, as always, to our publisher ECW Press for supporting this series five years running — with particular shout-outs to Erin, Michelle, Laura, and the production trio of Rachel, Troy, and Lynn for toiling on this volume. The kickass cover illustration is by Risa Rodil (RisaRodil.com) — we've long been fans of her work and are grateful to have this doppelgänger tribute grace our cover. Editor Gil Adamson once again proved her uncanny ability to divine what we mean even in the most garbled of nonsense sentences *and* she encourages a higher joke per page rate. Thank you for always being so keen to take on this diversion from your literary pursuits.

Carrie Raisler, Robyn Ross, and Price Peterson — you guys know how much we love you, and thank you for being a part of our Katherine memorial. This volume of the Love You to Death series has more interviews than any before it, and that's thanks to Julie Plec and Caroline Dries, and to Tom Farrell, without whom we literally could not have done this. Thanks also to Celeste Vasquez, Missy Woodward, Danny Tolli, and Bayan Wolcott for their help and responsiveness.

And to the forthcoming and eloquent and unfailingly charming *TVD* family members who took the time (for the most part while on hiatus) to answer our questions: Brett Matthews, Caroline Dries, Darren Genet, Garreth Stover, Joshua Butler, Julie Plec, Holly Brix, Kellie Cyrus, Marc Pollon, Matthew D'Ambrosio, Melinda Hsu Taylor, Michael Allowitz, Michael Karasick, Neil Reynolds, Paul Wesley, Rebecca Sonnenshine, and Tony Solomons. Know that it took every ounce of professionalism we possess to not inundate you with compliments — you bring an impressive body of experience to *TVD*, and it shows in the work that you each do. Kevin Williamson, know that we lost any and all cool when you kindly agreed to do the foreword for us. (And we have the iMessage freakout to prove it.) Thank you for taking the time from your insanely busy schedule to write from the heart about a show that means so much to us all.

On a bittersweet note, this season marks the swan song of Vampire-Diaries.net, which played a huge role in bringing us together as cowriters and, more importantly, as friends. There is no way to properly express the magnitude of love we have for Adam "Red" Birchall, Abby Graham, Kate

Welsh, and Holly Easley for helping anchor the site and always being the biggest and best cheerleaders and friends we could possibly ask for. Thanks also to the thousands of readers who called V-D.net home for over five years. Your support and dedication has meant the world.

And thanks to Heather's parents, who listened to stress-filled ramblings and gave her support, and to Crissy's mom, who made her step away from the laptop when her eyes went buggy, and to Crissy's dad, who just offered to write half the book for us. (Any errors or omissions you can blame on him.) Parents, siblings, and friends: we love you to death.

About the Authors

Crissy Calhoun is an editor and has written or co-written 11 pop culture non-fiction books, including the five volumes of Love You to Death. Find her online at CrissyCalhoun.com and @CrissyCalhoun. Heather Vee is the co-editor of *A Visitor's Guide to Mystic Falls*, was featured in *TVD*'s season one special features DVD/Blu-Ray, and ran the top *TVD* fansite for five years. Find her online at HeatherVee.com or @DiesLaughing.

GET THE eBOOK FREE! At ECW Press, we want you to enjoy *Love You to Death — Season 5* in whatever format you like, whenever you like. Leave your print book at home and take the eBook to go! Purchase the print edition and receive the eBook free. Just send an email to ebook@ecwpress.com and include:

- the book title
- the name of the store where you purchased it
- your receipt number
- your preference of file type: PDF or ePub?

A real person will respond to your email with your eBook attached. And thanks for supporting an independently owned publisher with your purchase!